STUDY GUIDE

TO ACCOMPANY
DORNBUSCH
AND FISCHER
MACRO
ECONOMICS

STUDY GUIDE

TO ACCOMPANY
DORNBUSCH
AND FISCHER
MACRO
ECONOMICS

RICHARD STARTZ

University of Washington

Fourth Edition

**McGRAW
HILL
BOOK
COMPANY**

New York • St. Louis • San Francisco
Auckland • Bogotá • Hamburg
London • Madrid
Mexico • Milan • Montreal
New Delhi • Panama • Paris
São Paulo • Singapore • Sydney
Tokyo • Toronto

STUDY GUIDE

TO ACCOMPANY
DORNBUSCH-FISCHER
MACROECONOMICS

3 4 5 6 7 8 9 0 H A L H A L 8 9 2 1 0 9

ISBN 0-07-017778-3

This book was set in Baskerville by Automated Composition Service, Inc.
The editor was Joseph F. Murphy;
the designer was Jo Jones;
the cover was designed by Joseph Gillians;
the production supervisor was Diane Renda.
The drawings were done by J & R Services, Inc.
Arcata Graphics/Halliday was printer and binder.

CONTENTS

v

TO
THE STUDENT

The *Study Guide* is designed for use with Dornbusch and Fischer's *Macroeconomics*. The only sensible reason for the existence of a study guide is to *make learning easier*.

FORMAT

Most of the twenty chapters have the following sections:

- Focus of the Chapter: gives a quick peek at the most important topics of the chapter.
- Section Summaries: summarize each section of the text briefly.
- Graph It: asks you to plot data, complete a graph, or fill in a chart. Most of these are quite simple. Think of the Graph Its as being like warm-up exercises before a run or limbering-up scales for piano practice. Taking a pencil in hand gets your mind loosened up *and* gets your mind focused on the subject at hand.
- Key Terms: list the most important technical terms used in the chapter.
- Review of Technique: (see below).
- Fill-In Questions: test the most important ideas and concepts of the chapter.
- True-False Questions and Multiple-Choice Questions: test the detailed

concepts of the chapter and sometimes require you to work out some simple problems.

- Problems: finish up each chapter. These require you to apply the concepts of the chapter to a specific problem.
- Answers: to every question in the *Study Guide* appear at the back of the book.

At the back of the *Study Guide* you will also find a glossary with definitions of many of the terms used in the text and the *Guide*. You may find them especially helpful with working on the fill-in questions. In addition, there are some reference tables at the back of the book; these give various kinds of annual economic data for the United States. You may want to refer to these data to get a feeling for what the real numbers in the economy are.

HOW TO STUDY MACROECONOMICS

Do not! It wastes too much time. Instead—

Practice Macroeconomics

Practice, do not study. Having taught several hundred students from the first edition of *Macroeconomics*, I have seen diligent students come in with the same problem over and over. They have read and reread the text several times, underlined all the important points, and spent hours and hours trying to memorize facts and theories. But they realize that somehow they have not quite caught on. As the authors of the text say, *active learning* is the only way to learn the material. Do not waste valuable hours trying to remember masses of material. Instead, spend a small amount of time trying to *focus* on the structure of the material. Since this is easier said than done, we have created this *Study Guide* to give you very specific questions to practice on. The questions in the *Study Guide* are not just lists of points to remember. Most questions have been picked to illustrate a basic principle. If you answer a question incorrectly, decide whether you have merely missed a minor point or whether you have overlooked a basic principle involved. The early questions in each chapter are quite easy, and later questions become progressively more difficult. Some of the problems are quite advanced. While you may be able to answer all the fill-in questions in 2 minutes, the problems take time to work through. When it becomes necessary to choose between rereading the text for the third time and spending 20 minutes doing a hard problem, do the problem.

Use this Study Guide *to learn more in less time.*

Review of Technique

A special feature of the *Study Guide* is the Review of Technique found in each chapter. Each one presents a quick review of some useful technical trick. Some of these are really very simple. Some are just a little bit advanced. You will probably find that you already know most of the material in each Review, but a few years may have passed since you last had to use it. The Reviews allow you to brush up at your own leisure. They are not directly related to the material in the chapters in which they appear. When you have time, browse through all the Reviews to find those most useful to use.

ACKNOWLEDGMENTS

First, thanks must go to Professors Dornbusch and Fischer for, among other things, teaching me a great deal about macroeconomics. Susann Bizzari typed the original manuscript (and retyped it faster than I could edit). Professors William Zahka, of Widener College, and Stephen Van der Ploeg, of Florida Atlantic University, provided very helpful reviews, as did several Wharton students.

Comments and (corrections!) on the *Study Guide* will be most appreciated.

For the Third Edition—Further Acknowledgments and Hints

Thanks continue to go to Professors Dornbusch and Fischer for continuing to teach me about macroeconomics. Thanks also go to the number of students who have sent corrections and suggestions. In response to several suggestions, this edition of the *Study Guide* is just a smidgen less technical than the earlier edition.

Here are two hints—the result of teaching several hundred students with the text and *Study Guide*.

1   Don't become overwhelmed by the details. Concentrate instead on the overall structure. The text has literally thousands of important details, but only a dozen or so major themes. You can think of the themes as big branches and the details as leaves on a tree. It's much easier to trace down a specific detail by running out along the right branch than it is to build up an entire tree from a pile of leaves.

2   Study with a pencil in your hand and scribble in the margins or on scrap paper as you go. Pictures show structures better than words do. When the *Study Guide* describes how two curves interact, scribble an example graph right there in the *Study Guide*. The picture you draw sticks much better than any words we can use.

For the Fourth Edition—Yet Another Acknowledgment and Hint

All the hard work in preparing this edition was done by Nick Pealy. Thanks to Nick, you'll find that this edition's coverage of the text material is even more thorough than in the past.

Hint: After the teaching of another thousand or so students, a bit more useful advice is available. The text has an enormous amount of detail but only a half dozen or so major themes. To test your understanding of the text, pretend to explain what you've learned to someone at a cocktail party.* Remember, you are supposed to explain how the entire economy works *without using any technical terms.*

*Now you know how economists get the reputation for being boring. However, like most suggestions made by economists, this is a darn good one!

Richard Startz

PART ONE

1

INTRODUCTION

FOCUS OF THE CHAPTER

- Our study of macroeconomics commences with an introduction to the principal concepts of macroeconomics and an overview of the textbook. We look at the questions of gross national product, unemployment, inflation, and economic growth.

● SECTION SUMMARIES

1. *Gross national product* (GNP) is the value of all goods and services produced in the economy in a year. *Real, or constant dollar,* GNP is the basic measure of economic activity. *Nominal, or current dollar,* GNP is the number of dollars needed to buy the entire gross national product. When prices go up, nominal GNP goes up even if real GNP doesn't change. In both the text and the *Study Guide*, ''GNP'' means ''real GNP'' unless we explicitly use the word ''nominal.'' In order to measure the real value of goods and services—wiping away price changes—we often measure the value of goods in terms of ''1982 dollars.''

From 1960 through 1985, GNP grew an average of 3.1 percent per year, though of course some years were good and some were bad. Trend growth in

GNP is due to increased amounts of labor and of capital and to increased efficiency in using these factors of production. Year-to-year movements around trend depend on how much of the available resources are used. When unemployment is high, less is produced.

Macroeconomic performance is judged on the *inflation* rate, the *growth* rate of GNP, and the *unemployment* rate. Macroeconomics is largely the study of how these three economic variables behave, how they can best be controlled, and what limits we face in our attempts to control them.

Full-employment output, or *potential output*, is the level of GNP that the economy would produce if all resources were being used at just the right level. Actual output fluctuates around this level. The difference between potential output and actual output is called the *output*, or *GNP, gap*.

2.   Output growth and unemployment are related by *Okun's law*. The trend growth of GNP is roughly 3 percent per year. If output grows faster than trend, unemployment falls. Okun's law suggests that GNP must grow about 2½ percent per year above trend to lower unemployment by 1 percentage point.

Inflation is the rate of increase in prices. When prices are going up, the level of inflation is positive. When (on those rare occasions) prices are going down, the level of inflation is negative.

The *Phillips curve* describes a relation between inflation and unemployment: the higher the rate of unemployment, the lower the rate of inflation. This relation is fairly reliable in the short run (say, 2 years). In the long run, there is no tradeoff worth speaking about between inflation and unemployment.

3.   Policy makers can affect the economy through *monetary policy* and *fiscal policy*. The primary instruments of monetary policy, controlled by the Federal Reserve, are the stock of money and, through the stock of money, the interest rate. The primary instruments of fiscal policy, controlled by Congress and the President, are tax rates and government spending. The Federal Reserve and Congress and the President use *stabilization policy* to smooth out fluctuations in the economy. Stabilization policy is also called *countercyclical policy*. Political use of policy instruments to reduce unemployment right before an election leads to the idea of the *political business cycle*.

Economists can, to some extent, be divided into *monetarists* and *activists*. Monetarists believe that the money supply is the most important determinant of the state of the economy and usually believe that the government should interfere in the economy as little as possible. *Activists* look to many other factors in addition to money and believe that the government ought to manage actively the level of economic activity.

The overall concepts in studying unemployment, growth, and inflation are *aggregate demand* and *aggregate supply*. Basically, aggregate demand tells how much GNP consumers, business, and the government choose to buy given the overall level of prices. Aggregate supply tells how much output is produced at a given price level. Figure 1-1 (text Figure 1-9) shows that the aggregate supply curve is flat at low levels of production and quite steep as production approaches potential GNP. In the flat region, changes in output occur with little price change. In the steep region, it is difficult to increase GNP; prices rise instead.

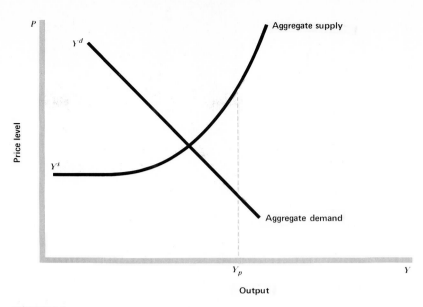

FIGURE 1-1

4.   Chapters 3 through 6 concentrate on aggregate demand. Later chapters consider aggregate supply as well as aggregate demand. You should think of the lessons of these early chapters as applying best at high levels of unemployment, that is, on the flat region of the aggregate supply curve.

Remember: In Chapters 3 through 6, GNP *really means aggregate demand for a given price level.*

5.   The easiest way to study macroeconomics is to break the subject into smaller pieces. You may find it helpful to think of some chapters as "forest" (broad overview) chapters and others as "tree" (sophisticated detail) chapters. Chapter 2 describes national income accounting; it's a tree chapter in that it provides detail about national income accounting, but a forest chapter in that it provides an overview of how the economy is put together. Chapters 3, 4, and 5 (forest) give the "big picture" about aggregate demand. Chapter 6 (forest) is an introduction to the international economy. Chapter 7 (forest) gives a broad overview of how aggregate demand combines with aggregate supply. Chapters 8 through 11 are tree chapters: they take an in-depth look at the sectors contributing to aggregate demand. Chapter 12 is a tree chapter since it looks at the details of policy making, but it also talks about the broad subject of how history and ideas interact. Chapters 13 and 14 (tree) examine the details of aggregate supply. Chapters 15 through 17 (tree) take a closer look at a number of policy issues. Chapter 18 (tree) goes into more depth about the interaction of events and ideas. Long-term growth is the subject of Chapter 19 (mostly tree, but some forest). Chapter 20 (tree) completes our examination of the international economy.

KEY TERMS

Monetarists	Inflation
Keynesians	Growth
New classical macroeconomist	Unemployment
GNP, nominal and real	Business cycle
Trend or potential output	Phillips curve
Peak	Monetary policy
Trough	Fiscal policy
Recovery or expansion	Stabilization policies
Recession	Activists
Output gap	Aggregate demand and supply
Okun's law	

GRAPH IT

The easiest way to see whether the economy is doing well is to chart real GNP. If GNP is going up by more than its usual trend, the economy is doing well— and vice versa. In Chart 1-1 you are asked to graph the annual rate of change in GNP from 1962 through 1985. Over this period, GNP grew about 3.3 percent each year *on average*, though some years had faster growth and some lower.

In order to fill out the chart, you must first calculate the rates of change of GNP and then plot them. For example, GNP was 1,873.3 billion dollars in

CHART 1-1

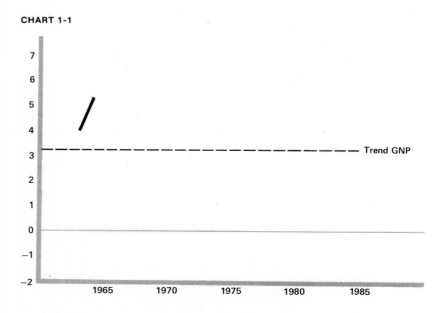

781 - 4555
- 1688

TABLE 1-1

Year	GNP	Percentage change from previous year
1962	1,799.4	
1963	1,873.3	4.01
1964	1,973.3	5.34
1965	——	——
1966	——	——
1967	——	——
1968	——	——
1969	——	——
1970	——	——
1971	——	——
1972	——	——
1973	——	——
1974	——	——
1975	——	——
1976	——	——
1977	——	——
1978	——	——
1979	——	——
1980	——	——
1981	——	——
1982	——	——
1983	——	——
1984	——	——
1985	——	——

1963 and 1,799.4 billion dollars in 1962. So the 1963 annual growth rate was
$100 \times [(1,873.3 - 1,799.4)/1,799.4]$, or 4.0 percent. We've filled in several
years on the calculation table and chart. You do the rest.

REVIEW OF TECHNIQUE 1
How to Review for This Course

Each person has a method of study which works best for her- or himself. In this
Review, we present some suggestions for breaking your studying up into
manageable chunks. In each chapter, form a picture of the "forest" for that
chapter before looking at the "trees." In this way, you have a framework on
which to hang the details of the chapter. The text is far too rich for you to try to
memorize a long list of unrelated facts and theories. Think of the difference in
putting together a jigsaw puzzle when you know the general picture as compared
with assembling it when you have no idea of the meaning of the big heap of
pieces!

Figure 1-2 presents one outline you can use for studying a chapter. You can
start at the top with any of the suggestions for initial reading and work your way
down to the RELAX box.

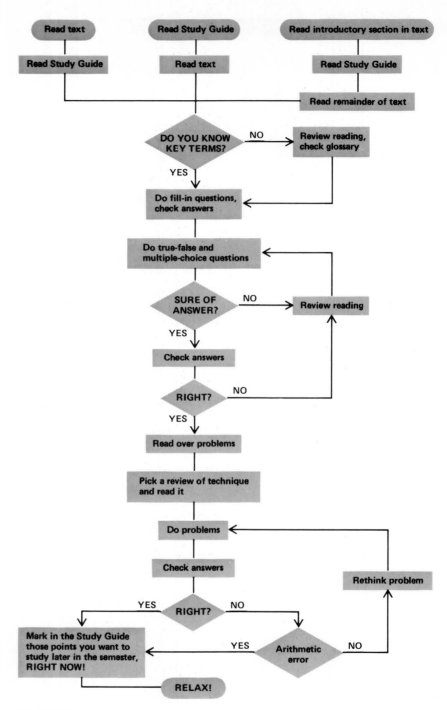

FIGURE 1-2

FILL-IN QUESTIONS

1. The value of production when all inputs are fully employed is _____ _____.

2. The difference between production with fully employed inputs and actual production is the _____.

3. The bottom of the business cycle is called the _____.

4. Economic policy makers may try to improve economic performance by changing government spending and taxes, which are types of _____ _____ policy.

5. Or they may try to do so by changing the money supply or interest rates, which are examples of _____ policy.

6. Both (4) and (5) are examples of _____.

7. GNP and unemployment are related through _____.

8. A time of high economic growth is called _____.

9. Times of economic weakness and contractions are termed _____ _____.

10. The first half of the text is devoted to the study of _____.

TRUE-FALSE QUESTIONS

T F 1. GNP growth and increases in the unemployment rate are positively related.

T F 2. In the first half of the text, prices are taken as being given.

T F 3. Chapter 1 is a "trees" chapter.

2

NATIONAL INCOME ACCOUNTING

FOCUS OF THE CHAPTER

- Under the heading "National Accounting," we consider the several different ways in which the national economic pie can be sliced into its component parts.
- While we are taking apart GNP, we are also really learning how the different sources of aggregate demand can be added together to determine total national income.

SECTION SUMMARIES

1. *Gross national product* (GNP) measures the value of all final output of the economy. We measure only the value of final goods because counting both the value of a car and the value of the steel in the car would be double-counting. GNP includes the value of current production. It excludes the sales of existing goods from inventory. Goods are valued at their market price. To be precise, *gross domestic product* (GDP) measures the value of goods produced within a country, while GNP measures the value of goods produced by domestically owned factors of production. *Net national product* (NNP) is GNP minus *depreciation*; in other words, it is total current production minus an allowance for equipment that has worn out.

2. Because prices change from year to year, we distinguish *real GNP* from *nominal GNP*. Real GNP is a measure of physical production. Nominal GNP is the cost of that production at prevailing prices. The words "real" and "nominal" emphasize that real GNP is the useful measure of the economy's output.

Wherever the text or *Study Guide* uses the term GNP, we mean *real* GNP unless we specifically state nominal GNP.

GNP is measured only imperfectly, especially in regard to items such as government services and housework, which are difficult to value because they are not generally sold in the open market. The Total Incomes System of Accounts (TISA) attempts to correct such deficiencies. GNP measurement is also made difficult by quality changes of goods and by the existence of the underground economy.

3. The three most important measures of the general price level are the *GNP deflator*, the *consumer price index* (CPI), and the *producer price index* (PPI). The GNP deflator equals the ratio of nominal GNP to real GNP. The CPI measures costs for a "typical" urban family. The PPI tracks prices of a range of goods used in production.

4. For the nation as a whole, income must equal output. When one person buys an item, the money paid for it is part of another person's income. There are two qualifications to this. Replacement of worn machinery does not add to anyone's income even though it requires production. Therefore, income should be identified with NNP rather than GNP. Sales tax and other indirect taxes also have to be deducted from the value of production since these payments are not directly part of anyone's income.

National income can be viewed as the sum of all payments to factors of production: wages, profits, and so on. National income can be further broken down into personal income and *disposable personal income* by subtracting those elements of income (principally taxes) that are not actually available for individuals to spend.

Disposable personal income must be either consumed or saved.

5. GNP can also be divided up according to the various demands for purchasing output. The four sources of demand for purchasing output are personal consumption, private domestic investment, government purchases of goods and services, and net exports. Note that government transfers of income to individuals do *not* constitute part of demand for GNP. Nor are taxes directly part of GNP.

6. Several important identities summarize the conventions of national income accounting. You *should memorize* the simple identities below. Be sure to learn the identities in terms of the economic concepts represented, not just as a set of abstract symbols.

$$Y \equiv C + I + G + NX \qquad \text{fundamental identity of aggregate demand}$$
$$YD \equiv Y + TR - TA \qquad \text{sources of disposable income}$$
$$YD \equiv C + S \qquad \text{uses of disposable income}$$
$$BD \equiv (G + TR) - TA \qquad \text{budget deficit}$$

$$Y = \text{GNP}$$
$$C = \text{consumption}$$

$$I = \text{investment} \qquad TR = \text{transfers}$$
$$G = \text{government purchases} \qquad TA = \text{taxes}$$
$$NX = \text{net exports} \qquad S = \text{savings}$$
$$YD = \text{disposable income} \qquad BD = \text{government budget deficit}$$

All these are summarized by the *basic macroeconomic identity*:

$$C + G + I + NX \equiv Y \equiv YD + (TA - TR) \equiv C + S + (TA - TR)$$

KEY TERMS

Final goods

Value added

Market prices

Factor cost

Gross domestic product (GDP)

Net national product (NNP)

Depreciation

Measure of economic welfare (MEW)

Total Incomes System of Accounts (TISA)

The underground economy

GNP deflator

Consumer price index (CPI)

Producer price index (PPI)

National income

Factor shares

Personal income

Transfers

Disposable personal income

Consumption

Government purchases

Government expenditure

Investment

Net exports

Final sales to domestic purchasers

Consumer durables

Government budget deficit

GRAPH IT 2

Economists spend a lot of time drawing straight lines on graph paper. This chapter's Graph It asks you to draw a line just for practice. We've taken two possible relations between consumption and income from Chapter 8. We've graphed the first in Chart 2-1. You are asked to draw the second in Chart 2-2. The two possible relations are

$$C = 6 + 0.90Y \qquad \text{(ours)}$$
$$C = 47 + 0.73Y \qquad \text{(yours)}$$

One draws a straight line by finding two points on the line and then connecting them. The easy point is found by taking $Y = 0$, and so $C = 6$, and we put a dot at

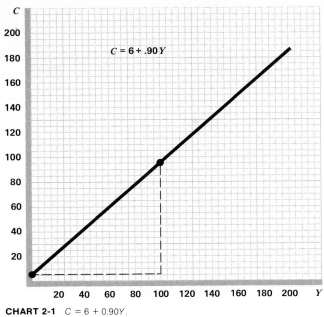

CHART 2-1 $C = 6 + 0.90Y$.

CHART 2-2 $C = 47 + 0.73Y$.

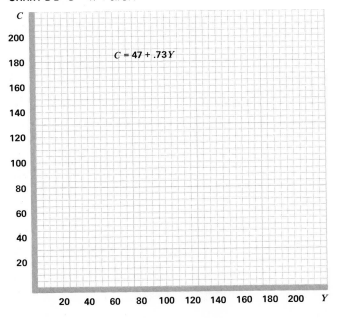

6 on the *C* axis. Since the *slope* of our relation is 0.90, consumption must go up 9 points for every 10 points that income goes up. From the first dot we counted off 10 positions to the right and then 9 positions up. We placed a second dot there and then drew the line connecting the two dots. Now you draw your relation on the blank graph.

REVIEW OF TECHNIQUE 2

Exogenous, Endogenous, and Policy Variables

Each subject in the text involves analyzing an economic model. A model is formed of one or more economic relationships that connect variables. Usually, these relationships are made specific by setting up one or more equations or graphs. At some philosophical level, everything studied in the book is all part of one large economic model. In practice, we break off small sectors of the economy to study in isolation.

Some variables are taken as inputs to a model. These are called *exogenous*. There are three general types of exogenous variables. Some economic variables are given by nature (the weather, for example), or at least are taken to be outside the scope of study of the model (investor psychology, for instance). Some economic variables can be set by policy makers. These are called *policy variables*. The rate of government spending and the level of the money stock are two important policy variables. Variables that may affect the reactions of the economy but that are not of any direct interest in and of themselves are called *parameters*. The marginal propensity to consume is an important economic parameter.

Endogenous variables are those that are determined internally by a given economic model. In supply-and-demand analysis, price and quantity are the endogenous variables. Whether a variable is endogenous or exogenous depends on context. When we study the simple multiplier model in Chapter 3, income and consumption are both endogenous. By contrast, in Chapter 8, where we study advanced theories of consumption, income is taken to be exogenous and consumption is endogenous.

Two points are helpful in thinking about economic models. The first is of fundamental importance. The second is a useful trick.

Exogenous variables determine the level of endogenous variables. The relation of exogenous to endogenous variables is one of cause to effect. Sensible questions are: "For a given change in an exogenous variable, what changes in the endogenous variables are expected?" and "In order to achieve a desired change in an endogenous variable, what change in a given exogenous variable would be required?" It is not sensible to ask about the effect of a change in an endogenous variable. A change in some endogenous variable is always the result of some more fundamental change in some exogenous variable.

When it comes time to find the solution of an economic model, try this procedure. Write down all the equations in the model. Next, write down a list of all the endogenous variables in the model. You should have the same number of equations and endogenous variables. If the numbers don't match, either some of the equations are just combinations of the other equations, or something fundamental has been omitted.

FILL-IN QUESTIONS

1. The value of all final goods and services produced in the economy is _____GNP_____.

2. It is necessary to adjust GNP for _____DEPRECIATION_____ in order to calculate net national product.

3. The difference between net national product and national income is the difference between measuring the value of production at _____MARKET PRICES_____ and at _____FACTOR COST_____.

4. A person's disposable income is (basically) either _____consumed_____ or _____SAVED_____.

5. The principal difference between national income and disposable income is the addition of _____TRANSFERS_____ and the subtraction of _____Personal taxes_____.

6. _____MEW_____ attempts to account for economic "fads" as well as economic goods.

7. The ratio of nominal to real GNP is a useful price index called the _____GNP Deflator_____.

8. The index we use to measure the cost of living is the _____CPI_____.

9. The excess of private savings over investment must equal _____Budget deficit_____ plus _____foreign trade surplus_____.

10. Net exports is the excess of _____EXPORTS_____ over _____imports_____.

TRUE-FALSE QUESTIONS

T ⓕ 1. Investment equals private savings.
T ⓕ 2. Sale of a home adds to GNP.
ⓣ F 3. The real estate agent's commission on the sale of a home adds to GNP.
ⓣ F 4. Depreciation expenses are part of GNP.
T ⓕ 5. Depreciation expenses are part of disposable income.
T ⓕ 6. Purchase of common stock is part of investment.
ⓣ F 7. Purchase of a jeep by a camping enthusiast is part of consumption.
ⓣ F 8. Purchase of a jeep by a logging company is part of investment.

(T) F 9. The difference between gross investment and net investment is the same as the difference between **GNP** and **NNP**.

(T) F 10. Exports are part of **GNP**.

MULTIPLE-CHOICE QUESTIONS

1. Which of the following is *not* part of aggregate demand?
    a. government spending   c. net exports
    b. taxes   d. investment

2. Which of the following is part of aggregate demand?
    a. indirect taxes   c. consumption
    b. transfers   d. imports

3. Social Security payments are counted as part of
    a. government expenditure   c. taxes
    b. transfers   d. consumption

4. Benefits paid to government employees are counted as part of
    a. government expenditure   c. taxes
    b. transfers   d. consumption

5. Suppose investment and three of the following four items remain fixed. Which of the four might have risen?
    a. government budget surplus c. net exports
    b. saving   d. tax rates

6. Suppose **GNP** and **NNP** both rise by the same amount while three of the following four remain fixed. Which of the four could have not risen?
    a. gross investment   c. consumption
    b. net investment   d. net exports

7. An increase in the price of bicycles will show up in
    a. the **GNP** deflator   c. the producer price index
    b. the consumer price index d. both a and b

8. If the price of apples goes up and the price of oranges goes down, this change would most likely be reflected in an increase in
    a. the **GNP** deflator   c. the producer price index
    b. the consumer price index d. none of these

9. Which of the following are part of national income?
    a. wages   c. both wages and profits
    b. profits   d. neither wages nor profits

10. Which of the following is not part of national income?
    a. rental income   c. salaries
    b. welfare payments   d. net interest

PROBLEMS

1. This is a problem in national income accounting. You are given the fol-
    lowing facts about the economy: consumption = $1,000; saving = $100;
    government expenditure = $300. The government budget is balanced. What
    is the value of GNP?
2. Suppose saving equals $200, the budget deficit is $50, and the trade deficit is
    $10. What is the level of investment?

#1.

$$BD = G + TR - TA = 0 \qquad G \equiv TA - TR = 300$$

$$YD = C + S = 1000 + 100$$
$$= 1100$$

$$YD = Y - TA + TR = 1100 \Rightarrow Y = 300$$

AGGREGATE DEMAND AND EQUILIBRIUM INCOME AND OUTPUT

FOCUS OF THE CHAPTER

- The heart of Keynesian macroeconomic analysis is the idea that national income and the level of unemployment depend on *aggregate demand*.
- Aggregate demand is not exogenously fixed. As an accounting identity, however, GNP must be the sum of consumption, investment, and government spending. The classic example works through the response of consumption to income. Higher government spending increases GNP, since government purchases are a direct source of aggregate demand. This increase in GNP causes consumption to rise, and this rise causes yet a further increase in GNP.
- In order to find the equilibrium of the economy, it is necessary to *combine* the aggregate demand identity and the consumption function.

SECTION SUMMARIES

1. The fundamental identity of aggregate demand, $Y \equiv C + I + G$, shows that the *actual* level of output must always equal the sum of all the different sources of aggregate demand. (Notice that we pretty much ignore the foreign sector until Chapter 6.) However, we can imagine a situation in which the *planned* level of output is not equal to the *planned* levels of consumption, investment, and government spending. When the planned and actual levels are

different, unintended inventory changes occur. When planned and actual levels are equal, the economy is in equilibrium. We use this fact to find the equilibrium of the economy by finding the level of GNP where planned output equals the sum of planned consumption, investment, and government spending.

2.   Increased income causes increased consumption. When an individual receives an additional dollar of income, a fraction of that dollar is consumed and the remaining fraction is saved. The fraction of each additional dollar that is consumed is called the *marginal propensity to consume*, abbreviated to *MPC*.

Since saving is just the difference between income and consumptions ($S \equiv Y - C$), a given consumption function implies a specific saving function. Saving and consumption cannot be looked at independently.

In order to determine the equilibrium level of output, we set income equal to planned consumption, which is itself a function of income, plus planned investment. The equilibrium of the economy is found by solving for income as a function of the autonomous components of consumption and investment. We can write aggregate demand as $AD = C + cY + I$, or letting $A = C + I$, as $AD = \bar{A} + cY$. For the economy to be in equilibrium, GNP must equal aggregate demand, or $AD = Y$.

The equilibrium level of GNP can be found by using the graphic technique illustrated in Figure 3-1 (text Figure 3-3). The 45° line represents $AD = Y$, and the second line is the graph of $AD = \bar{A} + cY$. The intersection of the two lines gives the value of GNP.

Alternatively, and equivalently, equilibrium may be found by equating investment and savings ($I = S$). (Both methods of finding equilibrium will require some minor modification when the public and foreign sectors are put back in the model.)

3.   A dollar increase in autonomous spending does not in general increase GNP by a dollar. The original increase adds directly to aggregate demand and also induces further spending. If the marginal propensity to consume is c, then a dollar increase in autonomous spending brings a further increase of c. But this further increase itself induces yet a further increase—this increase causes yet another increase and so forth. When all the increases are added up, the total addition to GNP is given by the *multiplier*. The value of the multiplier is $1/(1 - c)$. The change in GNP as a result of the original change in autonomous spending is

$$\Delta Y = \frac{1}{1 - c} \Delta \bar{A}$$

4.   Reintroducing the government sector requires two major modifications to our model. First, government spending belongs in the adding-up identity for GNP. Second, consumption truly depends on disposable income. If the government uses an income tax, the multiplier is reduced to

$$\frac{1}{1 - c(1 - t)}$$

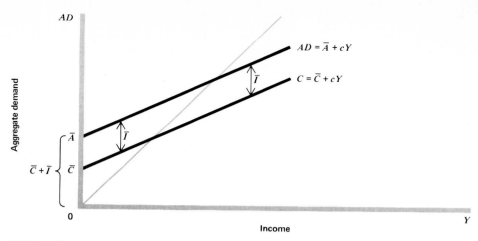

FIGURE 3-1

where the parameter t is the marginal income tax rate. As an example, if the MPC is 9/10 and the tax rate is 1/6, the multiplier will be 4. Because the multiplier is reduced, an income tax is called an *automatic stabilizer*. The multiplier for transfers is

$$\frac{c}{1 - c(1 - t)}.$$

5. The budget surplus is the difference between government income and government outgo. Symbolically, $BS = TA - G - TR$. The surplus responds to both exogenous changes in government expenditure and endogenous changes in tax collections due to changes in GNP.

6. The *full-employment budget surplus* measures what the surplus would be if the economy were at full employment, with current expenditure policy and current tax rates. The full-employment budget surplus responds to changes in government expenditure and in tax rates, but is immune to those changes in actual GNP that occur for other reasons, such as an increase in autonomous investment.

KEY TERMS

Aggregate demand

Equilibrium output

Unintended (undesired)
    inventory accumulation

Consumption function

Marginal propensity to consume

Marginal propensity to save

Multiplier

Planned aggregate demand

Automatic stabilizer

Budget surplus

Budget deficit

Balanced budget multiplier

Full-employment (high-
employment) surplus

GRAPH IT 3

For this Graph It, you are asked to use a graph to prove the following proposition: *For a given change in $\overline{A}$, a large marginal propensity to consume means a large change in GNP.* To prove this proposition requires a graph with five lines on it. We've provided the first three lines on Chart 3-1. You are asked to draw in the last two.

The first line we drew was the 45° line for $AD = Y$. Then we drew in the solid aggregate demand line for $AD = A_0 + cY$ and the dashed aggregate demand line for $AD = \overline{A}_1 + cY$, with $\overline{A}_1 > \overline{A}_0$. GNP is shown increasing from level E_0 to

CHART 3-1

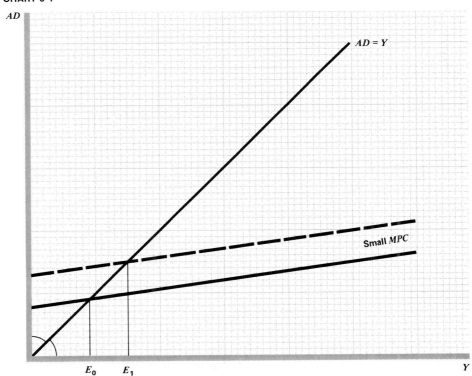

level E_1. Notice that both our aggregate demand lines were fairly shallow, indicating that the marginal propensity to consume is small.

Now you draw in a solid aggregate demand line that goes through point E_0 with a steep slope, indicating a large MPC. Then draw a dashed line parallel to your solid line, only moved higher by the same vertical distance as appears between the two lines we drew in. Mark the point where your dashed line hits the 45° line as E_2. You should be able to see that the distance from E_0 to E_2 is greater than the distance from E to E_1.

REVIEW OF TECHNIQUE 3

Solving Problems Backward

Most of the theories we develop tell us how a given change in an exogenous variable, such as government spending, will affect some endogenous variable, such as GNP. Sometimes it is necessary to reverse the question and ask what change in an exogenous variable would either cause or account for a given change in an endogenous variable.

Suppose you are asked to lower the government budget deficit by $100 by lowering government spending. Assume that the income tax rate is $33\frac{1}{3}$ percent and that the marginal propensity to consume is 0.9. Begin with the definition of the budget deficit.

Note: The symbol Δ (the Greek letter delta) is read "the change in."

$$BD = G - TA$$
$$\Delta BD = \Delta G - \Delta TA$$

ΔBD is -100, and ΔG is our final goal. We need to work backward to relate ΔTA to our final goal, ΔG. We know $TA = tY$. Since the tax rate t is constant, we can write $\Delta TA = \Delta tY = t\Delta Y$.

$$\Delta BD = \Delta G - t\Delta Y$$

Now we need to work backward from ΔY to ΔG. We can use the multiplier formula derived in the book for this purpose:

$$\Delta Y = \frac{1}{1 - c(1 - t)}\Delta G = \frac{1}{1 - 0.9(1 - \frac{1}{3})}\Delta G = 2.5\Delta G$$

Now substitute this into the formula for the change in the budget deficit:

$$\Delta BD = \Delta G - t \cdot 2.5\Delta G = \left(1 - \frac{2.5}{3}\right)\Delta G = \frac{1}{6}\Delta G$$

Thus, in this example, government spending must be decreased by $600.

In the questions that follow, we include a government sector but continue to omit the foreign sector.

FILL-IN QUESTIONS

1. When planned and actual spending are equal, the economy is in _____ _____.

2. The relation between consumption and income is called _____ _____.

3. A $10 increase in GNP induces an increase in consumption of $10 times the _____ (in the absence of an income tax).

4. The complement of the marginal propensity to consume is the _____ _____.

5. An initial increase in autonomous spending has an effect on GNP that is magnified by the _____.

6. The difference between government expenditure and taxes is the _____ _____.

7. An _____ is a program, such as the income tax, that reduces the impact of shocks to the economy without any direct government action.

8. The _____ is the difference between tax receipts at full employment and government expenditure.

9. The balanced budget multiplier equals _____.

10. In equilibrium, planned investment equals _____and _____.

TRUE-FALSE QUESTIONS

Assume that the autonomous components of spending remain constant except as specified.

T   F   1. Increasing transfers increases GNP.

T   F   2. Increasing the income tax rate increases GNP.

T   F   3. Increasing government purchases increases savings.

T   F   4. Increasing government purchases in the presence of a proportional income tax, increases the budget deficit.

T   F   5. Increased autonomous consumption, in the presence of an income tax, increases the full-employment budget surplus.

T   F   6. Increasing autonomous consumption increases savings.

T   F   7. An increase in the marginal propensity to consume reduces income.

T   F   8. In the absence of an income tax, an increase in government purchases, together with an equal decrease in transfers, will increase GNP by the amount of the increase in government purchases.

T F 9. In the presence of an income tax, an increase in government purchases, together with an equal decrease in transfers, will increase GNP by the amount of the increase in government purchases.

T F 10. The greater the marginal propensity to save, the greater the impact on GNP of a change in government purchases.

MULTIPLE-CHOICE QUESTIONS

1. If the marginal propensity to consume is 0.8, then, in the absence of an income tax, the multiplier is
   a. 1   c. 5
   b. 2   d. 10

2. If the *MPC* is 0.8, then, in the absence of an income tax, the multiplier relating changes in transfer payments to changes in national income is
   a. 4   c. 6
   b. 5   d. 8

3. In the presence of a *MPC* equal to 0.9 and a tax rate of 33⅓ percent, the multiplier is
   a. ½   c. 5
   b. 2½   d. 10

4. Using the same parameters as in question 3, a $30 increase in government spending leads to a change in the budget surplus of
   a. −$30   c. $5
   b. −$5   d. $30

5. Using the information in problem 4, the increase in the full-employment budget surplus is
   a. −$30   c. $25
   b. −$25   d. $30

6. If the *MPC* is 0.75, a $10 tax increase leads to a change in savings of
   a. −$30   c. $10
   b. −$10   d. $30

7. In equilibrium, investment equals
   a. private savings   c. the sum of a and b
   b. the budget surplus   d. neither a nor b

8. An increase in the income tax rate causes the full-employment budget surplus to
   a. increase   c. the answer depends on *t*
   b. decrease   d. the answer depends on *c*

9. In the presence of an income tax, the effect on GNP of equal and opposite changes in government purchases and transfers
    a. equals the change in government purchases
    b. depends on t
    c. depends on c
    d. depends on both t and c

10. Comparing the effect of government purchases on GNP in an economy with an income tax to the effect in an economy without an income tax, the effect in the former
    a. is greater   c. depends on MPC
    b. is less   d. cannot be determined

PROBLEMS

1. Government purchases and taxes are $500 and $400, respectively. Investment equals $200. The autonomous part of consumption is $100. The marginal propensity to consume is 0.9. What is the level of GNP?
2. The marginal propensity to consume is 0.9. The income tax is one-third of income. The government decides to increase spending in order to increase GNP by $750. How much should government spending increase? What happens to the budget deficit?
3. The MPC and the marginal income tax rate are 0.9 and one-third, respectively. The budget deficit is observed to increase by $15.
    a. What amount of change in investment would account for this?
    b. What amount of change in government purchases would account for this?

MONEY, INTEREST, AND INCOME

FOCUS OF THE CHAPTER

- *IS-LM* analysis is the core of modern macroeconomics.
- The simple model of Chapter 3 is extended to include the interaction of the money market with the goods market.
- The interest rate is now taken to be an endogenous variable.
- Our previous analysis of the goods market will lead to formation of the *IS* curve. We posit a simple *LM* curve, a relation expanded on in Chapters 10 and 11.

SECTION SUMMARIES

1. The *IS curve* represents equilibrium in the goods market. The *IS* curve shows all those combinations of income and interest such that the goods market is in balance. The formula for the *IS* curve is found by combining the consumption function and the investment function with the aggregate demand identity. We know from Chapter 3 that consumption depends on income. Chapter 9 shows that investment depends negatively on the interest rate. The simplest version of the *IS* curve is derived below.

$$Y \equiv C + I + G$$
$$C = \overline{C} + cY$$
$$I = \overline{I} - bi \quad [i \text{ is the interest rate}]$$
$$Y = \overline{C} + cY + \overline{I} - bi + G$$
$$Y = \frac{1}{1-c}(\overline{C} + \overline{I} + G) - \frac{b}{1-c}i = IS \text{ curve}$$

2. The *LM curve* represents equilibrium in the assets market. It shows all those combinations of income and interest such that the asset markets are in balance. The *LM* curve is the schedule which equates money supply and money demand. Money demand, which is studied in detail in Chapter 10, depends positively on income and negatively on the interest rate. Money supply is taken to be exogenous. In this chapter we also assume that prices are fixed. The *LM* curve is given by

$$\overline{M}/\overline{P} = kY - hi \quad (LM \text{ curve})$$
$\overline{M}/\overline{P}$ is the exogenously given real money supply

3. The *IS* and *LM* curves give us two independent relations between two endogenous variables, income and the interest rate. By solving the two equations simultaneously, the equilibrium levels of income and interest can be found. Figure 4-1 (text Figure 4-12) illustrates an *IS-LM* equilibrium. Figure 4-2 (text Figure 4-13) uses the *IS-LM* apparatus to show the effects of an increase in autonomous spending. Note that an expansion in autonomous demand,

FIGURE 4-1

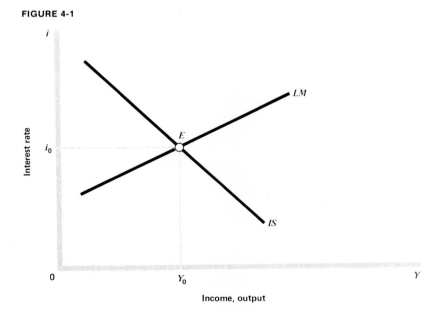

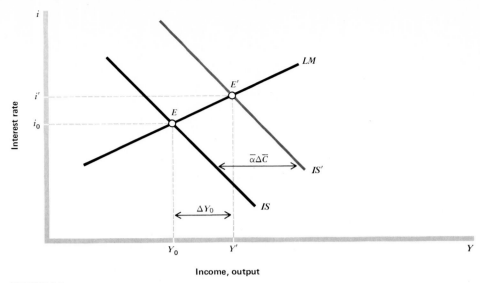

FIGURE 4-2

such as an increase in government purchases, increases both income and interest rates.

4.   At any point other than the intersection of the *IS* and *LM* curves, the economy is out of equilibrium. The economy moves toward equilibrium according to whether there is an excess supply or demand for money and an excess supply or demand for goods. It is often reasonable to assume adjustment in the money market is very fast, so that the adjustment path to equilibrium moves along the *LM* curve.

5.   When the Federal Reserve makes an *open market purchase*, it increases the money supply while reducing the outstanding supply of bonds. Notice that this operation reduces the interest rate but does not initially change private wealth. The lower interest rate induces increased investment, which means that GNP rises. The flatter the slope of the *IS* curve, the greater the impact of an increase of the money supply on GNP.

Figure 4-3 (text Figure 4-16) uses the *IS-LM* to show the effects of an increase in the money stock. Note that an expansion in the money stock increases income and decreases interest rates.

With a horizontal *LM* curve, called the *liquidity trap*, an increase in the money supply does not move the *LM* curve, and so income is unaffected. A vertical *LM* curve, called the *classical case* or quantity theory case, gives the maximum effect of an increase in the money supply.

6.   The 1979 policy switch provides a historical example of tight money. The Federal Reserve's tight money policy raised interest rates, lowering investment and GNP. In late 1980, the Fed drastically reversed directions.

Note the importance of lags between the change in interest rates and the drop in investment. Such lags can cause the Fed to miscalculate and increase the size of economic swings.

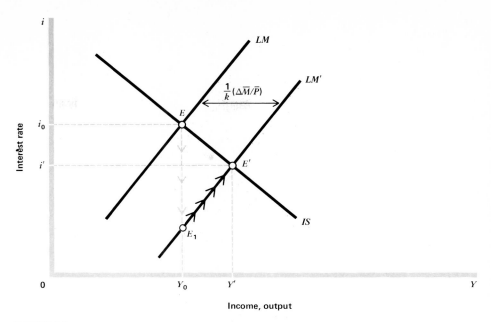

FIGURE 4-3

KEY TERMS

IS curve

LM curve

Bond

Money

Portfolio decisions

Real balances (real money balances)

Asset budget constraint
    (wealth constraint)

Open market operation

Transmission mechanism

Liquidity trap

Classical case

GRAPH IT 4

For this chapter's Graph It, we ask you to use graphs to demonstrate that an increase in the money stock generates a large increase in income if the *LM* curve is vertical (the *classical case*), a moderate increase in income if the *LM* curve has a moderate positive slope, and no change in income at all if the *LM* curve is horizontal (the *liquidity trap*). In Chart 4-1, we've provided three graphs, one under the other, with initial *IS* and *LM* curves filled in. On the middle graph, we've also drawn in a dashed line showing the *LM* curve moved a distance "Δ" to the right. Note the equilibrium moved from E_0 to E_2. Now you draw in new *LM* curves on the upper and lower graphs and show the new equilibria E_1 and E_3. You should find that the horizontal distance from E_0 to E_2 is less than the distance from E_0 to E_1 and greater than the distance from E_0 to E_3.

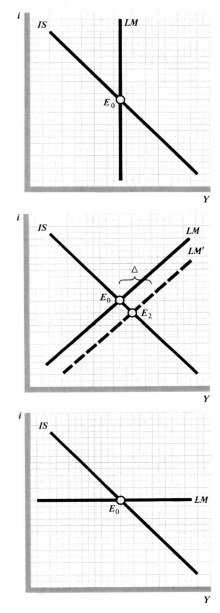

CHART 4-1

If you are out of practice in moving lines around on a graph, you might want to try the Review of Technique in this chapter and in the following chapter.

REVIEW OF TECHNIQUE 4

Graphing Equations

This Review gives you a chance to apply your talent at freehand sketching to drawing economic graphs. Solving economic questions by drawing graphs is often easier than finding an algebraic solution. This is especially true in three different cases: first, when a qualitative solution is sufficient, as opposed to a specific numerical answer; second, when we know the general relation of economic variables in an equation but don't have a specific formula; third, when nonlinear equations are involved. In this Review of Technique, we go over some useful "tricks" for graphing an equation. In Review of Technique 5, we use graphs to solve two simultaneous equations.

Suppose we have an equation such as

$$X = aY + bZ$$

X, Y, and Z are three economic variables. Both coefficients, a and b, are greater than zero. We graph the relation between two of the variables while treating the third as exogenous. In Figure 4-4, we show X as a function of Y. Since a is positive, X goes up when Y goes up; therefore, the line slopes upward from left to right.

The important fact we used was that X goes up with Y. Even if we have only a general functional form, we can draw a representative graph so long as we know the direction of the relation between X and Y. Figure 4-5 gives a representative graph for $X = f(Y, Z)$ using only the fact that X and Y are positively related.

Sometimes it is convenient to be able to draw the relation between two right-hand variables while treating the left-hand variable as exogenous. (We

FIGURE 4-4 $X = aY + bZ$ DRAWN FOR A FIXED VALUE OF Z

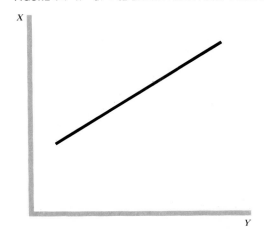

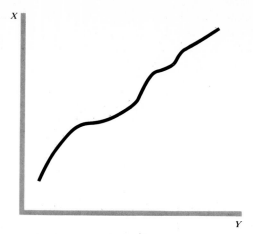

FIGURE 4-5 $X = f(Y, Z)$ DRAWN FOR A FIXED VALUE OF Z

do this when we draw the LM curve, for example.) Figures 4-6*a*, 6*b*, 6*c*, and 6*d* illustrate the four steps we use to decide whether the line should slope upward or downward.

a.   Pick any point that satisfies the equation.
b.   Draw an arrow representing an increase in the horizontal variable.

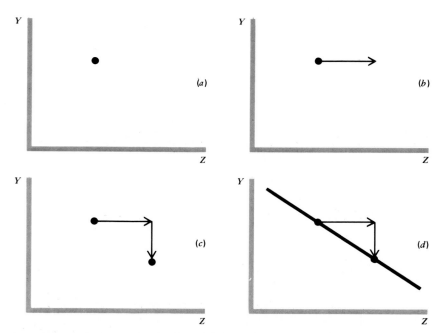

FIGURE 4-6   GRAPHING THE RELATION BETWEEN THE RIGHT-HAND SIDE VARIABLES WHILE HOLDING THE *LEFT*-HAND SIDE FIXED

c. Consider the point at the end of the arrow. The equation is out of balance at this point. Since b is positive, and since Z is higher than at the original point, the right-hand side must be too large. We ask the question: How must Y move in order to bring the right-hand side back into balance? Since a is positive, Y must decrease to bring the right-hand side back down to balance. Draw the arrow pointing down to show the decrease in Y.

d. Connect the original point to the end of the second arrow. In this case, the line slopes downward from left to right.

Frequently, we need to show how the graph shifts if the third variable changes. Suppose, in our example, that X increases. In which direction does the graph move? Figures 4-7a and 7b illustrate two different ways of figuring this out.

a. Pick any point on the original line. Since X is higher than before, we need to increase the right-hand side to return the equation to balance. This can be done by increasing Y. Draw a line above and parallel to the original line.

b. Alternatively, the right-hand side can be increased by increasing Z. Draw a line to the right and parallel to the original line.

Generally, the two methods are equivalent.

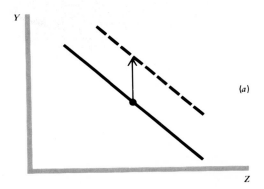

(a)

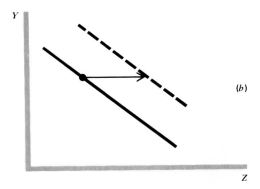

(b)

FIGURE 4-7 GRAPHING THE SHIFT OF A LINE

FILL-IN QUESTIONS

1. Both the *IS* curve and *LM* curve represent combinations of _____ _____ and the _____.

2. The *IS* curve represents equilibrium in the _____ market.

3. The *LM* curve represents equilibrium in the _____ market.

4. An _____ produces an increase in the money supply and an equal decrease in outstanding bonds.

5. The interest rate rises when there exists an excess _____ _____ money.

6. A flat region of the *LM* curve is known as the _____.

7. A vertical *LM* curve is called the _____.

8. The key sector of aggregate demand linking the money market and the goods market is _____.

9. The ratio of nominal money to the price level is called _____ _____.

10. The path leading from monetary policy to changes in GNP is called the _____.

TRUE-FALSE QUESTIONS

T F   1. Increased government spending moves the *IS* curve upward to the right.

T F   2. Increased money supply moves the *LM* curve downward to the right.

T F   3. For a given money supply, there is a positive relation between interest and income along the *LM* curve.

T F   4. For a given level of autonomous spending, there is a positive relation between interest and income along the *IS* curve.

T F   5. In the classical case, monetary policy has no effect on GNP.

T F   6. In the liquidity trap case, monetary policy has a large effect on GNP.

T F   7. Decreasing the money supply increases investment.

T F   8. Increasing government spending increases investment.

T F   9. Equal increases in government purchases or transfers have the same effect on the *IS* curve.

T F   10. Tax rates don't matter in the *IS-LM* model.

MULTIPLE-CHOICE QUESTIONS

1. Lower exogenous taxes lead to
   a. higher income
   b. higher interest
   c. both
   d. an increase in neither one

2. A lower money supply leads to
   a. higher income
   b. higher interest
   c. both
   d. an increase in neither one

3. An increase in the money supply increases
   a. interest rates
   b. investment
   c. both
   d. neither

4. An increase in government purchases increases
   a. interest rates
   b. investment
   c. both
   d. neither

5. The steeper the *LM* curve, the more an increase in the money stock
   a. increases GNP
   b. lowers interest rates
   c. both
   d. neither

6. Rapid adjustment in the money market means the economy is always on
   a. the *IS* curve
   b. the *LM* curve
   c. both
   d. neither

7. Expansionary fiscal policy tends to
   a. raise consumption
   b. lower investment
   c. both
   d. neither

8. A high *MPC* means a relatively
   a. steep *IS* curve
   b. flat *IS* curve
   c. steep *LM* curve
   d. flat *LM* curve

9. A high interest sensitivity of investment means a relatively
   a. steep *IS* curve
   b. flat *IS* curve
   c. steep *LM* curve
   d. flat *LM* curve

10. A high income tax rate means a relatively
    a. steep *IS* curve
    b. flat *IS* curve
    c. steep *LM* curve
    d. flat *LM* curve

PROBLEMS

1. The following equations describe the economy.

   $$C = 100 + .8Y \qquad \text{consumption}$$
   $$I = 200 - 1,000i \qquad \text{investment}$$
   $$L = Y - 10,000i \qquad \text{money demand}$$

   Initially, government purchases are $550 and taxes are $500. The real money supply equals $900.
   a. Derive the formulas for the *IS* curve and the *LM* curve.
   b. What are the initial levels of GNP, the interest rate, consumption, and investment?

Owing to a drop in investor confidence, the autonomous component of investment drops by $90.

c. By how much do income, the interest rate, and investment drop?

d. By how much should the money supply be changed in order to return GNP to its original level? What will the new interest rate be?

e. Draw three graphs to illustrate the equilibria in b, c, and d.

2. The following equations describe the economy.

$$C = 90 + 0.9Y \qquad \text{consumption}$$
$$I = 200 - 1{,}000i \qquad \text{investment}$$
$$L = Y - 10{,}000i \qquad \text{money demand}$$

There is a 33 percent proportional income tax. Government purchases equal $710. The real money supply is $500.

a. What are the initial values of investment and the budget deficit?

b. How large a change in the money supply would give the government a balanced budget?

5

FISCAL POLICY, CROWDING OUT, AND THE POLICY MIX

FOCUS OF THE CHAPTER

- The effectiveness of fiscal policy depends on the slopes of the *IS* and *LM* curves.
- The fiscal policy/monetary policy mix determines the composition of output as well as the overall size of aggregate demand.
- In the final section, we algebraically combine the *IS* and *LM* schedules to determine the equation for aggregate demand in terms of autonomous spending and the real money supply.

SECTION SUMMARIES

1. An increase in government spending increases GNP and the interest rate. The increased interest rate lowers investment. Thus, part of the increase in government spending is offset by a decrease in investment. This is called *crowding out*. In the quantity theory case, there is 100 percent crowding out; the increase in government spending is totally offset by a dropoff in investment, and so GNP does not increase at all. The flatter the *LM* schedule, the greater the increase in GNP. Thus fiscal policy has maximum power in the case of the liquidity trap and zero power in the quantity theory case.

Three rules summarize the effect of a fiscal expansion.

a. Income increases more, and interest rates increase less, the flatter the *LM* schedule.
b. Income increases more, and interest rates increase less, the flatter the *IS* schedule.
c. Income and interest rates increase more the larger the multiplier and thus the larger the horizontal shift of the *IS* schedule.

Will the large government budget deficits predicted for the 1980s crowd out investment? Not necessarily, since high budget deficits may be associated with higher income, and thus higher saving, rather than lower investment. In the real world the extent of crowding out depends on both the slope of the *LM* curve and the extent to which the Federal Reserve *accommodates* fiscal policy. The Federal Reserve accommodates fiscal policy when it increases the money supply (moves the *LM* curve right) to prevent interest rates from rising as the *IS* curve moves right.

2. Either fiscal or monetary policy can be used to expand aggregate demand. However, expansionary fiscal policy discourages investment, while expansionary monetary policy encourages investment. The choice of a policy mix, particularly between spending policy and tax policy, also depends on whether you favor a large government sector or a small one.

3. The 1964 tax cut combined expansionary fiscal policy with accommodating monetary policy. In 1968 and 1969, tight fiscal and monetary policy were used to contract the economy, but these steps failed to slow inflation. From 1979 to 1982, the Reagan administration used expansionary fiscal policy together with an extremely tight monetary policy. The tight monetary policy predominated, and the economy underwent the greatest contraction since the great depression of the 1930s. The inflation rate was reduced drastically.

The *real interest rate* is the *nominal interest rate* minus the inflation rate.

4. Since our *IS* and *LM* curves are both represented by linear equations, we can solve them together algebraically to find equilibrium income. The final equation for income in terms of all the exogenous variables is

$$Y = \frac{h\bar{\alpha}}{h + kb\bar{\alpha}} A + \frac{b\bar{\alpha}}{h + kb\bar{\alpha}} \frac{\bar{M}}{P}$$

For obvious reasons, the first fraction is called the *fiscal policy multiplier* and the second is called the *monetary policy multiplier,* $\bar{\alpha}$ is the multiplier from Chapter 3, $\frac{1}{1 - c}$ in the simplest model.

It is instructive to calculate the fiscal and monetary policy multipliers in the special cases of the liquidity trap and the classical case. The parameter h equals zero in the classical case, and so the fiscal policy multiplier equals zero and the monetary policy multiplier reaches its maximum value, $1/k$. In a liquidity trap, the parameter h approaches infinity, and so the fiscal policy multiplier approaches the simple multiplier α and the monetary policy multiplier goes to zero.

The final equation for the interest rate in terms of all the exogenous variables is

$$i = \frac{k\overline{\alpha}}{h + kb\overline{\alpha}} A - \frac{1}{h + kb\overline{\alpha}} \frac{\overline{M}}{P}$$

KEY TERMS

Crowding out

Monetary-fiscal policy mix

Monetary accommodation

Monetizing budget deficits

Composition of output

Investment subsidy

Monetary policy multiplier

Fiscal policy multiplier

Real interest rate

Nominal interest rate

GRAPH IT 5

Does tight monetary policy put people out of work? You might think that we could decide such a question just by graphing the unemployment rate against the real money stock. This would be a dangerous way to settle a scientific question because it ignores the influence of fiscal policy on unemployment. However, in recent years monetary policy seems to have been dominant, and so in this Graph It we are going to cast caution to the winds and graph the unemployment rate against the real money supply anyway.

TABLE 5-1

Year	Unemployment	M1	CPI	MIP
1972	5.60	252.00	125.30	2.01
1973	4.90	265.90	133.10	2.00
1974	——	——	——	——
1975	——	——	——	——
1976	——	——	——	——
1977	——	——	——	——
1978	——	——	——	——
1979	——	——	——	——
1980	——	——	——	——
1981	——	——	——	——
1982	——	——	——	——
1983	——	——	——	——
1984	——	——	——	——
1985	——	——	——	——

Source: Economic Report of the President, 1986.

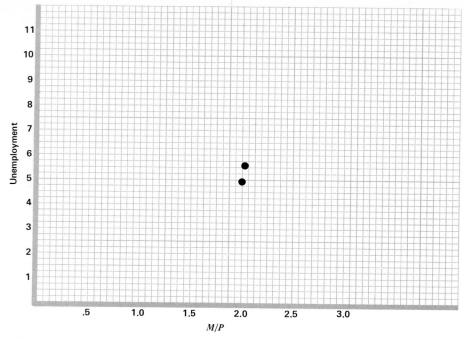

CHART 5-1

As a first step, you should collect data on the unemployment rate, $M1$, and the consumer price index for the years 1972 through 1985. Then calculate the real money supply by dividing $M1$ by the price level. Finally, plot unemployment against the real money supply on the graph provided. We've calculated the first two data points to get you started. What do you think? Will a big money supply reduce unemployment?

REVIEW OF TECHNIQUE 5

Graphic Solution of a Two-Equation Model

Many economic models can be reduced to a problem of two unknown variables described by two equations. *IS-LM* analysis and supply-and-demand analysis are the best known examples of such systems. In this Review of Technique, we use graphs to solve a two-equation model and then to show how the equilibrium of the system shifts when exogenous parameters shift.

Equations (5-1) and (5-2) are a pair of simultaneous equations. The unknown variables are X and Y. Q and Z are exogenous variables. The coefficients are all positive.

$$Y = a_1X + a_2Z \tag{5-1}$$
$$Y = -b_1X - b_2Z + b_3Q \tag{5-2}$$

Notice that these are totally made up equations. (We want you to work on technical tools for the moment and not use your economic intuition.) If you find algebraic coefficients such as "a" distracting, you can scratch them out and replace "a" with "7," "a_2" with "3," or whatever you like.

The two equations are graphed in Figure 5-1. The intersection of the two lines, the point (Y^*, X^*), is the one combination of X and Y that satisfies both equations.

We are frequently concerned with discovering how the solution to a system of equations is changed by a shift in one of the exogenous variables. Discovering the changes in income and the interest rate induced by an increase in government spending, which are predicted by the IS-LM model, is a typical example. We illustrate effects of increasing the exogenous variable Q in Figure 5-2. Equation (5-2) shifts upward to the right to the dashed line. At the new equilibrium (Y', X'), both X and Y are higher than at the original equilibrium. Notice that we are able to make very strong qualitative statements about the direction of change of the unknown variables even though we have very limited information about the two equations. In principle, we could find exact numerical solutions by drawing the graph with sufficient care. Practically speaking, we rarely do this. Graphs are used mainly for qualitative analysis.

If Z increases, both equations shift. As illustrated in Figure 5-3, Equation (5-1) shifts upward to the left and Equation (5-2) shifts downward to the left. (Go back to Review of Technique 4 if you are unsure why the motion is in the direction indicated.) Since both equations shift to the left, the equilibrium surely shifts to the left; in other words, X will be lower. On the other hand, since one equation shifts up and the other shifts down, the new intersection might be either above or below the original point. The change in Y might be either positive or negative. In order to know the change unambiguously, we would need to know the relative values of a_2 and b_2.

FIGURE 5-1

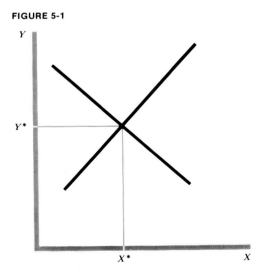

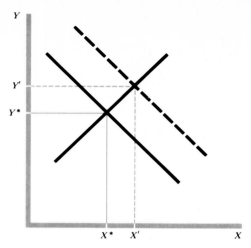

FIGURE 5-2 FINDING THE NEW INTERSECTION WHEN ONE RELATION SHIFTS.

The slope of Equation (5-1) determines how a shift in Equation (5-2) changes X and Y. A practical example of this is the question of how the slope of the IS curve determines the effectiveness of monetary policy. Figure 5-4 illustrates two different hypothetical versions of Equation (5-1). The dashed line represents a line with a higher value for a_1, and therefore a greater slope, than the original Equation (5-1). (Y^*, X^*) to (Y', X') is the change which would occur with the original value of a_1. The point (Y'', X'') illustrates the change caused by the hypothetically higher value of a_1. The higher slope of Equation (5-1') results in a larger shift in Y and a smaller shift in X.

FIGURE 5-3 FINDING THE NEW INTERSECTION WHEN BOTH RELATIONS SHIFT.

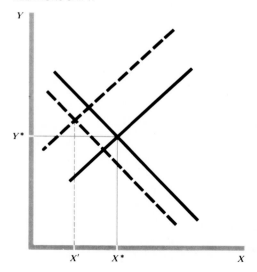

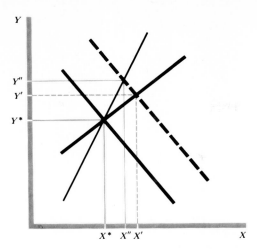

FIGURE 5-4 IMPACT OF A SHIFT IN ONE RELATION DEPENDS
ON THE SLOPE OF THE OTHER RELATION.

FILL-IN QUESTIONS

1. The increase in aggregate demand for a one dollar increase in the money
    stock is given by the _____.
2. The increase in aggregate demand for a one dollar increase in autonomous
    spending is given by the _____.
3. Because of _____, an increase in government pur-
    chases increases GNP by less than one might think after reading Chapter 3.
4. _____ provides a "good set of wheels" on which ex-
    pansionary fiscal policy can roll.
5. The choice of the proper _____ affects the division
    of aggregate demand between consumption and investment; that is, it af-
    fects the _____.

TRUE-FALSE QUESTIONS

T F 1. The effectiveness of monetary policy depends on the *LM* curve,
         not the *IS* curve.
T F 2. The effectiveness of fiscal policy depends on the *IS* curve, not the
         LM curve.
T F 3. In the liquidity trap, the demand for money responds a great
         deal to the interest rate.
T F 4. In the classical case, the demand for money does not respond
         at all to the interest rate.
T F 5. Expansionary monetary policy increases the budget deficit.

MULTIPLE-CHOICE QUESTIONS

1. Which of the following adminstrations employed restrictive fiscal policy.
   a. Kennedy-Johnson   c. Reagan
   b. Nixon   d. All of the above

2. The major postwar recession occurred in
   a. 1962–1963   c. 1973–1974
   b. 1968–1969   d. 1981–1982

3. A higher *MPC* increases
   a. the fiscal policy multiplier
   b. the monetary policy multiplier
   c. both
   d. neither one

4. A high interest sensitivity of investment increases
   a. the fiscal policy multiplier
   b. the monetary policy multiplier
   c. both
   d. neither one

5. A high interest sensitivity of money demand increases
   a. the fiscal policy multiplier
   b. the monetary policy multiplier
   c. both
   d. neither one

6. A high income sensitivity of money demand increases
   a. the fiscal policy multiplier
   b. the monetary policy multiplier
   c. both
   d. neither one

7. A high income tax rate decreases
   a. the fiscal policy multiplier
   b. the monetary policy multiplier
   c. both
   d. neither one

8. According to the model in this chapter, a balanced budget increase in taxes and spending generally increases **GNP**
   a. not at all
   b. by less than the amount of the increase
   c. by exactly the amount of the increase
   d. by more than the amount of the increase

9. Increased transfer payments increase
   a. the interest rate
   b. the budget surplus
   c. both
   d. neither one

10. Expansionary fiscal policy together with tight monetary policy produces
    a. high GNP—interest rates might go up or down
    b. low GNP—interest rates might go up or down
    c. high interest rates—GNP might go up or down
    d. low interest rates—GNP might go up or down

PROBLEMS

1. Find the transfer policy multiplier in terms of h, b, etc., assuming that
   a. transfers are not taxed.
   b. transfers are taxed, like all other income, at the rate t.

2. Suppose that government purchases rise 1 billion dollars while transfers fall 1 billion dollars. (Assume that transfers are not taxed directly, but that there is an income tax at rate t on all income.)
   a. What happens to GNP?
   b. What happens to the budget surplus?

3. In 1985, the interest rate on treasury bills was 7.48 percent. The consumer price index rose from 315.5 in December 1984 to 327.4 in December 1985.
   a. What was the inflation rate over 1985?
   b. What was the real interest rate?

6

INTERNATIONAL LINKAGES

FOCUS OF THE CHAPTER

- All countries engage in international trade, exporting some goods to foreign countries and importing other goods from abroad. Most countries also engage in international finance, borrowing or lending from other nations. A country that engages in international trade or finance is said to have an open economy.

- The U.S. economy is linked to other nations by the exchange rate, the value of other currencies relative to the U.S. dollar. When the value of other currencies is relatively high, the United States exports more and imports less. The U.S. economy is also linked to other nations by the relative level of domestic and foreign interest rates. When U.S. interest rates are relatively high, foreigners invest capital in the United States.

- We extend the *IS-LM* framework to include the effects of international trade. We also add a new consideration, the position of the balance of payments surplus or deficit.

- Exchange rates may be either fixed (set by central bank intervention) or floating (determined in the marketplace). Capital may be mobile (easily moved to the country with the highest interest rate) or relatively immobile. The effect of fiscal and monetary policy in an open economy varies considerably according to these two factors.

SECTION SUMMARIES

1. The *balance of payments* measures the difference between total payments leaving the country and total payments entering the country. The two principal parts of the balance are the *current account* and the *capital account*. The current account is made up of *trade balance*, the difference between exported goods and imported goods, plus net exports of services and net transfers abroad. The *capital account* is the difference between U.S. investment abroad and foreign investment in the United States, including both real and financial investment. Throughout most of the 1960s, our current account was in surplus, though this reversed itself dramatically by the early 1980s. The U.S. capital account ran a large deficit until the 1980s, when it moved to a surplus.

Foreigners usually want to be paid in their own currency, not dollars. When our balance of payments is in deficit, more dollars leave the country than return, and so the Fed and foreign central banks must turn these excess dollars into foreign currency. These *official reserve transactions* must just match the overall balance of payments deficit.

The exchange rate is the price of one currency in terms of another. If there are four deutschmarks (DM) per dollar, we say the German exchange rate is 0.25, or that each deutschmark is worth 25 cents. Under a *fixed exchange rate* regime, the central banks *intervene* in market to peg the prices of different currencies. The German central bank can buy or sell any amount of deutschmarks at 25 cents each. If a country is in persistent deficit, it may run out of the reserves needed to keep buying up its own currency. In this case, the bank must either borrow reserves from other central banks or lower the value of its currency.

Under *flexible exchange rates*, the prices of different currencies are decided by the laws of supply and demand. The price of deutschmarks changes continually in the same manner as the price of stocks on the stock exchange. Under fixed exchange rates, countries usually keep the value of their currency constant for a number of years. In a *clean floating* system, the central banks allow supply and demand to operate without interference. In practice, the world operates on a system of *managed* or *dirty floating*, in which central banks intervene in a limited way.

The exchange rate can be defined either as the value of foreign currency in terms of American dollars or as the value of American dollars in foreign currency. The text, as a matter of convention, always uses the former, and so the German-American exchange rate is, for example, $0.40 per DM. A *depreciation* of the exchange rate means that the dollar becomes worth less, and so the exchange rate rises, for example, from $0.40 to $0.60. An *appreciation* of the dollar means that the exchange rate falls. *Devaluation* (*revaluation*) refers to a depreciation (appreciation) deliberately brought about by the government under a fixed exchange rate system.

2. A bilateral exchange rate measures the price of a foreign country's currency in terms of the dollar. The effective or multilateral exchange rate measures the price of a representative basket of foreign currencies, the price being stated in "units of foreign currency per dollar." Each currency receives

a weight which reflects its importance to the United States in international trade.

The real exchange rate measures the prices of goods produced in a foreign country relative to the prices of those same goods produced at home. The real exchange rate is given by the expression

$$R = \frac{e \cdot P_f}{P}$$

where R is the real exchange rate, e is the currency exchange rate, and P_f and P are the foreign and domestic price levels.

3.   We return now to our *IS-LM* model and *add back in* net exports NX. We differentiate between spending by domestic residents and total spending on domestic goods.

$$\text{Spending by domestic residents} \equiv A \equiv C + I + G$$
$$\text{Spending on domestic goods} \equiv Y \equiv A + NX$$
$$\equiv (C + I + G) + NX$$

At first glance, it may appear that purchases of imported goods are omitted from spending by domestic residents. Remember that all purchases are already counted in consumption and the other sectors of aggregate demand.

We use X and Q to represent exports and imports, respectively. Exports depend positively on foreign income, Y_f, and positively on the real exchange rate, R. Imports depend positively on domestic income, Y, and negatively on the real exchange rate. The text defines functions $A(\ )$, $Q(\ )$, $X(\ )$, and $NX(\ )$.

$$A = A(Y, i)$$
$$NX = X(Y_f, R) - R \cdot Q(Y, R)$$
$$NX = NX(Y, Y_f, R)$$

We can combine these to find goods market equilibrium, the *IS* curve.

$$Y = A(Y, i) + NX(Y, Y_f, R)$$

This *IS* curve can be combined with the *LM* curve of Chapter 4 to find overall equilibrium. Once we know equilibrium GNP, we can compare exports and imports to find the overall trade surplus. Figure 6-1 (text Figure 6-3) shows the equilibrium of the economy at point E and also the level of GNP at which $NX = 0$. Since point E is shown to the left of the $NX = 0$ line, the economy has a trade surplus.

We can use this extended *IS-LM* diagram to explore the impact of several economic changes on GNP and the trade balance. Consider an increase in autonomous spending on domestic goods, for example, the use of expansionary fiscal policy. This moves the *IS* curve as shown in Figure 6-2, (text Figure 6-4), increasing GNP and reducing the trade surplus.

Consider now an increase in exports. As shown in Figure 6-3 (text Figure

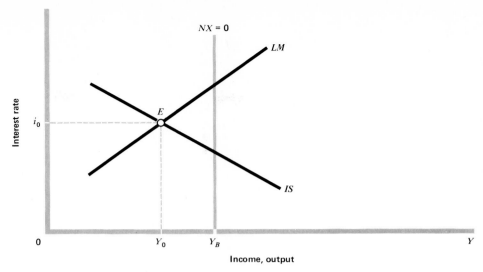

FIGURE 6-1 GOODS AND MONEY MARKET
EQUILIBRIUM.

6-5), this moves the *IS* curve to *IS'* and also moves the $NX = 0$ line right, since it now requires more imports (and therefore higher income) to have balanced trade. GNP increases. The trade surplus also improves as shown.

Just as our model of the U.S. economy depends on our exports to Germany, so too the state of the German economy depends on our imports from Germany. Thus all nations are interdependent. If U.S. income rises, we import more from Germany. This leads to an expansion of German GNP, leading to more purchases of American goods by Germany and a further increase in American GNP. This is called the *repercussion effect*.

FIGURE 6-2 THE EFFECTS OF AN INCREASE IN
DOMESTIC SPENDING.

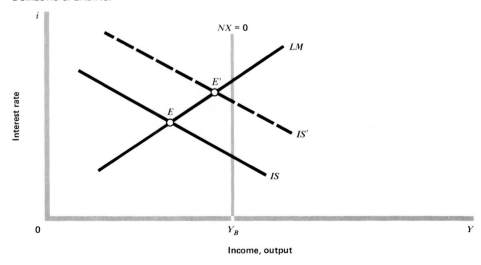

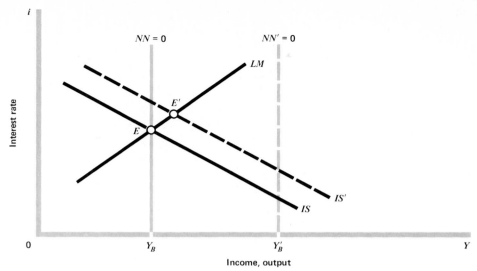

FIGURE 6-3 THE EFFECTS OF AN INCREASE IN EXPORTS.

4. Policy makers need to watch both internal balance, keeping the economy close to full employment, and external balance, keeping the balance of payments close to even.

Interest rates, adjusted for exchange rate risk, tend to be equalized across countries with well-developed capital markets. Investors move money out of low-interest-rate countries into high-interest-rate countries until rates are brought into line. Changes in the interest rate induce capital flows so that a policy that creates current account balance may be associated with capital account imbalance. When the interest rate in the United States is increased above comparable world rates, capital flows into America.

In the short run, by using both fiscal and monetary policy, we can choose both a level of GNP and a rate of interest. By choosing the appropriate rate of interest, we can have a capital account surplus that just offsets a current account deficit. Under fixed exchange rates, we should expand income through fiscal policy whenever there is unemployment and use tight monetary policy whenever there is a balance of payments deficit. In addition to the problems of fiscal and monetary policy discussed in Chapter 12, a country is not indifferent to the makeup of the balance of payments. After all, if you run a large permanent capital account surplus, eventually someone else owns your country.

5. When capital is perfectly mobile, domestic and foreign assets are perfect substitutes. Consequently, interest rate differentials between domestic and foreign assets cannot persist. Were yields on similar assets different from one another, investors would shift all of their investments to the asset with the highest yield.

When exchange rates are fixed, a country cannot pursue an independent monetary policy. If the domestic interest rate were above the world interest rate, investors would move their investment into domestic assets. In order to buy domestic assets, foreigners must exchange their own currencies for dollars. Central banks, including the Federal Reserve, are required to supply the dollars to meet the demands of these investors at the established exchange rates. The final result is that the influx of dollars into the domestic economy increases the domestic money supply and shifts the *LM* curve outward.

An understanding of the interaction between perfect capital mobility and a worldwide regime of fixed exchange rates leads us to conclude that fiscal policy can be used to increase domestic GNP, but that monetary policy is completely ineffective.

6. The Mundell-Fleming model is a tool for evaluating the relative effectiveness of domestic fiscal and monetary policy when capital is perfectly mobile and exchange rates are flexible.

Flexible exchange rates imply that the balance of payments must be zero. Perfect capital mobility implies that the domestic interest rate must equal the world interest rate.

A disturbance in the goods market, such as an increase in foreign demand for domestic goods, shifts the *IS* curve outward, as in Figure 6-4 (text Figure 6-9). Consideration of the domestic goods market alone would suggest that E' is the equilibrium. But at E' i exceeds i_f so that investors wish to increase their holdings of domestic assets. The increased demand for dollars raises the exchange rate (the price of dollars) and the relative price of domestic goods rises. The *IS* shifts leftward as the foreign demand for domestic goods falls and as the domestic demand for imports rises.

An increase in the domestic money stock (Figure 6-5, text Figure 6-10), on the other hand, will have powerful effects on domestic income. As the *LM* shifts to the right, the domestic interest rate falls below the world interest rate, capital flows out, and the dollar depreciates. Domestic goods become cheaper to

FIGURE 6-4 THE EFFECTS OF AN INCREASE IN THE FOREIGN DEMAND FOR DOMESTIC GOODS WHEN THE EXCHANGE RATE IS FLEXIBLE AND CAPITAL IS PERFECTLY MOBILE.

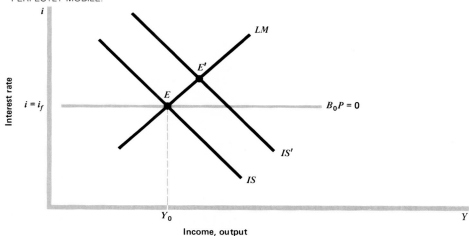

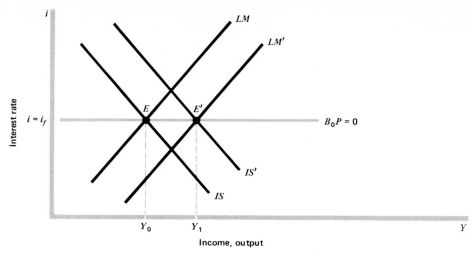

FIGURE 6-5   THE EFFECTS OF AN INCREASE IN THE
MONEY STOCK WHEN EXCHANGE RATES ARE
FLEXIBLE AND CAPITAL IS PERFECTLY MOBILE.

foreigners and imports become more expensive at home. Net exports rise,
which shifts the *IS* rightward. The economy ends up at E'.

On occasion, an individual country will engage in a beggar-thy-neighbor
policy of depreciating its currency. The domestic balance of payments will improve at the expense of the country's trading partners. Trading partners may
counter the home country's depreciation with a competitive depreciation of
their own.

KEY TERMS

Exchange rate	Real exchange rate
Current account	Depreciation
Capital account	Appreciation
Balance of payments	Repercussion effects
Fixed exchange rate	Capital mobility
Floating exchange rate	Internal and external balance
Intervention	Mundell-Fleming model
Dirty floating	Beggar-thy-neighbor policy

GRAPH IT 6

Does an increase in the exchange rate really cut exports? *By how much?* In this
Graph It, we ask you to prepare a graph with exports on the vertical axis and
the value of the U.S. dollar ($1/e$ in the textbook's terms) on the horizontal axis.

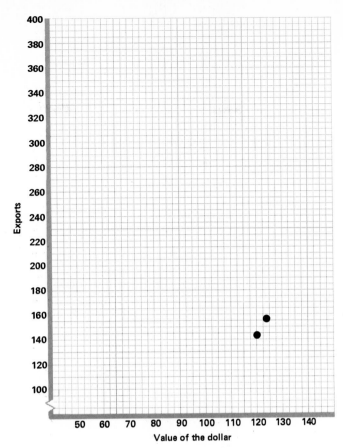

CHART 6-1

TABLE 6-1

Year	Real exports	Value of the dollar
1967	143.6	120.0
1968	155.7	122.1
1969	165.0	122.4
1970	178.3	121.1
1971	179.2	117.8
1972	195.2	109.1
1973	242.3	99.1
1974	269.1	101.4
1975	259.7	98.5
1976	274.4	105.6
1977	281.6	103.3
1978	312.6	92.4
1979	356.8	88.1

REVIEW OF TECHNIQUE 6

Solving Two Equations Algebraically

Some students find that a little algebra adds precision to economic arguments . . . and then some students find that it doesn't help at all. The text uses very little algebra, though there are spots such as the end of Chapter 5 where algebra comes in handy. This review provides some algebra practice for those who want it.

In the Review of Technique 5, we solved a system of two equations in two unknowns by using a graph. Now we will solve the same system algebraically. The equations are:

$$Y = a_1X + a_2Z$$
$$Y = -b_1X - b_2Z + b_3Q$$

Since the equations come in a form with the same variable on the left-hand side, the simplest method is to set one equation equal to the other.

$$a_1X + a_2Z = -b_1X - b_2Z + b_3Q$$

Equation (6-1) gives the final formula for X in terms of the exogenous variables.

$$X = -\frac{a_2 + b_2}{a_1 + b_1}Z + \frac{b_3}{a_1 + b_1}Q \tag{6-1}$$

We find the final equation for Y by substituting the value for X above into either of the original equations and collecting common terms.

$$Y = -b_1\left[-\frac{a_2 + b_2}{a_1 + b_1}Z + \frac{b_3}{a_1 + b_1}Q\right] - b_2Z + b_3Q$$
$$Y = \left[\frac{b_1(a_2 + b_2)}{a_1 + b_1} - b_2\right]Z + \left[\frac{-b_1b_3}{a_1 + b_1} + b_3\right]Q$$
$$Y = \frac{b_1a_2 - a_1b_2}{a_1 + b_1}Z + \frac{a_1b_3}{a_1 + b_1}Q \tag{6-2}$$

We can use Equations (6-1) and (6-2) to answer the same questions about changes in Q or Z as we did in the Review of Technique 5. If Q increases, then both X and Y increase, since the coefficient on each is positive. If Z increases, X definitely falls, since the coefficient in Equation (6-1) is negative. On the other hand, Y might either rise or fall, as $(b_1a_2 - a_2b_1)$ might be either positive or negative. These answers are the same as those obtained from the graphical analysis. Of course, if we had exact values for each coefficient, we could make precise calculations for X and Y.

FILL-IN QUESTIONS

1. The hypothesis that people plan consumption based on their wealth and all future income is called the _____ theory.

2. Estimates of long-term consumption opportunities based on previous and current income are called _____ income.

3. The hypothesis that current consumption depends on peak income is called the _____ theory.

4. Using up wealth to provide for consumption is called _____ _____.

5. The long-run average propensity to consume is about _____ _____.

6. The long-run marginal propensity to consume is about _____ _____.

7. The immediate response of GNP to a change in autonomous aggregate demand depends on the _____ multiplier.

8. The eventual response of GNP to a change in autonomous aggregate demand depends on the _____ multiplier.

9. The marginal propensity to consume depends on the number of _____ _____ years compared with the number of _____ _____ years.

10. When exchange rates are fixed and capital is perfectly mobile, the money supply is _____ .

11. When capital is perfectly mobile and exchange rates are fully flexible, the _____ always balances.

TRUE-FALSE QUESTIONS

T   F   1. Expansionary fiscal policy increases the trade surplus.

T   F   2. Expansionary monetary policy increases the capital account surplus.

T   F   3. Devaluation improves the trade balance.

T   F   4. Devaluation increases GNP.

T   F   5. Devaluation increases the domestic cost of living.

T   F   6. An increase in U.S. GNP generates a drop in German GNP.

T   F   7. An increase in U.S. interest rates leads to an increase in German interest rates.

T   F   8. The central bank can meet a temporary balance of payments deficit through using up reserves of foreign currency and gold.

T   F   9. The central bank can meet a permanent balance of payment deficit through using up reserves of foreign currency and gold.

1. High U.S. GNP leads to
   a. high U.S. exports
   b. high U.S. imports
   c. both high exports and imports
   d. neither one

2. High German GNP leads to
   a. high U.S. exports   c. both
   b. high U.S. imports   d. neither one

3. Contractionary fiscal policy increases
   a. the current account surplus
   b. the capital account surplus
   c. both types of surplus
   d. neither type of surplus

4. Contractionary monetary policy increases
   a. the current account surplus
   b. the capital account surplus
   c. both types of surplus
   d. neither type of surplus

5. Beginning with an increase in autonomous U.S. spending, the repercussion effect through the German economy
   a. leads to a further increase in U.S. GNP
   b. leads to a further decrease in GNP
   c. produces no further changes in U.S. GNP
   d. completely offsets the initial change in U.S. GNP

6. If the deutschmark is initially worth 25 cents and Germany revalues her currency by 50 percent, the German exchange rate
   a. rises
   b. falls
   c. remains unchanged
   d. cannot be determined from the information given

7. In an open economy, the simple multiplier is _____ in a closed economy.
   a. larger than that   c. no different from that
   b. smaller than that   d. any of a, b, or c

8. Combined expansionary fiscal and monetary policy, used so as to keep the interest rate constant, causes the current account surplus to
   a. increase   c. decrease
   b. remain unchanged   d. do any of a, b, or c

9. Combined expansionary fiscal and monetary policy, used so as to keep the interest rate constant, causes the capital account surplus to
   a. increase
   b. remain unchanged
   c. decrease
   d. do any of a, b, or c

10. An increase in foreign income when capital is perfectly mobile and exchange rates are fixed causes
    a. domestic output to rise
    b. foreign income to rise again
    c. a only
    d. both a and b

PROBLEMS

1. Initially, the deutschmark is worth 25 cents. Suppose the dollar is devalued by 50 percent and then by an additional 20 percent. What is the new exchange rate?

2. The domestic import schedule is given by $Q = R \cdot (a \cdot R + b \cdot Y)$, where a and b are constants. If an increase in R is to reduce Q in a fixed exchange rates world, what is the sign of a?

3. The marginal propensity to consume is 0.9, investment and exports are autonomous, and imports are as described below. What is the multiplier on government spending?

$$Q = \bar{Q} + 0.1Y \text{ (American imports)}$$

4. Suppose the American economy is as described in problem 2, and that the German economy has an MPC of 0.8, investment is purely autonomous, and German imports are as given below. Further assume that all trade between Germany and the United States is bilateral. What is the multiplier of U.S. government spending on U.S. GNP? What is the multiplier of U.S. government spending on German GNP?

$$Q_G = \bar{Q}_G + 0.2Y_G \text{ (German imports)}$$

5. With perfect capital mobility and fixed exchange rates, how will the domestic economy be affected by an increase in government spending and an increase in the money stock so as to maintain interest rates constant?

6. When capital is perfectly mobile and exchange rates are perfectly flexible, by what mechanism does an increase in the money stock raise GNP?

7

AGGREGATE SUPPLY AND DEMAND: AN INTRODUCTION

FOCUS OF THE CHAPTER

- *Aggregate supply* and *aggregate demand* each give a relationship between the overall price level and output. Together, the aggregate supply and demand schedules determine GNP and the price level.
- The aggregate supply schedule describes how much output firms are willing to supply at a given price level.
- The aggregate demand schedule summarizes the *IS-LM* equilibrium of Chapters 4 and 5, with the *LM* curve repositioned for changing price levels.
- Aggregate supply and demand schedules are not related to the ordinary supply and demand schedules of microeconomics, though they look alike.

SECTION SUMMARIES

1.   The slope of the aggregate supply schedule splits movements of the aggregate demand schedule into changes in prices and changes in output. If the aggregate supply schedule is steep, as in Figure 7-1a (text Figure 7-3), then an increase in aggregate demand mostly increases prices and leaves GNP relatively unchanged. If the aggregate supply schedule is relatively flat, as in Fig-

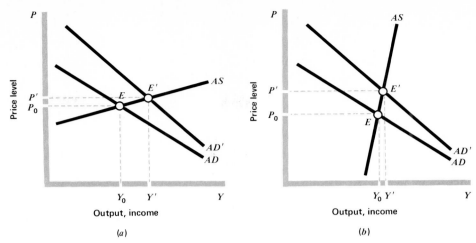

FIGURE 7-1

ure 7-1*b*, then an increase in aggregate demand mostly increases GNP and leaves prices relatively unchanged.

2. The two special cases of aggregate supply are the *Keynesian case*, a perfectly horizontal aggregate supply curve, and the *classical case*, a perfectly vertical aggregate supply curve.

3. The aggregate demand curve summarizes the *IS-LM* model for given fiscal and monetary policy, but changing price levels. At a high price level, the real money supply is low, and so aggregate demand is low. Thus the aggregate demand curve slopes downward. The slope of the aggregate demand curve is determined by the *monetary policy multiplier* of Chapter 5. If the monetary policy multiplier is large, then the aggregate demand curve is relatively flat, and vice versa. Expansionary fiscal or monetary policy shifts the *IS-LM* equilibrium out at a given price level and thus shifts the aggregate demand curve to the right.

4. With a Keynesian-case aggregate supply curve, prices are constant, and the conclusions of the first five chapters of the text hold without modification. With a classical aggregate supply curve, prices rise when aggregate demand increases. In the case of expansionary fiscal policy, there is full crowding out and interest rates rise so much that investment falls by an amount equal to the increase in government spending. With expansionary monetary policy, the price level rises in proportion to the increase in the money supply, and so the real money supply and GNP are unchanged.

5. The *quantity theory* emphasizes the idea that changes in the money supply are responsible for most changes in the price level. Money is said to be *neutral* if an increase in money increases prices but leaves all real variables— GNP, unemployment, and the interest rate—unchanged. The pure quantity theory is equivalent to the notion that the velocity of money is constant and that real GNP is unaffected by changes in money—neither of which is true. Modern quantity theorists believe that the aggregate supply curve is vertical in the long

run, but sloped in the short run. Thus the money supply will affect GNP in the short run but not in the long run.

6. The classical theory of aggregate supply is refuted by the facts. Output is not always at its full employment level, and changes in the money supply are associated with changes in GNP (at least in the short run).

Modern Keynesians seek explanations for why the aggregate supply curve might be relatively flat in the short run and, thus, why changes in fiscal and monetary policy might be associated with short-run changes in GNP. Explanations include long-term contracts, problems in coordinating price changes to respond to fluctuations in aggregate demand, and efficiency wages.

The imperfect information–market clearing theory of aggregate supply is based on the assumptions that markets always clear but that an individual seller cannot always determine whether or not a change in the seller's price is a change *relative* to the general price level, or simply a change in the general price level alone. The perception that the price change is a change in relative prices will lead the seller to alter supply. If the change turns out to be a movement in the general price level, the seller will only alter supply temporarily.

Real business cycle theory argues that real disturbances are the driving force behind business cycles. Real shocks mainly occur on the supply side.

KEY TERMS

Aggregate supply curve

Aggregate demand curve

Keynesian aggregate supply curve

Classical aggregate supply curve

Full crowding out

Quantity theory of money

Neutrality of money

Monetarism

GRAPH IT 7

The aggregate schedule represents the solutions of the *IS-LM* system at different price levels. Chart 7-1 shows an *IS-LM* diagram drawn above an aggregate demand diagram. We've drawn on an *IS* curve and an *LM* curve based on a price level P_0. The equilibrium income is E_0. We've marked off this same income level on the aggregate demand diagram at price P_0. This gives us one point on the aggregate demand schedule. Now you draw in two new *LM* curves, one based on $P_1 < P_0$ and another based on $P_2 > P_0$. Mark the points E_1 and E_2 and drop vertical lines to mark the points on the aggregate demand diagram. Connect the three points on the aggregate demand diagram and mark the line *AD*.

REVIEW OF TECHNIQUE 7

Logarithms

Logarithms turn out to be extremely useful for "back-of-the-envelope" economic calculations. Logarithms are intimately related to the calculation of percentage changes. The formal, and not very important, definition of logarithm is that

$$X = \log Y$$

if and only if

$$Y = e^x$$

where e is an irrational number (pi is another irrational number) approximately equal to 2.71828. (Technically, this is a natural logarithm, as distinguished from logarithms based on numbers other than e.) Before the days of calculators, tables of logarithms were used to speed calculations.

If you look up the logarithm of 100 and 110 in a table, or press the appropriate buttons on your calculator, you will find log $100 = 4.605$, log $101 = 4.615$, and log $110 = 4.700$. Notice that the log 101 minus log 100 is approximately 1 percent (more precisely, .00995). The log of 110 minus log 100 is about 10 percent (more precisely, .0953). As you can see, *the change in the logarithm of a variable approximately equals the percentage change in the variable itself.* Several useful points to remember about logarithms are:

$$\log (X \cdot Y) = \log X + \log Y$$
$$\log (X/Y) = \log X - \log Y$$
$$\log (X^Y) = Y \cdot \log X$$
$$\log (1 + x) \approx x \text{ for very small } x$$
$$(\approx \text{ means "approximately equal to")}$$

Today, logarithms are no longer needed to speed calculation. However, knowing the facts above allows us to solve many problems by inspection, never actually calculating a logarithm. See Review of Technique 13 for a very useful example of this.

FILL-IN QUESTIONS

1. The aggregate demand function depends on _____.
2. It also depends on _____.
3. The aggregate demand function represents those combinations of income and price level found through _____ analysis.
4. The displacement of investment by government spending is called _____.

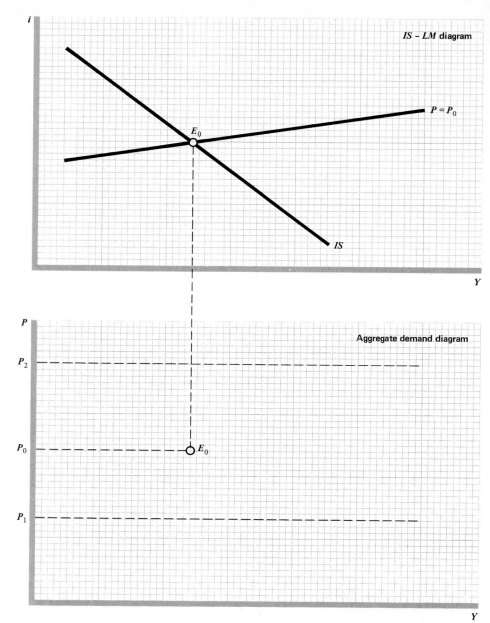

CHART 7-1

5. The proposition that proportional changes in the nominal money supply and the price level have no real effect is referred to as _____.

6. The relation between output and prices that summarizes the economy's ability to produce goods and services is the _____ schedule.

7. The relation between output and prices that summarizes the various possible *IS-LM* equilibria is the _____ schedule.

8. In the Keynesian model, the aggregate supply curve is _____.

9. In the classical model, the aggregate supply curve is _____.

TRUE-FALSE QUESTIONS

T F 1. Movements up and left along the aggregate demand schedule correspond to decreasing interest rates in the *IS-LM* equilibrium.

T F 2. A flat aggregate demand schedule results from a low *MPC*.

T F 3. A flat aggregate demand schedule results from a low interest sensitivity of money demand.

T F 4. A flat aggregate demand schedule results from a low interest sensitivity of investment.

T F 5. Aggregate demand (*AD*) is increased by increased government spending.

T F 6. Combinations of *IS* and *LM* curves can be used to trace out the aggregate supply curve.

T F 7. Increased government spending increases interest rates if the aggregate supply curve is Keynesian.

T F 8. Increased government spending increases interest rates if the aggregate supply curve is classical.

T F 9. Increased nominal money supply decreases interest rates if the aggregate supply curve is Keynesian.

T F 10. Increased nominal money supply decreases interest rates if the aggregate supply curve is classical.

MULTIPLE-CHOICE QUESTIONS

The price level is held constant in questions 1, 2, and 3.

1. Increasing the money supply
   a. increases aggregate supply
   b. decreases aggregate supply
   c. increases aggregate demand
   d. decreases aggregate demand

2. Increasing government spending
   a. increases aggregate supply
   b. decreases aggregate supply
   c. increases aggregate demand
   d. decreases aggregate demand

3. There is a positive relation between GNP and the price level along
   a. the aggregate demand curve
   b. the aggregate supply curve
   c. both these curves
   d. neither of these curves

4. There is a negative relation between GNP and the price level along
   a. the aggregate demand curve
   b. the aggregate supply curve
   c. both these curves
   d. neither of these curves

5. There is a negative relation between GNP and the interest rate along
   a. the aggregate demand curve
   b. the aggregate supply curve
   c. both these curves
   d. neither of these curves

6. A high marginal propensity to save implies
   a. that the aggregate supply curve is relatively flat
   b. that it is relatively steep
   c. that it is relatively flat only if *MPS* is greater than ½
   d. nothing about aggregate supply

7. If the nominal money supply doubles, eventually the price level will
   a. remain unchanged
   b. double
   c. increase by a factor of less than 2
   d. increase by a factor of more than 2

8. If autonomous spending doubles, eventually the price level
   a. will remain unchanged
   b. will double
   c. will more than double
   d. cannot be determined without more information

9. An increase in the nominal money supply will cause investment to increase in
   a. the long run
   b. the short run
   c. both the short and the long run
   d. neither one

10. An increase in government spending will cause investment to decrease in
    a. the long run   c. both the short and the long run
    b. the short run   d. neither one

PROBLEMS

Use the following equations for each of the questions below:

$$Y = 2A + 4(M_{-1}/P_{-1})$$ aggregate demand
$$P = P_{-1}[1 - .8(1 - (Y/Y_p))]$$ aggregate supply
$$I = 1,000 - 2,000i$$ investment

In the long run, assume the supply curve is classical and $P = P_{-1}$. Also, note that we assume there is a one-period lag before monetary policy works.

Potential GNP is 4,000. Initial levels are $A = 1,000$, $M = 50,000$, and $P = 100$. Consumption is a function only of current income.

1. Suppose government spending increases by 500. What are the levels of GNP and the price index in the year of the increase? In the 2 following years?
2. What is the price level in the long run? By how much does investment change? The interest rate?
3. Suppose, instead of increasing government spending, the money supply had been doubled. In the long run, what would be the level of the price index, the change in investment, and the change in the interest rate?

PART TWO

8

CONSUMPTION AND SAVING

FOCUS OF THE CHAPTER

- Consumption is the largest sector of aggregate demand.
- Consumption this year depends not only on disposable income this year, but also on income in the past and expectations of future income.
- People try to spread their available lifetime resources over their entire lifetime. A transitory change in income makes little difference to lifetime resources and thus does not much affect consumption. A permanent change in income makes a great difference to lifetime resources and thus greatly affects consumption.

SECTION SUMMARIES

1. The *life-cycle* theory is based on the notion that individuals plan in order to spread their available income over their entire lifetime. In particular, people save during their working lives in order to provide for retirement. Consumption is a function of wealth and of lifetime disposable income. Instead of simply stating a marginal propensity to consume, we can calculate

the *MPC* based on the number of years a person has remaining until retirement and on life expectancy.

2. The *permanent-income* theory argues that people gear consumption to their long-term consumption opportunities. This is the same basic theme as the life-cycle theory, but is made operational by assuming that, as a practical matter, people estimate their long-run opportunities by making a projection based on current and past income. This assumption suggests that a transitory change in income will have little lasting effect on consumption, but that a permanent change will have a large effect on consumption.

3. Researchers have found that household consumption systematically responds too much to changes in current household income, forcing macro-economists to qualify the claim that consumers behave precisely according to the permanent-income/life-cycle hypothesis. This *excess sensitivity* may be the result of liquidity constraints on households, whereby households are unable to borrow or lend freely so as to smooth consumption over time.

4. The household savings rate in the United States is the lowest among the group of countries that also includes the U.K., Japan, Canada, Italy, and France. The U.S. national savings rate, which includes corporate and government saving as well as household saving, is the lowest in this group.

Arguments have been made that policy measures to increase interest rates on savings will increase household saving, but empirical evidence suggests that changes in interest rates have little effect on savings in the United States.

The Barro-Ricardo hypothesis is the claim that a tax cut, matched by an increase in government borrowing to hold government expenditures constant, will have no effect on the interest rate. According to the Barro-Ricardo hypothesis, consumers view the increase in government debt as an increase in future taxes and, therefore, save their current tax cut for payment of future taxes.

5. The more sophisticated consumption function of this chapter can be put back in the *IS-LM* framework. The slope of the *IS* curve and the values of the fiscal policy and monetary policy multipliers now depend on the time frame of a policy action. Because the short-run *MPC* is less than the long-run *MPC*, the short-run multipliers are less than the long-run multipliers.

We can also see that a rise in the value of the stock market increases wealth and thus consumption, though the magnitude of this effect is fairly small.

KEY TERMS

Life-cycle hypothesis	Relative-income hypothesis
Dissaving	Dynamic multiplier
Permanent income	Excess sensitivity of consumption
Rational expectations	Barro-Ricardo hypothesis
Liquidity constraints	

TABLE 8-1

	GNP	Consumption
Group 1	50	49
	60	54
	70	59
Group 2	10	13
	20	18
	30	23
Group 3	80	76
	90	81
	100	86

GRAPH IT 8

Graph It 8 asks you to replicate one of the most important scientific investigations of postwar macroeconomics, the discovery of the life-cycle/permanent-income theory of consumption. As you know from Chapter 8, the marginal propensity to consume seems fairly low when we look at consumption over 2 or 3 years, but the *MPC* is quite high when looked at over decades. In this Graph It you will replicate this result.

Table 8-1 presents (made-up) consumption and income data for three

CHART 8-1

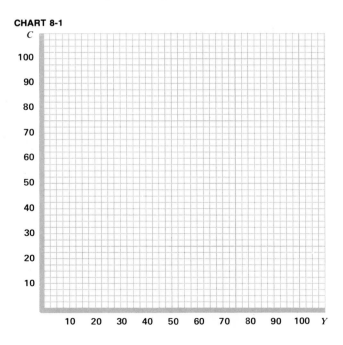

groups of three years. Ignore for the moment all but the first group. Plot the three points on the blank graph. Draw a straight line that fits the three points as well as you can. What's the slope (MPC) of the line?

Now do the same for each of the two other groups. Do you get the same slope for each line? (You should.) Think of these as short-run consumption functions measured in three different decades.

Now draw a single consumption function line for all nine points. (It won't fit exactly, of course). This represents a long-run consumption function. What's your estimate of the long-run MPC?

REVIEW OF TECHNIQUE 8

Dynamic Simulation

As soon as lags are introduced into an economic model, the model becomes *dynamic* instead of *static*. This shift makes it necessary to keep track of all the variables as they change over time. In this Review, we present a simple chart that makes this easy. Suppose we have the following economic model:

$$Y = C + I + G$$
$$C = 0.6Y + 0.3Y_{-1}$$
$$I = 100$$

Initially, G equals 20 and Y has been 1,200 for several years. Suppose G now increases to 40 for one period and then returns to 20. We can use Table 8-2 to trace out the impact on GNP for the next several periods. Note first of all that

$$Y = 0.6Y + 0.3Y_{-1} + I + G$$
$$Y(1 - 0.6) = 0.3Y_{-1} + I + G$$
$$Y = 0.75Y_{-1} + 2.5I + 2.5G \tag{8-1}$$

On Table 8-2a we have filled out all the information we have before beginning the problem. The entire trick is to recognize that Y_{-1} in period 1 is the same as Y was in period 0. (That, after all, is what the subscript "-1" tell us.) In Table 8-2b we have indicated this relation by the diagonal line connecting the two numbers. Using this fact, we can employ Equation (8-1) to find Y in period 1.

$$Y = 0.75(1,200) + 250 + 2.5(40) = 1,250$$

TABLE 8-2a

Period	Y	Y_{-1}	I	G
0	1,200	1,200	100	20
1			100	40
2			100	20
3			100	20

TABLE 8-2b

Period	Y	Y$_{-1}$	I	G
0	1,200	1,200	100	20
1	1,250	1,200	100	40
2	1,237.5	1,250	100	20
3	1,228.125	1,237.5	100	20

We can repeat the same "trick," noting that Y_{-1} in period 2 is the same as Y in period 1.

$$Y = 0.75(1,250) + 250 + 2.5(20) = 1,237.5$$

Table 8-2b runs the simulation up through period 3.

Now we repeat the same problem, except that G is increased from 20 to 40 permanently. Table 8-3a sets up the problem for you. Using Equation (8-1), fill in the rest of the table *before* you look at the answer. Table 8-3 is filled out.

TABLE 8-3a

Period	Y	Y$_{-1}$	I	G
0	1,200	1,200	100	20
1	_____	_____	100	40
2	_____	_____	100	40
3	_____	_____	100	40

TABLE 8-3b

Period	Y	Y$_{-1}$	I	G
0	1,200	1,200	100	20
1	1,250	1,200	100	40
2	1,287.5	1,250	100	40
3	1,315.625	1,287.5	100	40

FILL-IN QUESTIONS

1. The hypothesis that people plan consumption based on their wealth and all future income is called the _____ theory.
2. Estimates of long-term consumption opportunities based on previous and current income are called _____ income.
3. Using up wealth to provide for consumption is called _____ .
4. The long-run average propensity to consume is about _____ .
5. The long-run marginal propensity to consume is about _____ .

6. The immediate response of GNP to a change in autonomous aggregate demand depends on the _____ multiplier.

7. The eventual response of GNP to a change in autonomous aggregate demand depends on the _____ multiplier.

8. The marginal propensity to consume depends on the number of _____ _____ years compared with the number of _____ _____ years.

9. The gradual adjustment of output to a shock illustrates a _____ _____ lag.

TRUE-FALSE QUESTIONS

T   F   1. The permanent-income theory suggests that the long-run marginal propensity to consume is less than the short-run marginal propensity to consume.

T   F   2. Modern consumption theory suggests that consumption is proportional to long-run income.

T   F   3. A worker aged 20 who expects to retire at 65 and who has a life expectancy of 50 years should have a marginal propensity to consume out of income of 0.9.

T   F   4. A worker aged 20 who expects to retire at age 65 and who has a life expectancy of 50 years should have a marginal propensity to consume out of wealth of 0.02.

T   F   5. The long-run MPC and APC are approximately equal.

T   F   6. If a simple linear consumption function has a positive intercept, then the average propensity to consume falls as income rises.

T   F   7. Temporary changes in income produce relatively small changes in consumption.

T   F   8. The decision to leave an inheritance increases current consumption.

T   F   9. A growing population will have higher per capita savings than a static population.

T   F   10. The permanent-income theory and the life-cycle theory are fundamentally the same.

MULTIPLE-CHOICE QUESTIONS

1. According to the life-cycle theory, an individual's marginal propensity to consume out of permanent labor income
   a. rises over time
   b. falls over time
   c. remains constant
   d. may be either a, b, or c, depending on circumstances

2. According to the life-cycle theory, an individual's marginal propensity to consume out of transitory labor income
   a. rises over time
   b. falls over time
   c. remains constant
   d. may be either a, b, or c, depending on circumstances

3. The weights used on income and all the lagged income to estimate permanent income should probably add up to
   a. 0
   b. between 0 and 1
   c. 1
   d. more than 1

4. If the marginal propensity to consume out of permanent income is 0.9 and the weight on current income in estimating permanent income is two-thirds, the short-run simple Keynesian multiplier is
   a. 1
   b. 2.5
   c. 3
   d. 10

5. The life-cycle and permanent-income theories are associated with the
   a. Keynesian school
   b. monetarist school
   c. both
   d. neither

6. According to the life-cycle theory, wealth during the working years
   a. rises over time
   b. remains constant
   c. falls over time
   d. may either rise or fall, depending on the MPC

7. During a temporary recession, the average propensity to consume
   a. falls
   b. remains constant
   c. rises
   d. is neither a, b, nor c

8. During a temporary boom, the average propensity to save
   a. falls
   b. remains constant
   c. rises
   d. is neither a, b, nor c

9. The role of the stock market in determining consumption is shown most directly through the
   a. simple linear consumption function
   b. permanent-income theory
   c. life-cycle theory
   d. b and c both

10. When the expansionary effects of a permanent tax cut are compared with those of a temporary tax cut, the former tax cut
    a. is more expansionary
    b. has the same effect
    c. is less expansionary
    d. is either a, b, or c, depending on the MPC

PROBLEMS

1. Assume the typical consumer expects to work for 40 years and to live for 50. Assume consumers have perfect foresight. Disregarding any multiplier effects, how does consumption change this year as a result of a $100 annual tax cut on workers' income that
   a. is permanent, and will begin immediately?
   b. will last only for the current year?
   c. is permanent, but will not go into effect until next year?

2. Assume that the typical consumer has a marginal propensity to consume of 0.8. Consumers must use historical information to estimate permanent income. Research has shown that they estimate permanent income by using a weight of 0.75 on current disposable income and 0.25 on lagged disposable income. Disregarding any multiplier effects, how does consumption change as a result of a $100 tax cut that
   a. is permanent—how much the first year? How much the second year?
   b. is effective only for 1 year—how much the first year? How much the second year?

9

INVESTMENT SPENDING

FOCUS OF THE CHAPTER

- The second key sector of aggregate demand is investment spending.
- Investment is less than 20 percent of GNP, but investment is very volatile, and thus changes in investment account for much of the changes in GNP.
- Investment demand is especially important because it contains the main link through which monetary policy affects aggregate demand.
- Increased interest lowers investment because capital becomes more expensive.
- Decreases in expected sales lead manufacturers to reduce investment, thereby reducing aggregate demand.
- The three investment subsectors are *business fixed investment, residential investment,* and *inventory investment.*

SECTION SUMMARIES

1. Unintended inventory accumulation occurs when sales fall unexpectedly. On the other hand, when sales are expected to fall, firms intentionally reduce inventories. This intentional reduction feeds back very quickly to accelerate movements in aggregate demand. This is the *inventory cycle.*

2. Businesses use machinery, equipment, and structures in the course of producing final output. These make up the *stock* of *business fixed capital.* We de-

77

velop a theory of the *desired capital stock*. *Investment* is a *flow* that is the addition of new machinery to the existing capital stock. Investment closes the gap between the desired capital stock and the existing capital stock.

Manufacturers decide on how much capital they want by considering three factors: how much output they expect to sell; what the *marginal product of capital* is; and how much capital costs to use, or the *rental* or *user cost of capital*. The more output that must be produced, the more the required amount of capital. The higher the rental cost, the less capital will be used, since capital is more expensive. The most important component of the rental cost is the interest rate. Several other components are discussed below.

More capital always means that greater output can be made, but each additional unit of capital adds less and less additional production. However, each additional unit of capital costs as much to add as the previous unit. Thus, there is declining marginal product but constant marginal cost. The intelligent business manager adds just enough capital so that the last unit produces just as much as it costs.

Firms base their expectations of future sales on a period comparable to the life of the machinery. Current sales affect capital demand to the extent that they change expectations of sales over the life of the machinery.

The rental cost of capital is basically the market interest rate, since this is the opportunity cost of using funds to buy capital instead of "investing" in bonds. However, capital wears out over time. This depreciation cost must be covered in order to keep machines in working condition. If depreciation is d percent per year, then the cost of capital is

$$rc = i + d.$$

In the presence of inflation, we distinguish the *real interest* rate from the *nominal interest* rate. The difference is the expected rate of inflation, denoted gp^*. Since, on average, the price of goods produced will go up at the rate of inflation, the rental cost of capital properly depends on the real rate of interest. This leads to the following formula for the rental cost of capital:

$$rc \equiv r + d \equiv i - gp^* + d$$

The rental cost of capital must be adjusted to account properly for taxes. Under the *investment tax credit*, the government pays some portion τ of the cost of new equipment to the firm in the form of a tax rebate. This rebate lowers the effective cost of equipment and therefore increases the demand for capital. The *corporate income tax* is essentially a proportional tax on corporate profits. Because of the complexities of the tax code, theory alone leaves the effects of the corporate income tax ambiguous.

The rate of investment depends on the difference between the desired and actual capital stock. An important element of the way firms plan to adjust their capital stock is the gradual adjustment hypothesis. Each period firms close some portion of the gap between desired capital, K^*, and the capital available at the beginning of the period, K_{-1}. If the fraction of the gap closed each period is λ, then the investment function can be written:

$$I = K - K_{-1} = \lambda(K^* - K_{-1})$$

The timing of investment with respect to changes in the investment tax credit is especially important. A temporary investment tax credit means that a firm gets a tax break on any investment done now, but none on any done in the future. It pays the firm to invest right away not only because capital is cheaper, but also because any investment planned for the future should be made immediately instead. This means that a temporary tax credit has a much larger effect on current investment than a permanent tax credit.

3. In practice, firms rarely think of calculating a desired capital stock as such. Rather, they use a *discounted cash flow analysis* to compare the cost of adding a machine with the present value of the flow of profits the machine will provide. High interest rates mean future profits have a lower value today, thus making adding an additional machine less desirable. Discounted cash flow analysis and computation of a desired capital stock are really just two different ways of looking at the same problem.

The *accelerator* model states that the desired capital stock is proportional to income and that investment is proportional to the change in income. The accelerator model is a special case of investment theory with instantaneous adjustment to the desired capital stock and a constant ratio of desired capital to income.

4. The price and quantity of housing depend on the supply and demand for homes. Investment in housing occurs when the demand for homes rises above the available stock. The demand for housing falls when interest rates, especially mortgage rates, rise. The ability of people to buy new homes depends on the availability of mortgage money. Most home mortgages are made available through thrift institutions. These institutions raise money through savings accounts. When interest rates rise above the rate allowed by law on savings accounts, consumers pull their money out of savings, cutting off the flow of mortgages. This is called *disintermediation*. New types of savings instruments appear to have made disintermediation a less serious problem than in the past.

Appendix. The chapter appendix explains the relation between coupon rates, yields, and the prices of bonds. On a *Consol*, or perpetual bond, the yield is the coupon payment divided by the price of the bond. More generally, the price of a bond is the present discounted value (*PDV*) of all the payments on the bond. The *PDV* is found by reducing the value of future payments according to the interest rate and the time when the payment is due.

KEY TERMS

Business fixed investment	Real interest rate
Residential investment	Gradual adjustment hypothesis
Inventory investment	Discounted cash flow analysis
Desired capital stock	Accelerator model of investment
Marginal product of capital	Disintermediation
Rental (user) cost of capital	Inventory cycle
Cobb-Douglas production function	Present discounted value
q-theory	

GRAPH IT 9

Chapter 9 explains that investment forms a relatively small part of aggregate demand, but that changes in investment are responsible for much of the changes in aggregate demand. Another way to say this is that investment is a small but volatile sector. In this Graph It, you are asked to demonstrate both parts of the relationship. In Chart 9-1, you are asked to plot 13 years of GNP and investment data. You will see from this graph that GNP and investment are related, but only moderately. In Chart 9-2, you are asked to plot the annual change in GNP and the annual change in investment. This second graph shows that the relation between investment volatility and aggregate demand volatility is very strong.

Table 9-1 provides data on GNP and gross investment. We've also left space for you to fill in the annual change data you'll need for plotting the second chart.

By the way, if you are also taking a statistics course, you might compare

TABLE 9-1

Year	GNP	I	$Y_t - Y_{t-1}$	$I_t - I_{t-1}$
1972	2,608.5	465.4		
1973	2,744.1	520.8	135.6	55.4
1974	2,729.3	481.3		
1975	2,695.0	383.3		
1976	2,826.7	453.5		
1977	2,958.6	521.3		
1978	3,115.2	576.9		
1979	3,192.4	575.2		
1980	3,187.1	509.3		
1981	3,248.8	545.5		
1982	3,166.0	447.3		
1983	3,277.7	503.4		
1984	3,492.0	661.3		
1985	3,573.5	650.6		

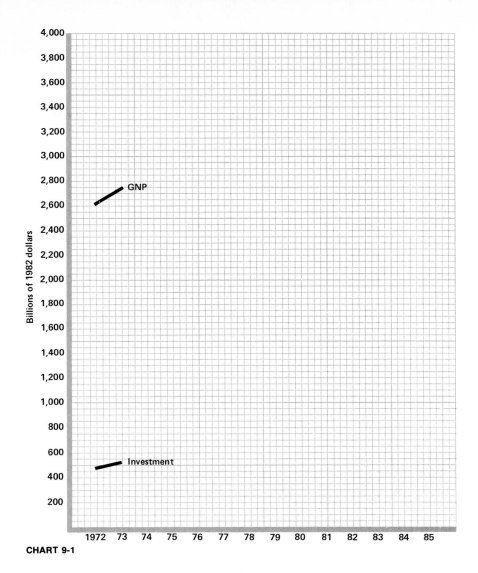

CHART 9-1

the correlation coefficient of GNP and investment versus the change in GNP and the change in investment.

REVIEW OF TECHNIQUE 9

Units of Measurement

We generally write our equations and variables without specific reference to the units by which we measure economic quantities. However, care must be taken to see that units of measurement are consistent throughout an equation.

We typically measure most quantities in dollars. However, behind this convenience we have carefully matched units. Speaking loosely, we say, "Investment is the change in the capital stock." To be precise, it is necessary to remember that investment is a rate of change per unit of time. If we go from a stock of 25 machines to 75 machines in 1 year, investment would be 50 machines per year. If the same change takes place over a 6-month period, we would say that the rate of investment is 100 machines per year.

The variable whose units of measurement are most frequently confused is the interest rate. Interest rates are typically quoted at an annual percentage rate. We can write an interest rate as "5 percent" or ".05" or even as "500 basis points." (A basis point is 1/100 of a percentage point.) It is understood, though, that the rate is 5 percent *per year*. Obviously, which manner we choose doesn't matter so long as we are consistent.

A frequent source of confusion is the statement that the "interest rate rose 20 percent." If the original rate was 5 percent, what is the new rate? The careless answer is 25 percent, 5 plus 20. The correct answer is 6 percent. Obviously, 20 percent of 5 is 1. So a 20 percent increase of a 5 percent interest rate is one percentage point, raising the interest rate from 5 to 6.

CHART 9-2

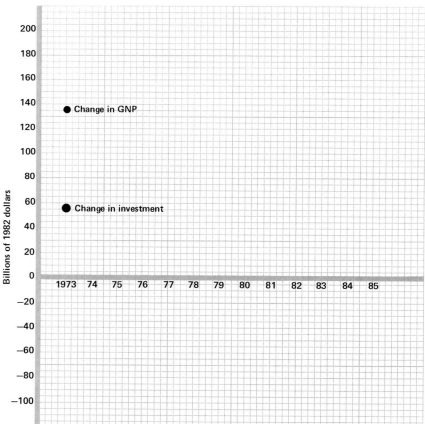

FILL-IN QUESTIONS

1. The three principal investment sectors are _____, _____, and _____.

2. Investment is a _____ devoted to maintaining the _____ of capital.

3. The contribution of an extra unit of capital to a firm's profits is the _____.

4. The cost of using capital for a year is the _____.

5. In planning how much capital to have, firms must estimate _____ sales.

6. The government gives firms a rebate for new capital; it is called the _____.

7. The difference between gross and net investment is _____.

8. The government rule limiting interest on bank accounts is _____.

9. The flight of money from savings institutions during periods of high interest rates is called _____.

10. The cycle of aggregate demand fluctuation that causes inventory fluctuation, causing more aggregate demand fluctuation, is called the _____.

TRUE-FALSE QUESTIONS

T F 1. Increased interest rates cause increased investment.
T F 2. Rising GNP causes increased investment.
T F 3. A permanent increase in the investment tax credit decreases current investment.
T F 4. High mortgage rates lead to increased investment.
T F 5. In the short run, the supply of housing is more or less fixed.
T F 6. A surprise sales boom leads to a drop in inventories.
T F 7. An expected sales boom leads to a drop in inventories.
T F 8. Changes in investment are directly proportional to income, according to the accelerator model.
T F 9. The actual capital stock adjusts gradually to the desired capital stock.
T F 10. Restrictive monetary policy decreases investment.

MULTIPLE-CHOICE QUESTIONS

1. The effect of an increase of the corporate income tax on investment
    a. is an increase
    b. is a decrease
    c. is nonexistent
    d. theoretically is any of a, b, or c

2. Comparing the impact on current investment of a permanent versus a temporary increase in the investment tax credit, we find that a permanent increase is
    a. more effective
    b. less effective
    c. the same
    d. theoretically either a, b, or c

3. Empirically it has been found that an increase in the desired capital stock causes investment to
    a. rise instantly, then gradually drop off
    b. respond in an upside-down U-pattern
    c. rise, then return immediately to zero
    d. fall gradually

4. An increase in the depreciation rate causes net investment to
    a. rise
    b. remain the same
    c. fall
    d. theoretically do any of a, b, or c

5. An increase in the depreciation rate causes gross investment to
    a. rise
    b. remain the same
    c. fall
    d. theoretically do any of a, b, or c

6. If the nominal interest rate is 12 percent and the inflation rate is 6 percent, the real interest rate is
    a. 18 percent   c. 6 percent
    b. 2 percent   d. 8.4 percent

7. According to the simple accelerator model, the response of investment to a permanent increase in GNP is to
    a. rise, then return to zero
    b. rise gradually, then fall gradually
    c. rise to a new permanent level
    d. remain unchanged

8. Net investment is the change in the capital stock
   a. according to the flexible accelerator
   b. according to the simple accelerator
   c. always
   d. never

9. The response of the housing stock to economic conditions is
   a. very rapid
   b. quite slow
   c. slow during a boom, quick during a downturn
   d. quick during a boom, slow during a downturn

10. The response of the stock of inventories to economic conditions is
    a. very rapid
    b. quite slow
    c. slow during a boom, quick during a downturn
    d. quick during a boom, slow during a downturn

11. The price of a bond increases
    a. with the market interest rate
    b. with the coupon payment
    c. both
    d. neither one

PROBLEMS

1. Assume that the demand for capital is determined by the equation $K^* = 0.25\, Y/rc$. The nominal interest rate is 12 percent (that is, $i = 0.12$), the inflation rate is 6 percent, and capital depreciates at 10 percent per year.
   a. Initially, income is $16,000. What is the desired capital stock?
   b. Now income doubles. What is the new desired capital stock?
   c. Given the simple accelerator model of investment, what is the rate of net investment? Gross investment?

2. Suppose the desired capital stock jumps from $2,000 to $3,600. If companies close half the gap between existing and actual capital each year, and if depreciation is 10 percent, what are the values of gross and net investment for each of the 3 years following the change?

3. A friend offers to lend you $1,000. You agree to pay him $220 in 1 year and to make a final payment in 2 years. The prevailing interest rate is 10 percent. You and your friend wish to agree on a fair final payment. How large should the final payment be?

THE DEMAND FOR MONEY

FOCUS OF THE CHAPTER

- We all hold money—either currency in our pockets or on deposit at a bank. In studying the demand for money, we try to discover exactly how much money a rational person will hold.
- Our basic goal is to find out how much money will be demanded for a known level of income and a known interest rate. (You will remember that we need this relation to form the *LM* curve, which we used in Chapter 4.)
- The evidence, both theoretical and empirical, is that higher income causes greater money demand and higher interest rates cause lower money demand.

SECTION SUMMARIES

1.   The most important characteristic of money is that we can use it directly to pay for things we buy. The assets in our economy that most closely fit this definition are cash and checking accounts. Together, these form *M*1. Savings accounts are good substitutes for checking accounts because you can get use of the savings deposit very quickly, even though you cannot actually make a payment by handing someone your savings passbook. Sometimes we use broader definitions of money that include time and savings deposits. The official

definitions of money have been expanded to include assets that are economically, but not legally, the same as checking accounts.

2.   Money has traditionally been defined by four functions.

a.   Serving as a *medium of exchange* is far and away the most important function of money. When you buy something, you pay for it with money rather than barter with some other merchandise.

b.   Being a *store of value* means that money retains its value over time. You would hardly be willing to accept money in payment if you didn't think that someone else would accept the money from you tomorrow.

c.   Saying that money is the *unit of account* just means that prices are quoted in dollars and cents. (A grocery could post a sign showing that 3 apples cost 2 oranges.)

d.   *Standard of deferred payment* means that when someone owes a debt, the payment is specified in terms of money.

3.   This section considers why people hold money. At first it seems strange to think that such a question ever needs to be asked. After all, we're all most happy to have money. The question we really need to answer is why people hold money instead of some better investment. Cash pays no interest at all and checking and savings accounts usually pay less than is available in other safe investments. John Maynard Keynes gave three broad motives for holding money instead of some other investment:

> Transactions motive
>
> Precautionary motive
>
> Speculative motive

The *transactions motive* arises from the cost of cashing in part of an investment each time you make a purchase. For example, it's much more sensible to draw a week's worth of pocket money at a time rather than go to the bank each morning. The most famous transactions model is the *Baumol-Tobin* theory. The development of the theory has three steps.

a.   If we know how many times a month a person replenishes her cash, what will her average balance be? Suppose the person begins with $100 and is going to spend it at a steady rate. If she takes it all in cash on the first day and spends it down to zero by the end of the month, the average cash balance will be $50. Suppose, instead, she takes only $50 for the first half of the month and after using it up gets the other $50. The average will be $25. The pattern follows so that if the person begins with Y_N dollars and makes n transfers, the average cash balance is $\frac{1}{2}Y_N/n$. (The subscript N stands for "nominal.")

b.   Cash doesn't earn any interest, and so the opportunity cost lost by holding money is $i\frac{1}{2}Y_N/n$. In addition, the cost of each transfer is tc. So:

$$\text{Total cost} = ntc + \frac{iY_N}{2n}$$

The more transfers, the higher the total costs of transactions and the less the interest lost. The better number of transfers is that which minimizes total costs. (The exact formula can be found by using calculus.)

c. Once we know the right number of transfers, we can find the average cash balance directly. The famous square-root formula turns out to be:

$$M^* = \sqrt{\frac{tcY_N}{2i}}$$

This formula implies that the income elasticity of money demand is one-half and that the interest elasticity is minus one-half, as the Reviews of Technique 7 and 11 through 13 demonstrate.

The *precautionary motive* arises from the notion that we never know our spending plans exactly. It pays to keep a little extra money on hand in case the urge for a hot fudge sundae hits at a time when it's inconvenient to cash in an investment. The greater the uncertainty about our spending plans, the more money we would be wise to keep around just in case. Just as with the transactions motive, the higher the interest rate, the greater the cost of holding money.

The *speculative motive* states that a person might sometimes want to keep money in a savings account for investment purposes. Because other investments are risky, even though they offer higher average returns, people will hold some money as a hedge against risk. The speculative demand for money is actually a demand for a safe asset.

4. Empirical research has settled four key points about money demand.

a. When the interest rate goes up, the demand for money goes down.
b. When income goes up, the demand for money goes up, but less than proportionately.
c. It takes time for money demand to adjust fully to changes in income and interest.
d. If the price level doubles, the number of dollars of money demanded will double.

5. Sometimes, instead of discussing the money demand equation, economists look at *velocity*. Velocity is the ratio of income to money. (You can think of it as the number of times a dollar passes from hand to hand in a year.) Higher interest rates mean lower money demand and therefore higher velocity. Higher income increases money demand but by less than the increase in income, so that velocity increases with increased income.

KEY TERMS

Real balances	Transactions demand
Money illusion	Inventory-theoretic approach

$M1$	Square-root formula
$M2$	Precautionary demand
Liquidity	Speculative demand
Medium of exchange	Income velocity of money
Store of value	Quantity equation
Unit of account	Quantity theory of money
Standard of deferred payments	Hyperinflation

GRAPH IT 10

Most people find themselves ready for a relaxing exercise about halfway through the text. Graph It 10 asks you to demonstrate the essential principles of the precautionary demand for money by drawing some random wiggles on the graph provided. (Well, almost random.)

The idea behind the precautionary demand for money is that you want to hold enough money so that you rarely run out of money, but that you don't want to hold too much because of the opportunity cost. In Chart 10-1 we've drawn a solid wiggly line illustrating a random cash need. Now suppose your rule of thumb was that you wanted to run short of cash no more than twice during the period. We took a straightedge and drew a solid line as low as possible, but still consistent with the random wiggle peaking over the line only twice. The solid line shows the optimal precautionary demand for money.

Now you draw in a dashed line with the same number of wiggles, but with the cash needs generally having higher peaks. Then use a straightedge to draw in a new money demand line.

REVIEW OF TECHNIQUE 10

Balance Sheets

One of the most useful devices for keeping track of changes in the economy is the *balance sheet*. A balance sheet is nothing more than a chart showing both the assets and liabilities of some agent in the economy. The usefulness of balance sheet analysis comes from the simple fact that changes in balance sheets must always balance. When working quickly, it is very easy to leave out some part of a transaction. By completely writing out all the balance sheet changes, one can make two special checks—*vertical balance* and *horizontal balance*.

Vertical balance means that all the changes on a given balance sheet must balance. One possibility is that both assets and liabilities change by the same amount. The other possibility is that one asset (or liability) goes up by the same amount that another asset (or liability) goes down.

Horizontal balance means that the changes in the total amount of a particular asset must add to zero when added up across every balance sheet in the economy. The reason is that one person's asset is another's liability. This should

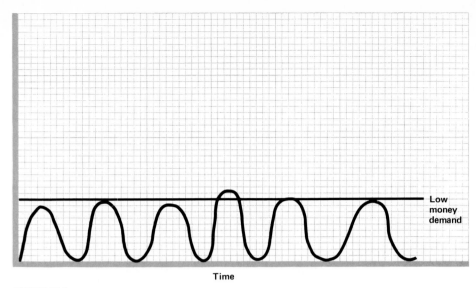

Time

CHART 10-1

be interpreted carefully. For example, if a person withdraws money from a bank, then it is true that the total in bank accounts is less. However, this is a decrease in the *assets* of the person and a decrease in the *liabilities* of the bank.

Remember that every transaction and every combination of transactions must show both vertical and horizontal balance.

As an example, consider the following problem. Mr. A owes Professor B money. In order to pay off $15 of the debt, Mr. A gives Professor B a $20 check and Professor B gives Mr. A back $5 in cash. Professor B deposits the check in her account. The bank credits her account and debits Mr. A's. The three balance sheets below show the transactions. Notice that we show only how the various levels change, not what their original levels were.

Mr. A		Prof. B		Bank	
Assets	Liabilities	Assets	Liabilities	Assets	Liabilities
④Cash +$5	⑥−$15 IOU	⑦IOU −$15			−$20 A's account ⑩
⑧Deposit −$20		⑤Cash −$5			+$20 B's account ⑪
		⑨Deposit +$20			
①−$15 −$15		②0 0		③0 0	

Points 1, 2, and 3 illustrate vertical balance. Points 4 and 5 illustrate horizontal balance in cash. Points 6 and 7 show horizontal balance in IOUs. Horizontal balance in bank deposits is shown by 8, 9, 10, and 11.

FILL-IN QUESTIONS

1. The study of the demand for money is the study of the demand for
   _____.

2. The assets forming $M1$ are _____.

3. The assets forming $M2$ are _____.

4. The Baumol-Tobin theory explains the _____ motive
   for the demand for money.

5. The number of times a dollar is turned over per year is called
   _____.

6. The ratio of income to the money stock is _____.

7. The _____ motive explains the need to hold money
   against unforeseen contingencies.

8. The need to hold money because it has a safe nominal value is called the
   _____ motive.

9. The one motive that plays little role in explaining the demand for $M1$ is the
   _____ motive.

10. In order to find the nominal demand for money, one multiplies the real
    demand for money by the _____.

TRUE-FALSE QUESTIONS

T F 1. If the number of dollars outstanding doubles and the price level goes up by one-half, then real balances have increased by one-third.

T F 2. If GNP and the money stock both fall by 50 percent, then velocity remains constant.

T F 3. Higher inflation generally leads to higher velocity.

T F 4. High inflation is associated with high nominal interest rates.

T F 5. In certain circumstances, $M2$ may be smaller than $M1$.

T F 6. An individual who ignores changes in the price level so long as all real variables remain constant is said to suffer from money illusion.

T F 7. According to the Baumol-Tobin theory, money demand is proportional to GNP.

T F 8. Velocity increases with real income.

T F 9. A shift of assets from checking to savings accounts increases $M2$.

T F 10. According to the precautionary theory of money demand, greater undertainty about spending plans results in higher money demand.

MULTIPLE-CHOICE QUESTIONS

1. An increase in real income from 100 to 110 will, according to the Baumol-Tobin theory, cause money demand to change by a
   a. 20 percent increase   c. 5 percent increase
   b. 10 percent increase   d. 5 percent decrease

2. An increase in the interest rate from 5 percent per year to 6 percent per year will, according to the Baumol-Tobin theory, cause money demand to change by a
   a. 0.5 percent decrease   c. 20 percent decrease
   b. 10 percent decrease   d. 0.5 percent increase

3. A shift of $100 from a checking account to a savings account means
   a. $M1$ up, $M2$ up   c. $M1$ down, $M2$ unchanged
   b. $M1$ down, $M2$ up   d. $M1$ down, $M2$ down

4. The most important function of money is as a
   a. medium of exhange
   b. store of value
   c. unit of account
   d. standard of deferred payment

5. The precautionary motive leads people to hold more money when
   a. the interest rate is high
   b. uncertainty about expenses is high
   c. both the rate and uncertainty are high
   d. neither the rate nor uncertainty is high

6. The demand for money is a theory of the demand for
   a. real balances   c. actual balances
   b. nominal balances   d. frictional balances

7. The demand for money depends on
   a. real income and real interest rates
   b. real income and nominal interest rates
   c. nominal income and real interest rates
   d. nominal income and nominal interest rates

8. Empirical evidence indicates that the income elasticity of money demand is
   a. greater than 1   c. between 0 and ½
   b. between ½ and 1   d. less than 0

9. Empirical evidence indicates that the interest elasticity of money demand is
   a. below −1   c. between 0 and −½
   b. between −½ and −1   d. above 0

10. The amount of demand deposits relative to currency is about
   a. 10 times as great   c. equal
   b. 3 times as great   d. one-third as great

11. The size of $M2$ as opposed to $M1$ is about
   a. equal   c. 4 times as great
   b. $2\frac{1}{2}$ times as great   d. 10 times as great

12. Money demand rises when
   a. income rises
   b. interest rates fall
   c. both income rises and interest rates fall
   d. neither income nor interest rates change

PROBLEMS

1. Assume that the Baumol-Tobin theory is true. If nominal GNP goes from $100 billion to $220 billion while the price level doubles, what is the increase in the real demand for money?

2. Suppose that we want to change the interest rate from 4 percent per year to 3 percent per year, while real GNP and the price level remain unchanged. By how much should we change the money stock if empirical investigation shows the interest elasticity to be -0.20?

11

THE MONEY SUPPLY, THE FED, AND MONETARY POLICY

FOCUS OF THE CHAPTER

- In previous chapters, the money supply has been taken to be exogenous. We now explore the process by which the Federal Reserve controls the money supply.
- We develop the connection between the monetary base, which the Federal Reserve controls directly, and the money supply.

SECTION SUMMARIES

1. $M1$ is checkable accounts plus currency in the hands of the public. $M2$ equals $M1$ plus liquid deposits at all depository institutions. The money supply is affected by the *currency-deposit ratio* chosen by the public and by the *reserve-deposit ratio* of banks. We denote the currency-deposit ratio as cu and the reserve-deposit ratio as re. The Fed directly controls the stock of *high-powered money*, also called the *monetary base* $\overline{H}$. High-powered money consists of currency plus reserves at the Fed.

2. The demand for high-powered money derives from the demand for currency plus the demand for reserves against deposits. The supply of money is limited by the supply of high-powered money and the *money multiplier mm*. The relation is given by

$$M = \left(\frac{1 + cu}{cu + re} \right) \overline{H} \equiv mm\, H$$

The term in parentheses is the *money multiplier*. Note that this formula ignores the distinction between demand and time deposits.

A high currency-deposit ratio implies a low money multiplier, as does a high reserve-deposit ratio.

3.   High-powered money is the principal liability of the Fed. Its main asset is government bonds. The Fed creates more money through an *open market purchase*, in which it buys bonds by writing a check on itself. The amount of the check is added to the total reserves available to the public and the banking system. The Fed may buy foreign exchange for American money, increasing the monetary base while engaging in *foreign exchange market intervention*. When the Federal Reserve wishes to buy foreign currency without increasing the base, it offsets its purchase of foreign exchange with an open market sale of U.S. government bonds. This operation, called *sterilization*, breaks the link between foreign exchange operations and the domestic money supply.

The *discount rate* is the interest rate the Fed charges banks for borrowing reserves. Since borrowed reserves are part of the monetary base, a high discount rate, which discourages borrowing, tends to reduce the base. In the past, the Federal Reserve used the discount rate to signal its intentions with respect to future changes in the money supply. More recently it has passively adjusted the discount rate to keep it in line with the general level of market interest rates.

It is commonly said that the government finances its deficit by printing money. When the Treasury sells bonds to the Fed rather than to the public, and receives high-powered money which the Treasury spends, the story is basically true. However, the Fed need not buy government bonds. Thus, the central bank can control the stock of high-powered money irrespective of the government budget deficit.

4.   The currency-deposit ratio depends on the tastes and habits of the public. Though it varies over time, it is convenient to treat it as a constant for illustrative purposes.

5.   The reserve-deposit ratio depends on the level of *required reserves* and of *excess reserves*. Required reserves are determined by Federal Reserve Board regulation. Banks hold excess reserves for reasons analogous to the consumer's precautionary demand for money. Excess reserves are available for making payments to other banks. Banks borrow reserves from one another at the *federal funds rate*. The higher the federal funds rate, the less excess reserves banks hold.

The Federal Deposit Insurance Corporation (FDIC) insures depositors' checking accounts up to $100,000. In addition, the FDIC usually steps in to aid failing banks with loans and other forms of assistance. The FDIC's role as an insurer of banks helps to maintain public confidence in the stability of the banking system.

6.   Commercial *bank credit* is the opposite side of the money supply coin. Banks are able to make credit available in the amount of their deposits minus reserves. When the base increases, banks are able to make more loans. These loans take the form of added deposits and more currency held by the public. The

bank that receives the new deposits can then make more loans. This adjustment process describes the *multiple expansion of bank deposits* which, when added across all the banks in the economy, yields the money multiplier.

7. The three main instruments of monetary control are open market operations (changes in the stock of high-powered money), the discount rate, and the required reserve ratio. Before 1986, Regulation Q was also used as an instrument of monetary control: higher deposit interest rates would lower the currency deposit ratio. Regulation Q expired in 1986.

8. Equilibrium in the money market is determined by setting money supply equal to money demand. Since the money multiplier responds to the interest rate, there is a small feedback effect which causes the money supply to change by slightly less than a simple constant money multiplier would indicate.

9. The Fed can control either the money supply or the interest rate, but not the two independently. The reason is that the money demand curve gives us a fixed relation between interest and the money stock.

10. In choosing between a money stock target and an interest rate target, the Fed has both economy-wide considerations and short-run technical considerations, the former being the more important. Consider the economy-wide fluctuations by looking at Figure 11-1a and 1b (text Figure 11-9a and 9b). In panel a, the *IS* curve moves around. If the interest rate is held constant, then no crowding out occurs (just like the model of Chapter 3). On the other hand, if the Fed controls the money supply, changes in the interest rate partially counteract movements in the *IS* curve. So with a volatile *IS* curve, the Fed should control the money supply rather than interest rates. In panel b, changes in money demand shift the *LM* curve around. If the money supply is held constant, then money demand changes shift the *LM* curve and thus GNP. If the interest rate is held constant, the *LM* may shift horizontally left or right—but

FIGURE 11-1

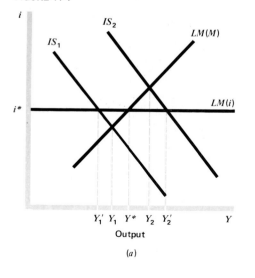

(a)

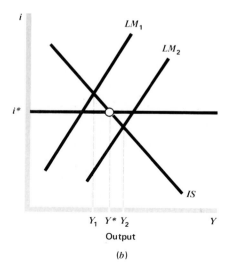

(b)

as long as the interest rate is constant, investment is constant, and GNP is constant. Thus unstable money demand argues for controlling the interest rate.

In the long run, the Fed can control the money supply quite accurately. On a day-to-day basis, it is easier to set the interest rate, and the Fed frequently uses day-to-day interest rate targets even though it is targeting the money stock on a week-to-week and month-to-month basis.

Monetarists, led by Milton Friedman, are highly critical of the Fed's monetary targeting procedures. In particular, they note that the Fed's targeting procedures lead to substantial *base drift*. The data, however, indicate that the Fed's record for controlling monetary growth over the last several years has been good. "Excessive growth" in one period is usually compensated for in the following period, keeping the money growth rate close to the target.

11. The use of publicly announced intermediate targets by the Fed helps to give the public (households and firms) an idea of what the Fed is trying to accomplish with its policies. That is, the Fed can be accountable to the public if the public knows the Fed's goals.

There is no firm agreement, however, concerning what the Fed's targets should be. In practice, the Fed sets intermediate targets for $M1$, $M2$, $M3$, and debt growth, as well as for different interest rates.

KEY TERMS

Currency-deposit ratio	Multiple expansion of bank deposits
Reserve-deposit ratio	Money supply function
High-powered money (monetary base)	Money stock and interest rate targets
Money multiplier	Intermediate targets
Discount rate	Ultimate targets
Excess reserves	Base drift
FDIC	Fan versus band

GRAPH IT 11

Graph It 11 asks you to use balance sheets to illustrate the multiple expansion of deposits. We'll assume that there is only one bank and one person, Professor B. As the problem opens, Professor B has $200 on deposit. The bank is holding the $200 as reserves. The reserve requirement is 10 percent, and so $20 is required reserves and $180 is excess reserves. The first set of balance sheets appears below.

FIRST BALANCE SHEET

Professor B				Bank			
Assets		Liabilities		Assets			Liabilities
Deposit $200		None		Reserves	$200		$200 Deposit
				(Required	20)		
				(Excess	180)		
		$200 Net worth					
	$200	$200			$180		$180

Professor B decides to borrow as much as possible from the bank, in order to finance advanced macroeconomic research. This being a worthy cause, the bank agrees to loan the entire $180 in excess reserves. Professor B signs the loan agreement, and the bank credits her account with the $180 dollars. Fill in the blanks in the second set of balance sheets.

SECOND BALANCE SHEET

Professor B				Bank			
Assets		Liabilities		Assets			Liabilities
Deposit $___		$180 Loan		Reserves	$200		$___ Deposit
				(Required	___)		
				(Excess	___)		
		$___ Net worth		Loan	___		
	$___	$___			$___		$___

Advanced macroeconomic research being as expensive as it is, Professor B decides to go for another loan. The bank again agrees to loan all its excess reserves. The bank increases the size of Professor B's loan balance and credits Professor B's account. Fill out the details in the third set of balance sheets.

THIRD BALANCE SHEET

Professor B				Bank			
Assets		Liabilities		Assets			Liabilities
Deposit $___		$___ Loan		Reserves	$___		$___ Deposit
				(Required	___)		
				(Excess	___)		
		$___ Net worth		Loan	___		
	$___	$___			$___		$___

Clearly, this process could go on for a long time. Using what you've learned about the money multiplier, fill out a final set of balance sheets reflecting the final multiple expansion of deposits and zero excess reserves.

FINAL BALANCE SHEET					
Professor B			**Bank**		
Assets	Liabilities		Assets		Liabilities
Deposit $__	$__ Loan		Reserves	$__	$__ Deposit
			(Required	__)	
			(Excess	0)	
	$__ Net worth		Loan	__	
$__	$__			$__	$__

REVIEW OF TECHNIQUE 11

Percentage Change

Looking at fluctuations in economic variables in terms of percentage changes is easy and convenient. Here we quickly review the calculations of percentage changes in preparation for the Reviews of Technique 12 and 13.

Percentage change is defined as the amount of the change in a variable divided by its original level. (For ease of expression, we generally multiply the change by 100.) The percentage change in X is

$$100 \cdot \frac{\Delta X}{X}$$

If X goes from 100 to 120, the percentage change is 20/100, or 20 percent. If X goes from 100 to 80, the change is $-20/100$, or minus 20 percent. Notice that if X goes back from 80 to 100, the change is 20/80, or 25 percent. For small changes in X, it doesn't matter whether we use the original level or the new level as a base. For example, if X drops from 100 to 99, the change is minus 1 percent. If it returns from 99 to 100, the percentage change is 1/99, or 1.01 percent.

FILL-IN QUESTIONS

1. Currency plus bank reserves form _____, or _____.

2. Total reserves of a bank are _____ reserves plus _____ reserves.

3. The interest rate charged by the Federal Reserve to member banks is the _____.

4. The interest rate charged by one bank to another for loans of deposits at the Fed is the _____.

5. The Federal Reserve lowers its holdings of bonds and decreases the money supply through an _____.

6. The ratio of the money supply to high-powered money is the _____.

7. _____ is the operation in which the Fed offsets the effects of foreign exchange operations.

8. In order to avoid disrupting the money supply process, the Treasury does most of its business through _____ accounts at commercial banks.

9. Public portfolio preferences affect the money supply through changing the _____.

10. The principal asset of the Federal Reserve is _____.

TRUE-FALSE QUESTIONS

T F 1. An increase in high-powered money increases the money supply.

T F 2. An increase in the public's preferences for currency vis-à-vis deposits increases the money supply.

T F 3. An increase in reserve requirements increases the money supply.

T F 4. An increase in bank preferences for excess reserves increases the money supply.

T F 5. An increase in income increases the money supply.

T F 6. The Federal Reserve increases the money supply when it buys foreign currency.

T F 7. The Fed uses Regulation Q to set the federal funds rate.

T F 8. After accounting for induced changes in the money multiplier, an increase in high-powered money works through money demand to lower the interest rate.

T F 9. An increase in bank borrowing from the Fed increases the money supply.

T F 10. For a given stock of high-powered money, higher interest rates increase the money supply.

MULTIPLE-CHOICE QUESTIONS

1. The money multiplier is
   a. negative
   b. between 0 and 1
   c. exactly 1
   d. greater than 1

2. The Federal Reserve does *not* set by regulation
   a. the federal funds rate
   b. the discount rate
   c. the rate on bank deposits
   d. either a, b, or c

3. An increase in Regulation Q lowers
   a. high-powered money
   b. the currency-deposit ratio
   c. bank borrowings from the Fed
   d. the discount rate

4. Repeated errors by the Federal Reserve might lead to an upward spiral of the money supply under the
   a. band
   b. fan
   c. both
   d. neither

5. If the currency-deposit ratio is one-half and the reserve-deposit ratio is 10 percent, the money multiplier is
   a. −0.75   c. 1
   b. 0.75   d. 2.5

6. The money multiplier reaches a maximum when the currency-deposit ratio equals
   a. 0   c. 1
   b. one-half   d. infinity

7. The money multiplier reaches a maximum when the reserve-deposit ratio equals
   a. 0   c. 1
   b. one-half   d. infinity

8. The money multiplier reaches a maximum when excess reserves
   a. equal required reserves   c. equal 0
   b. become negative   d. approach infinity

9. Deposits at commercial banks are insured by
   a. the Federal Reserve   c. the FDIC
   b. the Treasury   d. none of a, b, or c

10. Bank credit will increase following an increase in
    a. the reserve requirement   c. the discount rate
    b. the monetary base   d. all of a, b, and c

PROBLEMS

1. Suppose that the only deposits requiring reserves are checkable deposits; that the reserve requirement on checkable deposits is 10 percent; and that people always hold 40 percent as much currency as they hold checkable deposits.
   a. If high-powered money equals $100 billion, what is the level of $M1$?

b. If high-powered money is increased by $50 billion, by how much do checkable deposits increase?

2. Suppose that, in addition to the original conditions in problem 1, a 4 percent reserve requirement is put on time deposits, and that consumers always hold 2½ times as much in time deposits as in checkable deposits.
   a. What is the level of $M2$?
   b. What is the level of $M1$?

3. The demand functions for currency and checkable deposits are given below. The reserve requirement on checkable deposits is 10 percent, and no other assets require reserves. High-powered money equals $1,150; GNP equals $2,000. What is the interest rate?

$$CU = .5Y - 495i$$
$$D = Y - 50i$$

STABILIZATION POLICY: PROSPECTS AND PROBLEMS

FOCUS OF THE CHAPTER

● Preceding chapters have developed a macroeconomic model that would appear to solve the problems of economic policy making. Once we know our national goals and all the appropriate policy multipliers, we need only perform a few calculations to discover the best economic policy. The world is far more complicated than this. The controversy over what caused the great depression (the controversy is discussed in the first three sections of Chapter 12) is evidence of how complicated macroeconomic theorizing and policy making can be. In this chapter we discuss the three *handicaps of policy making:*

1. *Lags* in the effects of policy
2. The role of *expectations* in determining private sector responses to policy
3. *Uncertainty* about the effects of policy

SECTION SUMMARIES

1. During the early part of the great depression (1929–1933) the money stock fell rapidly; its composition changed as well, with the currency-deposit ratio rising from 18.5 percent in March 1931 to 40.7 percent two years later.

Large-scale bank failures resulted in the destruction of deposits, and banks that remained open increased their reserve holdings. The money multiplier fell, reducing the money stock as a result. The Fed did little to prevent bank failures and increase the money supply.

Although fiscal policy was stimulative prior to 1932, the presidential candidates of 1932 advocated a balanced federal budget. Federal, state, and local fiscal policies were contractionary throughout the mid-1930s.

During the period 1933 to 1937, the federal government created the Federal Deposit Insurance Corporation (FDIC), the Securities and Exchange Commission, and the Social Security Administration. These institutions were viewed as potentially stabilizing forces in the economy.

2. Early Keynesians believed that the depression was a consequence of contractionary fiscal policy. They pointed to the fact that the full-employment budget was in surplus during the early 1930s. They argued that expansionary monetary policy would not have produced an economic recovery because interest rates were already close to zero.

Monetarists, notably Milton Friedman and Anna Schwartz, claimed that it was precisely the Fed's failure to help struggling banks and its failure to increase the money stock that prolonged the depression.

3. Activism became the trademark of U.S. macroeconomic policy making during the 1960s. The approach was dubbed *The New Economics*.

Beginning in the Kennedy Administration, the Council of Economic Advisers (CEA) advocated the active use of tax incentives and other fiscal policy tools as means for encouraging economic growth. The performance of the U.S. economy during the 1960s seemed to be testimony to the potency of fiscal policy. The 1964 tax cut was major stimulus to economic growth. The U.S. economy did not experience a recession during the period 1961 to 1969.

4. The principal purpose of macroeconomic policy is to counteract the effects of *economic disturbances*. Anything that changes aggregate demand can move the economy away from full employment and/or change the price level. Thus anything that moves the *IS* or *LM* curve can be a source of disturbance. Anything that changes aggregate supply (a subject discussed in Chapter 7), such as the 1973–1974 oil embargo, will also move the economy away from full employment and/or change the price level. It is often argued that policy makers may deliberately disturb the economy for political gain. This possibility gives rise to the *political business cycle*.

5. In order to combat economic disturbances we need to know how much policy to use as well as what kind. *Econometric models* supply numerical estimates of multipliers. These models are also used to forecast GNP, interest rates, and inflation so that business may plan for the future. Large econometric models are fairly accurate, though hardly perfect.

6. The first difficulty in responding to a disturbance is determining whether the disturbance is permanent or temporary. If it is temporary, the disturbance will likely have passed before policy changes can become effective. If the timing of policy is poor, it may actually *destabilize* the economy.

Policy changes take time to become effective. This time is divided into the *inside lag*, the time necessary to undertake a policy change, and the *outside lag*, the time for the policy action to take effect. The inside lag is subdivided into the *recognition lag*, the *decision lag*, and the *action lag*. The recognition lag is the time required for policy makers to realize that a problem exists. The decision lag is the time spent between discovering the problem and deciding what to do about it. The action lag is the time needed to put decisions into effect. The recognition lag is the same for monetary and fiscal policy. Decision and action lags are generally much larger for fiscal than for monetary policy. Of course, *automatic stabilizers* have no inside lag at all.

The outside lag arises from the gradual response of the economy to policy changes. The *dynamic multipliers* of Chapter 8 are a prime example. The outside lag is a *distributed lag:* its effects are spread out over time. Fiscal policy generally has a shorter outside lag than does monetary policy.

7. *Expectations* of future economic conditions are critical in economic models. These expectations are extremely difficult to model accurately. Most econometric models approximate expectations with an average of past variables. This approach leads to serious errors when people know about the future impact of some event rather than having to rely solely on previous experience. In addition, expectations themselves depend on policy. Finding consistent models of expectations and policy rules is currently a major research problem. Lucas's *econometric policy critique* points out that many of today's macromodels lack this consistency.

8. There are three major sources of uncertainty in economic models. First, some events are unpredictable, such as natural disasters and simple changes in consumer tastes. Second, we recognize that we never know whether our models are exactly correct. Third, the true empirical values of the coefficients in our models are all uncertain.

9. Proponents of activist policy argue that we should use the tools of macroeconomics to reduce economic fluctuations. While some economists have argued against the use of activist policy entirely, active policy is appropriate so long as we recognize all the lags and uncertainty involved and are careful to be as modest as necessary in our attempts to offset disturbances.

KEY TERMS

Economic disturbances	Action lag
Political business cycle	Outside lag
Econometric models	Econometric policy evaluation critique
Macroeconometric models	Multiplier uncertainty
Inside lag	Activist policy
Recognition lag	Fine tuning
Decision lag	Rules versus discretion
New Deal	Dynamic consistency
New Economics	Policy rule

GRAPH IT 12

Economists make much of the distinction between stocks and flows. Capital, wealth, and the money supply are examples of stocks. Investment, GNP, and interest payments are examples of flows. A very much analogous distinction is made in business and in accounting between a balance sheet and an income statement. This Graph It gives you a balance sheet showing the stocks of assets and liabilities at a bank. You are then asked to prepare an income statement showing the bank's income and expense flows over the year and a new balance sheet showing the stocks at the beginning of the next year. The initial balance sheet appears below.

BANK BALANCE SHEET 1		
Assets		Liabilities
Reserves	$ 200	$2,000 Deposit
Treasury bills	400	
Loans	1,600	200 Paid in capital
	$2,200	$2,200

Assume that the bank receives no interest on reserves, 9.5 percent interest on Treasury bills, and 14 percent interest on loans. The bank pays 5.5 percent on deposits and pays a 20 percent dividend. Any profits left over after paying dividends are called retained earnings and are added to the paid in capital account. Fill in the details of the income and expense statement.

BANK INCOME STATEMENT		
Income		Expenses
Interest on reserves	$ 0	$ _____ Deposit interest
Interest on T-bills	_____	
Interest on loans	_____	_____ Stockholders' dividends
		_____ Retained earnings
	$ _____	$ _____

Assume that the bank invests its profits entirely in Treasury bills and that depositors withdraw all their interest. Show how the balance sheet looks at the beginning of the second year.

BANK BALANCE SHEET 2		
Assets		Liabilities
Reserves $ _____		$ _____ Deposit
Treasury bills _____		_____ Paid in capital
Loans _____		
$ _____		$ _____

REVIEW OF TECHNIQUE 12

Definition of Elasticity

The *elasticity* of X with respect to Y is the percentage change in X that results from a percentage change in Y. This can be written several ways.

$$\frac{\text{percentage change in } X}{\text{percentage change in } Y}$$

$$\frac{\dfrac{\Delta X}{X}}{\dfrac{\Delta Y}{Y}}$$

$$\frac{\Delta X}{\Delta Y} \cdot \frac{Y}{X}$$

The elasticity of a given relation is independent of the units of measurement of the variables.

It is worth noting that if X is proportional to Y, then X has unit elasticity with respect to Y. (The elasticity is 1.) This is true irrespective of the constant of proportionality. This is proved as follows: Suppose $X = aY$. If Y changes by ΔY, then X changes by $a\Delta Y$. The percentage change in X is $a\Delta Y/aY$, which equals $\Delta Y/Y$. The ratio of the percentage change in X to the percentage change in Y is $(\Delta X/X)/(\Delta Y/Y) = (a\Delta Y/aY)\,(\Delta Y/Y) = (\Delta Y/Y)/(\Delta Y/Y)$, which, of course, equals 1.

FILL-IN QUESTIONS

1. The time required for policy makers to counteract an economic disturbance is the _____.
2. The time required for a new policy to produce a change in the economy is the _____.

3. The three handicaps of policy making are _____,
_____, and _____.

4. The _____ is the period between the point when a new policy is chosen and the point when the policy is first put into effect.

5. The time required for an economic disturbance to be discovered is the _____.

6. The time necessary for policy makers to choose a new policy is called the _____.

7. A policy that requires no direct action on the part of policy makers is called an _____.

8. Economists who believe policy should be used to counteract economic disturbances are called _____.

9. The _____ lag is much longer for fiscal than for monetary policy.

10. The _____ lag is shorter for fiscal than for monetary policy.

PART THREE

AGGREGATE SUPPLY: WAGES, PRICES, AND EMPLOYMENT

FOCUS OF THE CHAPTER

- The frictionless classical model is a bench mark for the amount of production possible, potential GNP, when all prices are fully flexible.
- Money wages adjust slowly. When the wage differs from its long-run value, GNP differs from potential GNP.
- The Phillips curve describes the relation between wage change and unemployment. The aggregate supply curve is derived from the Phillips curve by looking at the relation of prices to wages and output to employment.
- The aggregate supply curve is inherently dynamic. In the long run it will move to bring the economy to full employment.
- Expectations of inflation are implicitly held constant in this chapter. This important assumption is reexamined in Chapter 14.

SECTION SUMMARIES

1. In the *frictionless neoclassical model of the labor market*, all firms are competitive and produce with a fixed amount of capital. Each firm's demand curve for labor slopes downward, a result of the fact that the marginal product of labor falls as additional workers are used in production. Firms hire labor up to

the point where the marginal cost of labor—the real wage—is equal to the marginal product of labor.

The supply curve of labor to the economy is an upward-sloping function of the real wage rate. As the real wage rises, more workers enter the labor force.

The economy-wide real wage rate is determined by the intersection of the aggregate demand curve for labor and the supply curve of labor to the economy.

Employment is always at its *full-employment level* in the frictionless neo-classical model. Any disturbance that causes the price level to rise or fall produces immediate pressure in the labor market for the money wage rate to rise by the same proportion. Output and employment immediately return to their full-employment levels. The aggregate supply curve is vertical.

Even at full employment there will be frictional unemployment. Frictional unemployment is associated with normal turnover in the labor market. The unemployment rate at full employment is called the *natural rate of unemployment.*

2.   Unemployment fluctuates much more than the frictionless neoclassical model implies should be the case. Furthermore, money wage rates respond slowly to shifts in aggregate demand, which, again, is inconsistent with the neoclassical model. Shifts in aggregate demand appear to affect output and employment well before they affect prices and money wages.

The Phillips curve

$$\frac{W - W_{-1}}{W_{-1}} = -\epsilon \, (u - u^*)$$

makes precise the notion that wages respond slowly to shifts in aggregate demand (unemployment). As u rises above u^* (the natural rate of unemployment), money wages fall. As u falls below u^*, money wage rates rise. The rate at which money wages change from last period's level depends upon ϵ as well as $u - u^*$. The larger is ϵ, the more rapidly wages change.

At one time it was argued that policy makers could choose any combination of inflation and unemployment along the Phillips curve. Friedman and Phelps argued that the Phillips curve was not stable over time and that in the long run the economy would return to the natural rate of unemployment. Econometric evidence supports Friedman and Phelps's argument.

3.   Using the definition of the unemployment rate

$$u = \frac{LF - N}{LF}$$

where LF is the size of the labor force and N is the actual level of employment, we can rewrite the Phillips curve in terms of the level of employment:

$$W = W_{-1}\left[1 + \epsilon \left(\frac{N - N^*}{LF}\right)\right]$$

Wages rise ($W > W_{-1}$) whenever employment is above full employment ($N > N^*$).

Wage employment contracts are renegotiated only periodically, since negotiation is costly. Renegotiation dates are usually staggered, so that at any point in time, only a fraction of all workers' wages are rising or falling in response to current changes in the cost of living or productivity. Wages in economies with low inflation rates are usually set in nominal terms, so that real wages do not adjust to changes in goods prices immediately. Therefore, nominal wage contracts cause real wages to fluctuate over time, even though nominal wages may remain fixed for long periods. Fluctuations in the real wage cause the terms on which employers can hire workers to change over time and, thus, produce fluctuations in employment.

4.   The aggregate supply curve relates prices and output. Prices depend on costs, which we can think of as unit labor costs $1/a$ times the money wage w plus a percentage markup z, to cover the costs of materials, capital, and profits.

$$P = w/a\,(1 + z)$$

Now we substitute in the wage adjustment equation, prices for wages and GNP for labor to get aggregate supply.

$$P = P_{-1}\left[1 + \epsilon\left(\frac{Y - YF}{YF}\right)\right]$$

Note three properties of aggregate supply.

a. If wage adjustment is slow, the aggregate supply curve is relatively flat.
b. The position of the aggregate supply curve depends on the past history of prices.
c. The aggregate supply curve shifts over time because today's price becomes yesterday's price tomorrow. (Reread the last sentence if necessary. It actually does make sense). A different P_{-1} tomorrow means that the aggregate supply curve has a new position tomorrow.

5.   Figures 13-1 (text Figure 13-11), 13-2, and 13-3 show the short-, medium-, and long-run response of the economy to an increase in the money stock. The aggregate demand curve shifts to the right. At first, prices rise very little and output goes up almost as much as the horizontal shift in aggregate demand. Since we are now above full employment, prices rise and the aggregate supply curve gradually shifts up. The aggregate supply curve keeps shifting up until output returns to potential GNP, at a higher price than when we started, as in Figure 13-3.

6.   An aggregate supply shock, an increase in the price of raw materials for example, shifts the supply curve up. This increases prices and reduces output. If potential GNP has not fallen (and it may have), the aggregate supply curve will eventually return to its initial position. Aggregate demand policy can be used to accommodate supply shocks, stabilizing output but raising prices.

Appendix.   The production function is a technological relation telling us how much output can be produced for a given combination of factor inputs. In the short run, when cooperating factors of production are in fixed supply, the marginal product of labor will be falling as more labor is added to the produc-

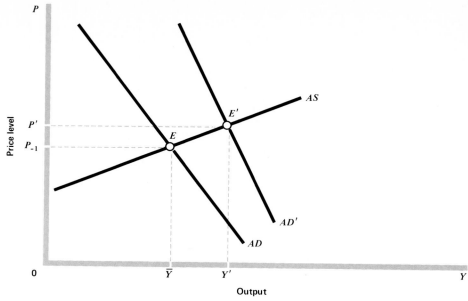

FIGURE 13-1

tion process. The marginal product of labor measures the contribution to total output of an additional unit of labor (another worker). Firms will hire a worker as long as the contribution to total output is greater than the cost of hiring, which is the real wage.

FIGURE 13-2

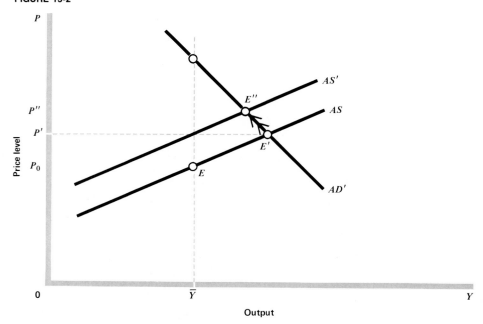

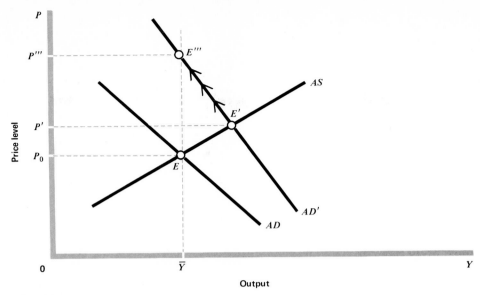

FIGURE 13-3

KEY TERMS

Frictionless neoclassical model   Unit labor costs

Frictional unemployment   Markup

Natural rate of unemployment   Sticky wages

Phillips curve   Adverse supply shock

Labor productivity   Accommodation of supply shocks

GRAPH IT 13

Graph It 13 asks you to implement fiscal policy (or at least to figure out how far to move the IS curve). Chart 13-1 shows IS and LM curves on the top diagram and aggregate supply and demand curves on the bottom diagram. Initially, equilibrium is at point E_0. Then a supply shock moves the aggregate supply curve up. The new equilibrium, with lower output and higher prices, is at point E_1. Draw in a new IS' curve that will move the economy to point E_2 and mark off the horizontal distance by which you moved the IS curve.

Hold it! Not so fast! Prices are higher at E_1 than at E_0. This means that real balances are lower and that the LM curve has already shifted left. Draw in the curve LM' corresponding to this movement along the aggregate demand curve. Then draw in IS' and measure the distance.

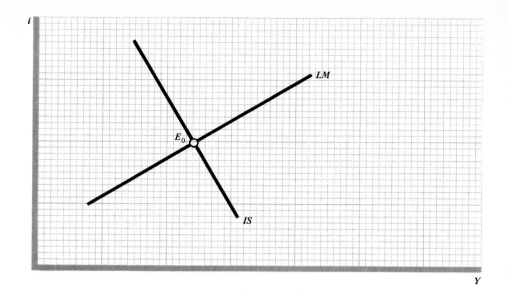

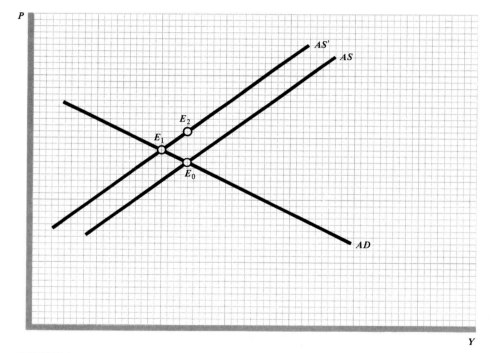

CHART 13-1

REVIEW OF TECHNIQUE 13

Constant Elasticity Formulas

Certain formulas show that one variable has a constant elasticity with respect to another. These formulas are extremely convenient because the variables involved always have the same relation in terms of percentage changes. The formula

$$X = AY^a Z^b$$

can be rewritten by taking logarithms of both sides.

$$\log X = \log A + a \log Y + b \log Z$$

Since the change in a log is the percentage change in the underlying variable, we can find directly the effect of a percentage change in Y or Z. Letting $\%\Delta$ mean percentage change,

$$\Delta \log X = a\Delta \log Y + b\Delta \log Z$$

or

$$\%\Delta\ X = a\%\Delta\ Y + b\%\Delta\ Z$$

In other words, if Y goes up by 1 percent, X goes up by a times 1 percent. By definition, then, the elasticity of X with respect to Y equals a and the elasticity of X with respect to Z equals b.

We have already seen several examples of this type of formula. For example, the Baumol-Tobin money demand formula can be written

$$\frac{M}{P} = (bY)^{1/2}(2i)^{-1/2}$$

The previous claim that the elasticity of money demand with respect to income equals one-half is thus seen to be true.

FILL-IN QUESTIONS

1. The fact that wages change slowly is due to _____.
2. The rate of _____ is the percentage change in the general price level per annum.
3. The _____ is the relation between inflation and un-employment derived from the aggregate supply curve.
4. According to the _____, prices are flexible and prices and output are determined by perfect competition.

5. The ratio of output to labor input is called _____ .
6. The theory that prices are set by a constant percentage over variable costs is the _____ theory.
7. Events that change costs or shift the supply or demand for labor are called _____ .

TRUE-FALSE QUESTIONS

T F 1. Average output per worker generally rises during a boom.

T F 2. The concept of diminishing returns indicates that additional labor leads to lower output.

T F 3. Aggregate supply (AS) is increased by increased potential GNP.

T F 4. AS is increased by an increased labor force.

T F 5. An increase in materials prices pushes the aggregate supply curve up.

T F 6. Unit labor cost is the inverse of labor productivity.

T F 7. The government should always accommodate an adverse supply shock.

T F 8. The frictionless classical model is a reasonably good short-run description of the economy.

T F 9. The frictionless classical model is a reasonably good long-run description of the economy.

MULTIPLE-CHOICE QUESTIONS

1. In the frictionless classical model, the real wage
   a. is unchanging over time
   b. equals the marginal product of labor
   c. equals the nominal wage
   d. is higher than in the Keynesian model

2. Adverse supply shocks
   a. increase prices and increase output
   b. decrease prices and increase output
   c. increase prices and decrease output
   d. decrease prices and decrease output

3. Movement of the aggregate supply curve moves the economy to potential GNP
   a. instantly   c. slowly
   b. quite quickly   d. never

4. An increase in the money stock increases GNP in
   a. the short run   c. both
   b. the long run   d. neither

5. A drop in autonomous spending decreases GNP in
   a. the short run
   b. the long run
   c. both
   d. neither

6. The position of the aggregate supply curve depends on
   a. potential GNP
   b. past prices
   c. both
   d. neither

PROBLEMS

1. Suppose that the fraction of the labor force that become unemployed for each percent deviation of GNP from potential GNP is 0.4. Further assume that nominal wages drop 2 percent for each 1 percent increase in unemployment. Initially, the economy is a full employment and the consumer price index (CPI) is 100. If the government increases GNP by 10 percent and maintains it at its new level, what will the CPI be after 1 year? After 2 years?

2. According to the aggregate supply curve theory developed in this chapter, what is the inflation rate when the economy is at full employment?

INFLATION AND UNEMPLOYMENT

FOCUS OF THE CHAPTER

- Modified to take account of inflationary expectations, the Phillips curve becomes a dynamic aggregate supply curve. When the expected inflation rate is equal to the actual inflation rate, output is at its full-employment level. For a *given* rate of expected inflation, the dynamic aggregate supply curve implies a tradeoff between output and inflation. In the long run, the tradeoff cannot persist because inflationary expectations will "catch up" with the actual inflation rate.
- Together with the dynamic aggregate supply curve, the dynamic aggregate demand curve determines the equilibrium level of output and inflation. In the short run, adaptive expectations imply that output may deviate from full employment as a result of monetary, fiscal, and other forms of shocks. In the long run, inflation is mainly a monetary phenomenon. Rational inflationary expectations imply that anticipated monetary and fiscal policy has no real effects.

SECTION SUMMARIES

1. The aggregate supply curve

$$P = P_{-1}[1 + \lambda(Y - Y^*)]$$

is derived by combining the Phillips curve, the inverse relationship between the unemployment rate and the level of output, and the markup pricing rule of firms.

An implication of markup pricing is that firms pass wage increases on to consumers directly. Thus, in our model, wages and prices always rise or fall at the same rate.

Using the aggregate supply curve we can write the wage Phillips curve as

$$\frac{W - W_{-1}}{W_{-1}} \equiv W = \lambda(Y - Y^*).$$

Friedman and Phelps argued that the simple wage Phillips curve incorrectly ignores the effect of expected inflation on wage rates. At the very least, workers will demand periodic wage increases to compensate for expected inflation. Workers care about real wages, not nominal wages. To take account of the role of expected (price) inflation on wage changes, we write the expectations-augmented wage Phillips curve

$$W = \pi^e + \lambda(Y - Y^*)$$

When Y is equal to Y^*, wages rise at the expected rate of inflation. When Y is below (above) Y^*, wages rise at a rate below (above) the expected rate of inflation.

Since π, the actual inflation rate, is equal to w, the rate of wage inflation, we can substitute into the expectations-augmented wage Phillips curve to derive the dynamic aggregate supply curve

$$\pi = \pi^e + \lambda(Y - Y^*)$$

2. There is a short-run (dynamic) aggregate supply curve corresponding to every level of expected inflation. For example, at an expected inflation rate of 5 percent (Figure 14-1, text Figure 14-3), the dynamic aggregate supply curve is *SAS*. At $Y = Y^*$, the actual inflation rate equals the expected inflation rate (5 percent), as should be the case. If expected inflation were to jump to 10 percent, the new short-run aggregate supply curve would be *SAS'*. Along each short-run aggregate supply curve there is a tradeoff between inflation and unemployment.

The short-run dynamic aggregate supply curve appeared to shift in the late 1960s as the public began to expect higher inflation rates. Higher actual inflation rates became associated with each level of GNP.

If the actual inflation rate remains stable for a long period of time, the public will begin to anticipate that particular level of inflation. The only level of output consistent with $\pi = \pi^e$ is full employment. When the economy is resting at full employment, prices and wages are rising at the rate expected by the public; the long-run aggregate supply curve is vertical.

3. It is not clear whether wage adjustments required by labor contracts reflect compensation for past inflation or expectations of current and future

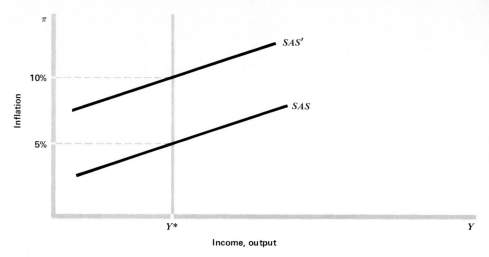

FIGURE 14-1   THE DYNAMIC AGGREGATE SUPPLY
CURVE.

inflation. The fact that many adjustments are based on last period's inflation rate gives wage changes the appearance of being compensation for past inflation.

If wage adjustments are based on last period's inflation rate, wages and prices change only gradually over time.

Anticipated inflation based on the past behavior of inflation is called *adaptive expectations*. For example, inflationary expectations are adaptive when

$$\pi^e = \pi_{-1}$$

According to the rational expectations hypothesis, people use all the relevant and (economically) available information to forecast the future behavior of the price level. The rational expectations hypothesis implies that the public does not make systematic mistakes in forecasting the inflation rate.

The dynamic aggregate supply curve under the adaptive expectations hypothesis is

$$\pi = \pi_{-1} + \lambda(Y - Y^*)$$

4.   The dynamic aggregate demand curve shows the relationship between the rate of inflation and the rate of change in aggregate demand for a fixed level of nominal money supply growth and a fixed rate of fiscal expansion. It is

$$Y = Y_{-1} + \psi(m - \pi) + \sigma \cdot f$$

where ψ and σ are positive constants, $m - \pi$ is the rate of change of real money balances, and f is the rate of fiscal expansion. The dynamic aggregate demand curve says that the rate of change in aggregate demand, $Y - Y_{-1}$, is positively related to the growth of real money balances and fiscal expansion.

We write the dynamic aggregate demand curve (derived from a simplified *IS/LM* model) as

$$\pi = m - \frac{1}{\psi}(Y - Y_{-1})$$

to highlight the relationship between actual inflation, the rate of growth of the nominal money stock, and the change in aggregate demand (assuming, for simplicity, that f is zero). Plotting π against Y (for a given m and Y_{-1}), the dynamic aggregate demand curve is downward-sloping, as in Figure 14-2 (text Figure 14-5). Holding the rate of growth of the nominal money stock fixed, a reduction in π causes real balances to grow more rapidly and spending to increase.

An increase (decrease) in the nominal growth rate of money causes the dynamic aggregate demand curve to shift up (down).

5.   The equilibrium inflation rate and level of output are determined by the intersection of the dynamic aggregate supply curve with the dynamic aggregate demand curve.

In the short run, holding the expected inflation rate constant, an increase in the growth rate of the nominal money stock will shift the dynamic aggregate demand curve rightward, raising the level of output. The inflation rate will increase, but not by as much as the growth rate of the money stock.

An exogenous increase in expected inflation will reduce output in the short run. Actual inflation will rise, but not by as much as the expected inflation rate.

When the economy is resting at full employment and the nominal money stock is growing at a positive rate (f assumed to be zero), the expected infla-

FIGURE 14-2   THE DYNAMIC AGGREGATE DEMAND
CURVE.

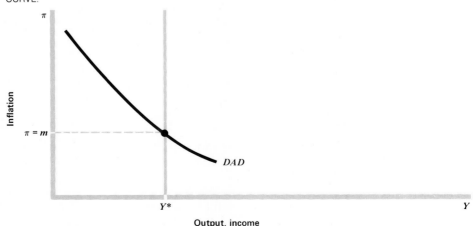

Output, income

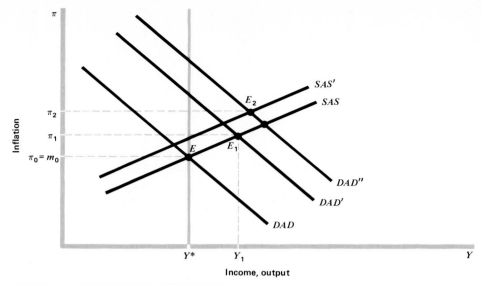

FIGURE 14-3 THE DYNAMIC ADJUSTMENT TO A
PERMANENT INCREASE IN THE GROWTH RATE OF
THE NOMINAL MONEY STOCK.

tion rate, the actual inflation rate, and the growth rate of the nominal money
stock are all equal. In the long run (''steady state''), the inflation rate is determined solely by the growth rate of the money stock.

In reality, the economy never reaches a steady state. However, over a long
period of time, macroeconomists would expect the average behavior of the
economy to approximate the steady state behavior predicted by our model.

6.   We consider the dynamic adjustment of the inflation rate and the level
of output to a permanent increase in the growth rate of the money stock under
the assumption that inflationary expectations are adaptive.

The economy is initially at point E in Figure 14-3 (text Figure 14-7),
where money growth rate is m_0 and inflation rate π_0. An increase in the growth
rate of money to m_1 shifts the aggregate demand curve upward; the inflation
rate is now π_1 and the level of output is Y_1 (point E_1). Expected inflation is still
last period's actual level of inflation, π_0.

Because output has increased from the its initial level, the dynamic aggregate demand curve shifts again. The aggregate supply curve shifts up now as
expected inflation rises to π_1; the economy moves to point E_2. The actual inflation rate has already risen above its eventual steady-state level, π_1. At some
point during the adjustment process the inflation rate must fall, but this can
only happen if the economy suffers a period of falling output, that is, a recession. The economy will go through a cycle, as shown in Figure 14-4 (text Figure 14-8).

During the process of adjustment to an increase in the growth rate of
money, the economy exhibits a period of stagflation and overshooting.

With perfect-foresight inflationary expectations—the equivalent of rational expectations when there is no uncertainty—

$$\pi = \pi^e$$

and the economy is at full employment always. Under rational expectations, unexpected changes in the growth rate of the money supply may cause temporary deviations of output from its full-employment level, but adjustment back to full employment will occur within one period.

7. A permanent fiscal expansion will temporarily raise output and increase the inflation rate. With an unchanged money supply growth rate, the economy must eventually return to its initial equilibrium, where Y equals Y^*, and $\pi = m_0$. During the adjustment process the economy exhibits overshooting—a recession—and since government spending exceeds its old level in the new equilibrium, some private spending has been permanently crowded out.

8. In fighting inflation, we choose between *gradualism*, in which we have a small recession for a long time, and *cold turkey policies*, where we have a shorter, deeper recession. The choice is difficult. However, the cold turkey policies have the advantage of being *credible*. If people really believe the government is going to reduce inflation, then π^e falls. For every point π^e falls, we get rid of one point of inflation without having to pay the unemployment price.

Two policies that have been suggested to reduce inflation without paying an unemployment price are *incomes policy* and *TIP* (*tax incentive policy*). Incomes policy means either formal or informal wage or price controls. TIP uses tax subsidies to companies that hold down price and wage increases to try to accomplish the same thing as wage and price controls without needing as much regulation. Both policies face two problems. First, relative price changes are necessary for efficient allocation of economic resources, and controls greatly interfere with the market's ability to change prices. Second, governments try to

FIGURE 14-4   THE FULL ADJUSTMENT PATH.

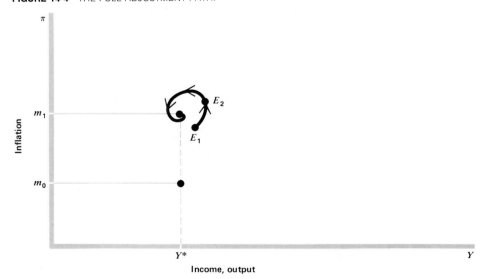

use these policies instead of controlling aggregate demand rather than using them together with controlling aggregate demand.

KEY TERMS

Expectations-augmented aggregate supply curve

Short-run aggregate supply curve

Long-run aggregate supply curve

Adaptive expectations

Rational expectations

Stagflation

Overshooting

Gradualism

Cold turkey

Credibility

Sacrifice ratio

Incomes policies

Wage and price controls

TIP

GRAPH IT 14

Graph It 14 asks you to calculate the opportunity cost differences between money, bonds, and capital. The purpose of this exercise is to see when you should look at the nominal interest rate and when you should look at the real interest rate.

Assume that money pays no interest. Bonds pay the nominal interest rate. Capital takes the form of seed corn. Every bushel of seed corn you have at the beginning of the year grows into 1.1 bushels by the end of the year. Initially, the general price level equals 1.0, and a bushel of corn costs $1. You start with $100 in money, $100 in bonds, and 100 bushels of corn.

Fill out Table 14-1 on the basis of the assumptions that the price level, of corn and everything else, rises to 1.02 by the end of the year and that the nominal interest rate is 7 percent.

Fill out Table 14-2 on the basis of the new assumptions that the price level rises to 1.12 by the end of the year and that the nominal interest rate is 17 percent.

You should be able to see that in both tables the opportunity cost of money (versus bonds) is approximately the nominal interest rate—whether the cost is measured by the real difference or the dollar difference. The opportunity cost of capital (seed corn) is approximately the real interest rate in both cases. At

TABLE 14-1

Asset	Beginning value	End dollar value	End real value	Dollar difference	Real difference
Money	$100	$100	$ 98.04	$7	_____
Bonds	$100	$107	_____		_____
Corn	$100	$112.2	$110.0	_____	_____

TABLE 14-2

Asset	Beginning value	End dollar value	End real value	Dollar difference	Real difference
Money	$100	————	————	————	————
Bonds	$100	————	————	————	————
Corn	$100	————	————	————	————

low inflation rates (such as in Table 14-1), the real and nominal interest rates are approximately the same, and so it doesn't matter terribly much which one we look at. At high inflation rates (such as in Table 14-2), the difference is crucial.

REVIEW OF TECHNIQUE 14

Infinite Geometric Series

Infinite geometric series have been used at least twice in the text. They were first used when we discussed the simple consumption function and multiplier, and second when we considered the multiple expansion of bank deposits. We now demonstrate how to calculate the sum of an infinite series. Suppose that c is a fraction between 0 and 1 and that S is the sum of the following series.

$$S = 1 + c + c^2 + c^3 + c^4 + \ldots$$

Notice then that

$$cS = c + c^2 + c^3 + c^4 + c^5 + \ldots$$

If we subtract the second line from the first, we get

$$S - cS = 1 + (c - c) + (c^2 - c^2) + (c^3 - c^3) + \ldots$$
$$S - cS = 1 + 0 + 0 + 0 + \ldots = 1$$
$$S(1 - c) = 1$$
$$S = \frac{1}{1 - c}$$

Notice that if c "happens" to be the marginal propensity to consume, then S is the simple multiplier.

FILL-IN QUESTIONS

1. ———————————————— occurs when the inflation rate rises above or below its steady-state level during the adjustment to a disturbance.

2. So long as people do not make systematic errors in predicting the future of the economy, they are said to have ————————————— .

3. In order to explain inflation, the _____ curve takes into account not only the current state of the economy but also people's expectations about future price changes.

4. The theory that in the long run the economy must return to full employment is shown by the long-run _____ curve.

5. Simultaneous high inflation and high unemployment is called _____ _____ .

6. A _____ government policy pronouncement is one that the public believes the government will act upon.

7. People are said to have _____ expectations when there is no uncertainty and they know the actual inflation rate precisely.

8. A provision in a wage contract that ties the wage rate to the inflation rate is called a(n) _____ clause.

TRUE-FALSE QUESTIONS

T F   1. Rational expectations theory says that GNP always equals potential GNP.

T F   2. Incomes policies have been mostly unsuccessful in the United States.

T F   3. In the early 1980s, the Reagan administration took the cold turkey approach to combating inflation.

T F   4. We can think of the Phillips curve as being vertical when expected inflation and actual inflation are equal.

T F   5. Inflation is increased by high expectations of inflation.

T F   6. Increased inflationary expectations lower the nominal interest rate.

MULTIPLE-CHOICE QUESTIONS

1. Initially, the general price level is 100. If, 6 months later, the general price level is 102, the annual inflation rate has been
   a. 2 percent   c. 5 percent
   b. 4 percent   d. 12 percent

2. If expected inflation rises one percentage point, in the short run the nominal rate will
   a. remain constant
   b. rise by less than one point
   c. rise by one point
   d. rise by more than one point

3. If expected inflation rises by one percentage point, in the long run the nominal interest rate will
   a. remain constant
   b. rise by less than one point
   c. rise by one point
   d. rise by more than one point

4. If expected inflation rises by one percentage point, in the short run the expected real interest rate will
   a. remain constant
   b. fall by less than one point
   c. fall by one point
   d. fall by more than one point

5. If expected inflation rises by one percentage point, in the long run the expected real interest rate will
   a. remain constant
   b. fall by less than one point
   c. fall by one point
   d. fall by more than one point

6. Assuming that real GNP grows at 3 percent per year and the money supply grows at 6 percent per year, then, if the income elasticity of the demand for money is ½, long-run inflation will be
   a. 3 percent   c. 6 percent
   b. 4½ percent   d. 7½ percent

7. An increase of 1 percent per year in the rate of growth of the money supply will increase inflation in the long run by
   a. 0   c. 1 percent
   b. 0.5 percent   d. more than 1 percent

8. A permanent increase in the rate of growth of money of 1 percent will permanently increase GNP by
   a. 0   c. 1 percent
   b. 0.5 percent   d. more than 1 percent

9. A permanent increase in government spending will generate
   a. temporarily increased inflation
   b. permanently increased inflation
   c. no change in inflation
   d. temporarily decreased inflation

10. A permanent increase in the level of money stock, with no change in the rate of growth, will generate
   a. temporarily increased inflation
   b. permanently increased inflation
   c. no change in inflation
   d. temporarily decreased inflation

PROBLEMS

Use the following equations for each of the questions below:

$$Y = Y_{-1} + 2f + 2{,}000(m_{-1} - \pi_{-1}) + 1{,}000\,\Delta\pi^e \qquad \text{Dynamic aggregate demand}$$

$$\pi = \pi^e + 0.8\left(\frac{Y - Y^*}{Y^*}\right) \qquad \text{Expectations-augmented Phillips curve}$$

$$\pi^e = \pi_{-1} \qquad \text{Inflationary expectations}$$

Initially, GNP equals 4,000, as does potential GNP. Initial $\overline{A}$ ($f = 0$) is 1,000, and both inflation and inflationary expectations have been zero for some time. The rate of growth of the money supply, m, is also initially zero.

1. Suppose the government permanently increases spending by 500. What is the level of GNP in the year of the increase? What is the inflation rate? What inflation rate will people expect for the next year? What actually happens to GNP and inflation the following year? The year after?
2. Suppose, instead, that the money supply is permanently increased by one-half, so that m equals 0.5 and then returns to 0 in the following year. Obviously, aggregate demand is not changed the first year, since money only affects income with a lag. What happens to GNP and inflation the next year? The year after? The year after that?
3. Suppose the government lets the money supply grow at 50 percent per year permanently. What happens to GNP and inflation in years 2, 3, 4, and 5 of the new policy?

THE TRADEOFFS BETWEEN INFLATION AND UNEMPLOYMENT

FOCUS OF THE CHAPTER

- After reviewing the available tradeoffs between unemployment and inflation, we study their relative costs.
- We study the *anatomy of unemployment*, its distribution among different groups in society, and the determination of the natural rate.
- We then look at the costs of inflation, with special emphasis on the difference between *anticipated* and *unanticipated inflation*.
- We conclude with a look at the politics of inflation and unemployment.

SECTION SUMMARIES

1. There are three central facts about unemployment in the United States. These facts help us to understand who bears the cost of unemployment.

a. There are substantial flows in and out of unemployment each month, and most people who become unemployed return to work very quickly.

b. Much of the total number of unemployed persons is made up of people who are unemployed for long periods.

c. Different groups in society have very different unemployment rates. Women are unemployed more than men. Teenagers are unemployed more than adults. Blacks are unemployed more than whites.

2. The *natural rate of unemployment*, also called the full-employment level of unemployment, is the unemployment rate at which flows in and out of unemployment just balance *and* at which expectations about prices and wages are correct. The natural rate of unemployment changes over time. Since the overall natural rate is a weighted average of natural rates of different groups in society, the natural rate has risen as groups with higher unemployment have become a larger part of the labor force.

3. Okun's law suggests that a one-point increase in the unemployment rate for 1 year costs society about 2½ percent of GNP. The burden of unemployment is not spread evenly over society. Most of it is borne by the individuals who find themselves out of work. A permanent one-point decrease in unemployment would save society about three-fourths of 1 percent of GNP each year.

4. In determining the costs of inflation, we make a critical distinction between *perfectly anticipated* and *imperfectly anticipated* inflation. If everyone knew how much inflation there would be, all agreements and contracts would be written to reflect this inflation. The only costs of anticipated inflation arise because the interest rate on currency cannot be adjusted to inflation (since there is no interest on currency) and because people have to spend a lot of time remarking price tags. Both costs are trivial. When inflation is *unanticipated* or *imperfectly anticipated*, people who owe nominal debts repay them with cheaper dollars and people who are creditors are paid off in cheaper dollars. Thus debtors benefit and creditors lose. Of course, most people are both debtors and creditors. Unanticipated inflation helps some individuals and hurts others. The effect of unanticipated inflation is mostly *distributional*.

5. The major areas where unanticipated inflation redistributes income are long-term nominal loans and long-term wage contracts. For example, most homeowners found their homes to be good investments in the 1960s and 1970s because the increase in home prices was as great as the mortgage interest rate. The homeowners effectively paid zero interest. Long-term wage contracts fix nominal wages over a period of several years. In order to avoid too great a change in the real wage should inflation differ from the rate expected when the contract was signed, many contracts include cost-of-living adjustments (COLAs) which index the wage rate to the rate of inflation.

6. Policy makers must choose the adjustment path of the economy, back to full employment, after a shock. They can increase aggregate demand rapidly, at the expense of high prices, or they can fight inflation, at the expense of a slow recovery. In a perfect society, political leaders would weigh the costs and benefits involved. It has been suggested (the so-called *political business cycle*) that politicians actually manipulate the economy in order to aid their own reelection.

KEY TERMS

Unemployment pool	Costs of cyclical unemployment
Layoffs	Okun's law
Involuntary quits	Anticipated inflation
Accessions	Redistribution of wealth
Separations	Fisher equation
Duration of spells of unemployment	Indexation
	COLA
Natural rate of unemployment	Extended Phillips curve
Targeted programs	Political business cycle

GRAPH IT 15

As you know, statistics can be misleading. When a statistic is a weighted average of underlying data, changes in the weights can easily lead us to guess wrong about what is going on in the economy. Graph It 15 illustrates this by looking at changes in the natural rate of unemployment.

The underlying information for Table 15-1 is the unemployment rate for men and women and the number of men and women in the labor force. From these figures we calculated the number employed. Then we added up the total labor force and the total employed and worked backward to get the overall unemployment rate, 3.67 percent [$3.67 = 1 - (1{,}156/1{,}200)$].

Now you fill in Table 15-2 and answer the following two questions. Has the overall unemployment rate risen? If so, what group is unemployed more?

TABLE 15-1 "THE OLD DAYS"

	Unemployment rate	Number in labor force	Number employed
Male	3.00	1,000	970
Female	7.00	200	186
Total	3.67	1,200	1,156

TABLE 15-2 "THE NEW DAYS"

	Unemployment rate	Number in labor force	Number employed
Male	2.80	1,000	＿＿
Female	5.50	800	＿＿
Total	＿＿	＿＿	＿＿

REVIEW OF TECHNIQUE 15

Constant Returns to Scale

A production function is said to *exhibit constant returns to scale* if whenever we double all inputs, the amount of output doubles. Notice that we emphasize that *all* inputs must be increased in a balanced way, not just one increased while another stays constant.

We can prove that the Cobb-Douglas production function has constant returns to scale. We need only show that for any combination of capital and labor K and N, if we multiply both K and N by any arbitrary constant b, and then plug these new levels into the production function, output Y will have been multiplied by the same b.

$$Y = AK^aN^{1-a}$$
$$? = A(bK)^a(bN)^{1-a}$$
$$? = Ab^aK^ab^{1-a}N^{1-a} = AK^aN^{1-a}(b^ab^{1-a}) = AK^aN^{1-a}(b)$$
$$! = bY$$

FILL-IN QUESTIONS

1. The problem of stabilization policy concerns the tradeoff between _____ _____ and _____.

2. The _____ is the permanently sustainable rate of unemployment.

3. Contracts can be adjusted in advance for _____ inflation.

4. Unforeseen inflation is called _____ or _____ _____.

5. The effects of unforeseen inflation are mostly _____.

6. The use of _____ will slowly bring down the rate of inflation.

7. On the other hand, a _____ policy will halt inflation immediately.

8. The short-run relation between unemployment and GNP is described by _____.

9. An unforeseen increase in prices benefits _____.

10. This group benefits at the expense of _____.

TRUE-FALSE QUESTIONS

T F   1. The natural rate of employment is determined by long-run aggregate demand policies.

T F   2. The effects of unanticipated unemployment are mostly distributional.

T F   3. The effects of unanticipated inflation are mostly distributional.

T F   4. The effects of anticipated unemployment are very large.

T F   5. The effects of anticipated inflation are trivial.

T F   6. Most people who become unemployed return to work quickly.

T F   7. Most unemployment is accounted for by people who are only briefly unemployed.

T F   8. Optimally, the unemployment rate would be zero.

T F   9. The natural rate of unemployment cannot be changed by government economic policies.

T F   10. Aggregate demand policies cannot be used to change inflation in the long run.

MULTIPLE-CHOICE QUESTIONS

1. The natural rate of unemployment is currently estimated at around
   - a. 0
   - b. 2 to 3 percent
   - c. 5 to 6 percent
   - d. 8 to 9 percent

2. Compared with white unemployment among groups of the same age and sex, black unemployment is
   - a. less
   - b. roughly the same
   - c. $1\frac{1}{2}$ to 2 times as great
   - d. nearly 4 times as great

3. The typical person who becomes unemployed either finds a new job or leaves the labor force in about
   - a. a week
   - b. a month
   - c. 6 months
   - d. a year

4. The natural rate of unemployment is the level at which
   - a. entry and exit from the unemployment pool balance
   - b. expectations about wages and prices are correct
   - c. neither a nor b occurs
   - d. both a and b occur

5. The natural rate of unemployment changes in response to
   - a. labor market policies
   - b. the composition of the labor force
   - c. neither a nor b
   - d. both a and b

6. Inflation could be brought to an abrupt halt by
   - a. a deep, short recession
   - b. a shallow, short recession
   - c. a big boom
   - d. neither a, b, nor c

7. Inflation could be brought to a gradual halt by
   a. a deep, long recession
   b. a shallow, long recession
   c. a big boom
   d. neither a, b, nor c

8. If the government commands total credibility and prices and wages are fully flexible, inflation
   a. can be stopped instantly, but with high unemployment
   b. can be stopped instantly, with no unemployment
   c. can be stopped gradually, with no unemployment
   d. cannot be stopped

9. Anticipated inflation largely transfers wealth from
   a. debtors to creditors
   b. creditors to debtors
   c. poor to rich
   d. none of a, b, or c

10. Unanticipated inflation largely transfers wealth from
    a. young to old
    b. poor to rich
    c. creditors to debtors
    d. none of a, b, or c

PROBLEMS

1. Suppose that the natural rate of unemployment is 5 percent for men and 8 percent for women. If women are 40 percent of the labor force, what is the overall natural rate? What would the natural rate be if the number of working women increased until women made up 50 percent of the labor force? Would full-employment GNP be higher or lower at this new natural rate?

2. Suppose that in a typical month, four people out of every hundred leave their jobs. If two of these people are out of work for 1 month, one is out of work for 2 months, and one is out of work for a year, what is the average duration of unemployment? What is the employment rate?

3. Assume you buy a 1-year bond at $100 with a 7 percent nominal interest rate and that over the year the inflation rate is 10 percent. What is your real gain over the year?

4. Assume people expect the inflation rate to be 10 percent. What nominal interest rate will they charge to obtain a 2 percent real return?

5. Suppose you own a piece of real estate that is gaining in value at 2 percent per year plus the inflation rate. If the inflation rate is 10 percent and the capital gains tax rate is 25 percent, what is your real after-tax return if you sell after 2 years?

BUDGET DEFICITS
AND
THE PUBLIC DEBT

FOCUS OF THE CHAPTER

- The budget deficit became a major economic and political question in the mid-1980s as the national debt grew more rapidly than GNP ever has during peace time.

SECTION SUMMARIES

1.   The *budget deficit* is the difference between government spending and tax receipts.

The U.S. Treasury can finance the deficit in either of two ways.

a.   It can sell government bonds to the public.
b.   It can borrow from the central bank by selling bonds to the Fed.

When the government borrows from the Fed, the Fed lends newly "printed" high-powered money. Deficit finance through sales of bonds to the public does not affect the money stock. Financing through borrowing from the Fed increases high-powered money by the amount borrowed from the Fed. For this reason, deficit finance through sales of the debt to the Fed is called *monetizing the debt*. In the United States, the Fed independently decides on how much of the national debt it wishes to buy up. Therefore, there is no necessary connection between the government deficit and the money supply.

2.   High and persistent budget deficits were a fact of economic life in the United States during the 1970s and early 1980s and will continue through the rest of the decade.

The deficit is composed of cyclical and structural components. The cyclical component represents the effects of the business cycle on the difference between government spending and revenues. Recessions are usually associated with an increase in the budget deficit as tax revenues fall in relation to spending. A rule of thumb is that each one percentage point increase in the unemployment rate is associated with a $25 to 30 billion increase in the budget deficit.

The progressive income tax system in the United States produces *fiscal drag*. The effect of real income growth on aggregate demand is dampened as households' larger incomes move them into higher tax brackets. Nominal income growth also moves households into higher tax brackets. An increase in nominal income exactly offset by an increase in the price level will move a household into a higher tax bracket when the tax system in not indexed to the inflation rate. In such circumstances, a household's real tax payments will rise. This phenomenon is known as *bracket creep*.

Bracket creep may partially eliminate the need to raise taxes to finance a deficit; the government's tax receipts automatically rise with an increase in households' nominal incomes. Prior to 1985, when tax rates in the United States became indexed, it was estimated that each one percentage point increase in nominal GNP would reduce the deficit by $34 to 38 billion.

Given constant tax rates and government spending that is not rising too rapidly relative to GNP, steady nominal GNP growth will eventually wipe out a deficit.

3.   Government expenditures consist of *mandatory* and *discretionary outlays*. Mandatory outlays, consisting mainly of entitlement programs, have doubled as a percentage of GNP since 1965. Discretionary expenditures, including defense outlays, have declined over the same period. Net interest payments have risen from 1.3 percent of GNP in 1965 to 3.3 percent in 1985. Federal government spending as a percentage of GNP has continually increased, reaching 24.0 percent in 1985.

Transfer payments, such as unemployment compensation, are not included in the definition of government purchases of goods and services, G, but do affect aggregate demand indirectly by altering household disposable income.

Most of the federal government's revenues are obtained from the personal income tax and social insurance taxes on wage earners. As a source of revenue, the corporate income tax has declined in importance over time.

Examination of government spending and revenue data over time indicates that our current deficit problem is a consequence of rising outlays, not falling revenues.

To highlight the significance of interest payments in generating a budget deficit, we decompose the total deficit into the *primary deficit*—noninterest outlays minus total government revenues—and interest payments. Since 1960, interest payments as a fraction of GNP have continued to rise, and since 1975, the noninterest budget has been in deficit. With a noninterest budget deficit, the total budget deficit will continue to grow as the government accumulates more debt just to pay the interest on previously outstanding bonds.

Taxes were cut below spending in the early 1980s, resulting in massive deficits. *Supply-siders* had argued that tax cuts could cause so large an incentive to work that the work force would increase greatly and that income would rise sharply. Therefore tax collections would actually be higher at the low tax rates than at the high tax rates. (No economist ever believed this theory.) A political argument was also made that spending could be controlled only by controlling tax revenues.

The 1985 Gramm-Rudman-Hollings Act imposes maximum deficit ceilings with the intention of reducing the federal deficit to zero by 1991. If the President and Congress cannot agree to a budget that meets the deficit reduction targets, all federal programs—with the exception of Social Security and a few others—will be subjected to (roughly) equal percentage cuts.

4.   Deficits can be either transitory or permanent and money-financed or debt-financed. Money-financed deficits cause a higher price level if transitory and a higher inflation rate if permanent. Transitory debt-financed deficits (which are more common in the United States than transitory money-financed deficits) partially crowd out private borrowing. A permanent real deficit cannot be financed purely by debt because interest payments would eventually become larger than GNP (unless the economy is growing faster than the debt).

One important question about debt financing is whether people regard government bonds as net wealth. Government bonds are certainly wealth to an individual, but consumers as a whole may feel their wealth is reduced by the future taxes they will have to pay to repay the debt. This latter idea is the basis of the *Barro-Ricardo* hypothesis, which states that a debt-financed tax cut cannot have any real effects on the economy.

The debt-to-GNP ratio is growing, remaining constant, or shrinking as

$$b\,(r - y) + x$$

is greater than, equal to, or less than zero. In the equation above, b is the debt-income ratio, r is the real interest rate, y is the growth rate of real GNP, and x is the noninterest budget surplus measured as a fraction of nominal income. The debt-income ratio cannot continue to rise indefinitely without special actions, such as tax increases, or a large unanticipated inflation that wipes out the real value of the debt. In 1986 the United States was not in a position where such drastic actions needed to be taken.

5.   The national debt, over $1.5 trillion, seems like a great burden. However, as a nation, we largely owe it to ourselves. (A portion of the debt is borrowed from people in other countries.) We also tend to forget that a large fraction of the debt is offset by government assets, such as buildings and dams. The debt is an indirect burden if it results in a lower investment and thus lower long-term growth.

6.   As the public sector has grown, reducing the size of the government has become an important political question. There are good economic reasons to prevent large permanent deficits. Beyond this, the choice of spending society's resources privately or through the government requires a value judgment of whether we prefer to consume public or private goods.

KEY TERMS

Budget deficit	Debt-income ratio
Public debt	Laffer curve
Debt finance	Gramm-Rudman-Hollings Act
Entitlement program	Barro-Ricardo hypothesis
Discretionary spending	Primary deficit
Bracket creep	Noninterest deficit
Tax indexation	Burden of the debt
Transfers	

GRAPH IT 16

In the 1980s interest payments on the national debt became a substantial portion of Federal government spending. Because a large part of the nominal interest payments go to cover inflation, rather than the real cost of interest, it can be hard to see how big the debt really is. Graph It 16 asks you to do a little inflation accounting to get a handle on this problem.

Tables 16-1 and 16-2 track the debt using five rows of information. The row "Spending deficit" shows how much the government spent on goods and services in excess of its revenues. (Assume the government does all its spending on the first day of the year.) The row "Beginning debt" is last year's beginning debt plus last year's interest plus this year's spending deficit. The "Interest" row shows the interest due on the beginning debt plus the spending deficit. "Price level" records the price at the end of the year. "Real debt" equals the spending deficit plus beginning debt plus interest, all deflated by the price level.

TABLE 16-1

Year	1	2	3	4	5
Spending deficit	100.00	100.00	100.00	100.00	100.00
Beginning debt	100.00	202.00	_____	_____	_____
Interest	2.00	4.04	_____	_____	_____
Price level, end of year	1.00	1.00	_____	_____	_____
Real debt, end of year	102.00	206.04	_____	_____	_____

TABLE 16-2

Year	1	2	3	4	5
Spending deficit	100.00	110.00	121.00	133.10	146.41
Beginning debt	100.00	222.00	————	————	————
Interest	12.00	26.64	————	————	————
Price level, end of year	1.10	1.21	————	————	————
Real debt, end of year	101.82	205.49	————	————	————

We want to know what difference inflation makes. Fill out the remainder of Table 16-1, which is based on zero inflation and a 2 percent interest rate. Then fill out Table 16-2, which is based on 10 percent inflation and a 12 percent interest rate. (Notice that the real spending deficit is the same in both cases.) What is the dollar difference in what the government owes by the end of year 5? How large is the real difference?

REVIEW OF TECHNIQUE 16

Marginal Product

You will remember from your introductory economics course that *marginal product* is the amount of *extra* output that can be produced with one *extra* unit of input. In general, there are two ways to calculate a marginal product. One way is to calculate output for the production function you are given, add one more unit of input, and recalculate. Alternatively, if you are at home with calculus, you can take the derivative of production with respect to the input. In this Review, we illustrate a simple way to use our previous work on logarithms to find the marginal product of capital for the Cobb-Douglas production function. Suppose we have the function

$$Y = AK^a N^{1-a} \qquad A = 1,000 \qquad a = 0.25$$

First, we directly calculate the marginal product for the case $K = 256$, $N = 81$. Initially, we calculate output.

$$Y = 1,000 \cdot (256)^{.25}(81)^{.75} = 1,000 \cdot (4) \cdot (27) = 108,000$$

Now, using a calculator, we recalculate with $K = 257$.

$$Y = 1,000 \cdot (4.004) \cdot (27) = 108,105$$

Thus the marginal product of capital is 105 ($108,105 - 108,000$).
We can calculate this much more generally by using a couple of tricks with logarithms. Taking logs of both sides of the Cobb-Douglas function:

$$\log Y = \log A + a \log K + (1 - a) \log N$$

Now take the change in the logs of both sides.

$$\Delta \log Y = a\Delta \log K$$

We know that the change in a log is a percentage change, so that for any variable X,

$$\Delta \log X = \frac{\Delta X}{X}$$

In this case,

$$\frac{\Delta Y}{Y} = \frac{a\Delta K}{K}$$

or $$\frac{\Delta Y}{\Delta K} \equiv MPK = \frac{aY}{K}$$

Note that 0.25 (108,000)/256 equals 105.

FILL-IN QUESTIONS

1. The _____ is the difference between government expenditures and receipts.
2. The _____ is the net accumulation over the years of the difference between government expenditures and receipts.
3. The sale of government bonds by the Treasury to the Fed is called _____ .
4. The method of government financing through sales of debt to the public is called _____ .
5. The method of government financing through sales of debt to the Fed is called _____ .
6. Increased tax collections due to inflation result from _____ _____ .
7. These tax increases could be prevented by _____ the tax system.
8. The part of the deficit not including interest payments is called the _____ or _____ .
9. In an attempt to reduce deficits in the second half of the 1980s, Congress passed the _____ .
10. The notion that the average person in the United States is responsible for $6,000 in government debt is known as _____ .

TRUE-FALSE QUESTIONS

T F   1. A budget surplus is a negative budget deficit.

T F   2. The government budget deficit is a flow.

T F   3. The national debt is a stock.

T F   4. A deficit necessarily leads to an increase in the money supply.

T F   5. The Fed buys bonds from the Treasury by "printing" more M_1.

T F   6. Inflation decreases real tax collection in a regressive tax system.

T F   7. Inflation increases real tax collections in a proportional tax system.

T F   8. Inflation increases real tax collections in a progressive tax system.

T F   9. Interest payments on the debt themselves increase the current deficit.

T F   10. State and local governments, like the federal government, can finance their deficits either by issuing bonds or by having the Fed print more money.

MULTIPLE-CHOICE QUESTIONS

1. If the nominal money supply is growing at 6 percent a year while the real money supply is constant at $100 billion, then the "inflation tax" is
   a. $100 billion   c. $6 billion
   b. $60 billion   d. 0

2. The deficit is $35 billion per year with an initial national debt of $700 billion. If no money is printed, what will the level of the national debt be in 3 years?
   a. $105 billion   c. $735 billion
   b. $700 billion   d. $805 billion

3. The Federal government is mostly paid for by
   a. the individual income tax
   b. the Fed
   c. the corporate income tax
   d. Social Security tax

4. If the budget surplus is $100 billion and the government sells $10 billion in bonds to the public, high-powered money
   a. increases by $100 billion
   b. remains constant
   c. falls by $100 billion
   d. falls by $110 billion

5. Since the 1960s, federal revenues, as a fraction of GNP, have
   a. fallen slightly
   b. remained about fixed
   c. risen slightly
   d. risen sharply

6. Since the 1960s, state and local expenditures, as a fraction of GNP, have
   a. fallen slightly
   b. remained fixed
   c. risen slightly
   d. risen sharply

7. Total federal expenditure, as a fraction of GNP, is about
   a. 10 percent
   b. 25 percent
   c. 40 percent
   d. 60 percent

8. The largest slice of the federal budget goes for
   a. defense
   b. benefit payments to individuals
   c. grants to state and local governments
   d. interest payments on the national debt

9. The most rapidly growing source of federal revenue has been
   a. individual income tax
   b. corporate income tax
   c. tariff revenue
   d. Social Security and similar taxes

10. Since World War II, the national debt, as a fraction of GNP, has
    a. dropped drastically, but has recently started to rise
    b. remained roughly constant
    c. risen drastically, then leveled off
    d. been level, but has recently risen rapidly

PROBLEMS

1. Since the U.S. economy is growing, some level of primary deficit is sustainable without causing the ratio of debt to national income to rise. Assume that over some long period of time the real interest rate in the United States is about 2 percent per year and that the rate of GNP growth is about 2.7 percent per year. How large a primary deficit (as a fraction of GNP) can the government run without an increase in the debt-to-income ratio?

2. Suppose that the government ran a budget deficit of $200 billion one year. Rather than paying it off the following year, the government borrows enough extra to pay the interest on the debt. The government keeps up this policy for 10 years and then pays off the entire accumulated debt. How much will it owe if it has been paying 2 percent interest per year? 5 percent interest per year? (Hint: See Review of Technique 17 on compound interest problems.)

MONEY, DEFICITS, AND INFLATION

FOCUS OF THE CHAPTER

- Very high inflation rates are due primarily to excessive money growth, but the link between money and inflation at low inflation rates is much weaker.
- We look at whether money growth raises or lowers interest rates.
- Budget deficits may generate money growth, but whether or not they actually do depends on Federal Reserve policy.
- We examine the relationship between hyperinflations and money growth.

SECTION SUMMARIES

1. The monetarist claim that monetary growth affects the price level, but not real variables, is essentially correct in the long run. In the short run, monetary and nonmonetary forces influence both the inflation rate and real variables.

In the model developed in Chapter 14, we found that growth in aggregate demand, $\Delta Y = Y - Y_{-1}$, depends on the rate of growth of real money balances, and that the rate of growth of real money balances equals the difference between nominal money growth and inflation.

$$\Delta Y = f(m - \pi)$$

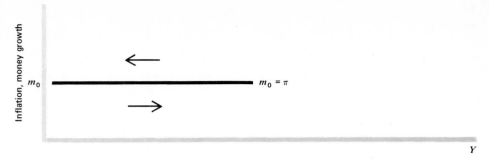

FIGURE 17-1a

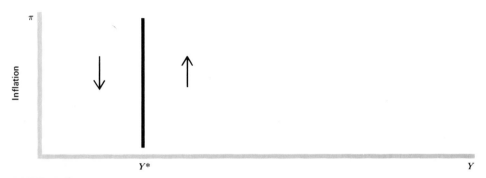

FIGURE 17-1b

Aggregate demand rises (falls) when nominal money growth is greater (less) than inflation. These scenarios are graphed in Figure 17-1a (text Figure 17-1a), where the arrows indicate the direction in which aggregate demand is changing at the specified inflation rate.

The aggregate supply curve is

$$\tau = \pi^e + \lambda(Y - Y^*)$$

If we assume adaptive expectations such as $\pi^e = \pi_{-1}$, then

$$\pi - \pi^e \equiv \pi - \pi_{-1} \equiv \Delta\pi = \lambda(Y - Y^*)$$

The inflation rate will be rising if the level of output, Y, exceeds the full-employment rate of output, Y^*, and will be falling if the opposite is true. These scenarios are pictured in Figure 17-1b (text Figure 17-1b), where the arrows indicate the direction in which the inflation rate is moving at the specified level of output.

We combine aggregate demand (Figure 17-1a) and aggregate supply (17-1b) into one figure (the upper portion of Figure 17-2, the upper portion of text Figure 17-2) that describes the dynamics of inflation and output. In region I, output and inflation are both rising; in region II, inflation is rising and

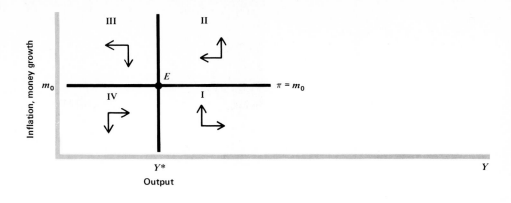

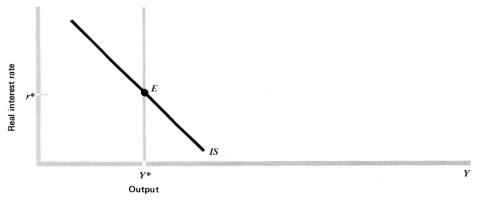

FIGURE 17-2

output is falling; in region III, inflation and output are both falling; and in region IV, output is rising and inflation is falling. In the lower portion of Figure 17-2 (same text figure), we graph the *IS* schedule for a given level of autonomous spending. The upper and lower portions of Figure 17-2 permit us to keep track of the real interest rate, the actual inflation rate and level of output, and the dynamics of inflation and output, all at once.

A permanent increase in the growth rate of the money stock shifts the $\pi = m$ schedule upward as in the upper portion of Figure 17-3 (same text figure). With adaptive expectations the expected inflation rate is last period's inflation rate, so the equilibrium real interest rate initially falls. With output above its full employment level, the inflation rate is rising. Output eventually returns to Y^*, the real interest rate returns to r^*, and the inflation rate rises to its new level, m', which is the new growth rate of the money stock. The adjustment path looks something like the path drawn in the upper portion of Figure 17-3.

In contrast, with the assumption of rational expectations, the economy will immediately jump to the new $\pi = m$ point at full employment.

The Fisher equation

$$r^* = i - \pi^*$$

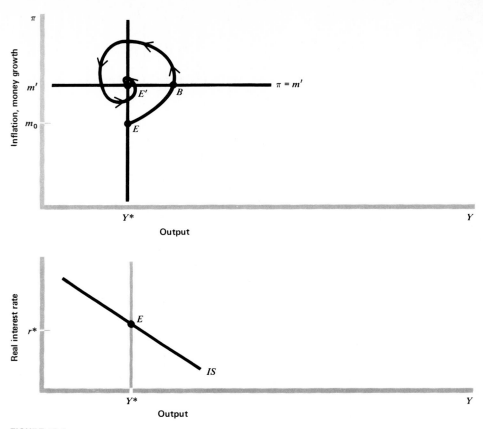

FIGURE 17-3

helps us track the nominal interest rate during the adjustment of the economy to a new equilibrium. If inflationary expectations are adaptive, the nominal interest rate adjusts slowly to changes in the growth rate of the money stock. If, for example, there is a permanent increase in the growth rate of the money, the nominal interest rate will initially fall by the same amount as the initial decline in the real rate, but eventually rise above its initial level by the amount of the increase in the steady-state inflation rate.

The declining phase of the nominal interest rate adjustment path is called the *liquidity effect* to denote the impact of increased real balances on the interest rate. The income effect—which causes the nominal and real interest rates to begin to rise—results from the fact that increased nominal income causes the real demand for money to rise. The Fisher or expectations effect denotes the adjustment of the nominal interest rate to changing inflationary expectations.

A sustained increase in the growth rate of the money stock must eventually reduce real money balances. In order for this to occur, there must be a period during the adjustment to the increase in which the price level rises more rapidly than the money stock.

2. Empirical evidence suggests that changes in the monetary growth rate are associated with changes in the inflation rate, though with a lag. The length of the lag is not constant but may range anywhere from a few months to several years.

For a given, stable money demand function, we have

$$\pi = m - \eta g^*$$

where η is the elasticity of real money demand with respect to output and g^* is the growth rate of real GNP. Data for different countries indicate that π does not follow the relationship above precisely. In all likelihood, shifts in the position of the money demand function have played an important role in determining the relationship between π and m. Furthermore, supply shocks may temporarily sever the link described by the equation above.

The nominal interest rate and the actual inflation rate tend to move together over time, but the relationship is not one-for-one. The actual real rate is not constant over time.

3. The government's budget constraint states that

Budget deficit = sales of bonds + increase in the money base

The Fed is said to monetize the deficit when it purchases a part of any new Treasury issues of debt to finance the deficit.

The Fed faces a dilemma in deciding whether or not to monetize the deficit. Fiscal expansion, unaccompanied by a monetary accommodation, will have the undesirable effect of raising interest rates. On the other hand, excessive monetary accommodation will have the longer-term effect of raising the inflation rate. Moreover, monetary accommodation can only stabilize interest rates temporarily. Evidence on whether or not the U.S. Federal Reserve partially monetizes deficits is mixed.

The creation of high-powered money serves as an alternative to taxation in financing a deficit. "Tax" revenue obtained by money creation is known as *seigniorage*. The government collects seigniorage by creating high-powered money that is used to pay for the government's purchases of goods and services.

The amount collected through the inflation tax is

Inflation tax revenue = inflation rate × real money base

The government cannot collect inflation tax revenue at arbitrarily high rates of inflation. Eventually, as the money growth rate becomes large, the real money stock will fall to zero. In practice, the amount of inflation tax revenue collected by governments in developed countries is small, although there have been examples where as much as 10 percent of GNP was collected through seigniorage.

4. A rough characterization of a hyperinflation economy would be one for which the annual inflation rate was 1,000 percent per year or more.

All hyperinflating economies suffer from large budget deficits and rapid monetary growth. Usually the tax collecting system has broken down, and the government has resorted to the collection of seigniorage. Countries that have been able to stop a hyperinflation have done so by balancing the government budget and (eventually) reducing the growth rate of the money supply.

Increasing nominal interest rates increases the size of the measured deficit, but the measured deficit gives a distorted picture of its true size. A better measure is the inflation-corrected deficit, which accounts for the fact that the real value of the government's outstanding debt falls with inflation.

KEY TERMS

Fisher effect	Hyperinflation
Liquidity effect	Inflation tax
Income effect	Seigniorage
Expectations effect	Inflation-corrected deficit
Monetization of deficits	

GRAPH IT 17

Graph It 17 gives you the opportunity to investigate the relationship between the level of (and change in) the U.S. government's inflation tax revenues and the size of (and change in) the U.S. budget deficit. Use the data in Table 17-1 to compute the federal government's annual inflation tax revenues for the period 1959 to 1985. Since Table 17-1 only reports $M1$, not the monetary base, you will need to compute the monetary base on your own. In your computations, assume that the money multiplier is equal to 3.00. (You should ask yourself how the value of the money multiplier affects the amount of inflation tax collected.) Now, on Chart 17-1a, graph the amount of inflation tax revenue against the budget deficit. On Chart 17-1b, plot the change in inflation tax revenue against the change in the budget deficit.* Can you draw any conclusions from these two diagrams?

REVIEW OF TECHNIQUE 17

Compound Interest

You may have heard of the "miracle of compound interest." When the interest on a debt is allowed to accumulate, together with the interest on the interest, and the interest on the interest on the interest, and so on, the total mounts up quickly. If you start off with P dollars and invest them at interest rate r for t

---

*The first two points are plotted for you in each diagram.

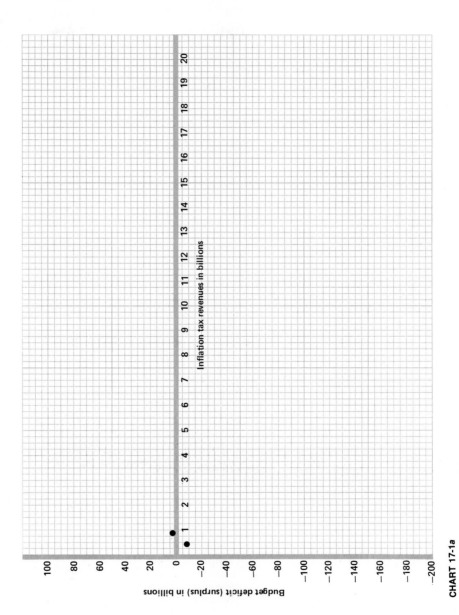

CHART 17-1a

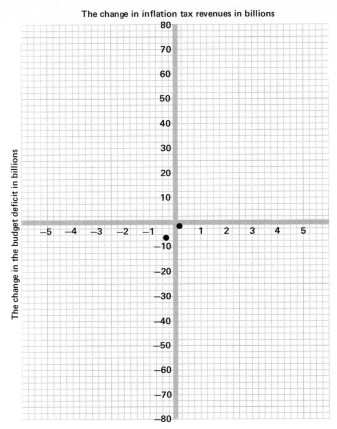

CHART 17-1b

years, you end up with a final value *FV* given by the formula

$$FV = P(1 + r)^t$$

For example, 1 dollar invested at 5 percent for 1 year will give you back $1.00 × 1.05 = $1.05. Invested for 2 years, it would yield $1.00 × 1.05 × 1.05 = $1.1025. If you didn't receive the interest on the interest, then after 2 years you'd have received 10 cents in interest, rather than 10 1/4 cents. (This is called "simple interest.") A fourth of a cent doesn't seem worth making much of a fuss about compound interest, but if you held the investment for 30 years, simple interest would return your dollar plus 2 dollars in interest while compound interest returns your dollar plus $3.32 in interest.

Sometimes you would like to know how long your money will take to double when invested at compound interest. A good rule of thumb is the "Rule of 72s." The approximate number of years required for an investment to double is found by dividing 72 by the interest rate. For example, at 5 percent an investment doubles in about 14 1/2 years; at 10 percent, in just over 7.

TABLE 17-1

Year	Deficit (billions)	M1 (billions)	Price level
1959	−1.1	141.0	87.3
1960	3.0	141.8	88.7
1961	−3.9	146.5	89.6
1962	−4.2	149.2	90.6
1963	.3	154.7	91.7
1964	−3.3	161.9	92.9
1965	.5	169.5	94.5
1966	−1.8	173.7	97.2
1967	−13.2	185.1	100.0
1968	−6.0	199.4	104.2
1969	8.4	205.8	109.8
1970	−12.4	216.6	116.3
1971	−22.0	230.8	121.3
1972	−16.8	252.0	125.3
1973	−5.6	265.9	133.1
1974	−11.6	277.5	147.7
1975	−69.4	291.1	161.2
1976	−53.5	310.3	170.5
1977	−46.0	335.3	181.5
1978	−29.3	363.0	195.4
1979	−16.1	389.0	217.4
1980	−61.3	414.8	246.8
1981	−63.8	441.8	272.4
1982	−145.9	480.8	289.1
1983	−179.4	528.0	298.4
1984	−172.9	558.5	311.1
1985	−197.3	624.7	322.2

FILL-IN QUESTIONS

1. An extremely rapid inflation is called a _____ .
2. Government revenue from printing money results in what is sometimes called an _____ .
3. The revenue the government receives from printing money is also known as _____ .
4. Official deficit figures can be adjusted for the drop in the value of the national debt due to inflation to obtain the _____ .
5. The _____ describes the connection between the nominal interest rate, the real interest rate, and the expected inflation rate.
6. The Federal Reserve has the discretion to _____ if it wishes.
7. An increase in the money supply moves the *LM* curve and thus initially lowers the interest rate through the _____ .

8. As nominal income starts to rise, interest rates start to rise because of the
_____ .

9. Another name for the Fisher effect is the _____ .

TRUE-FALSE QUESTIONS

T F 1. In the long run, growth of the money supply has a major effect on the price level.

T F 2. In the long run, growth of the money supply has a major effect on real output.

T F 3. In the long run, growth of the money supply has a major effect on nominal GNP.

T F 4. In the long run, growth of the money supply has a major effect on the nominal interest rate.

T F 5. In the long run, growth of the money supply has a major effect on the real interest rate.

T F 6. Hyperinflations are always caused by very rapid money growth.

T F 7. Hyperinflations are usually accompanied by very large budget deficits.

T F 8. The U.S. budget deficit is financed largely by the Federal Reserve's "printing money."

T F 9. The economy responds to money growth with a lag of uncertain length.

T F 10. The nominal interest rate and the inflation rate are tightly linked.

MULTIPLE-CHOICE QUESTIONS

1. If the nominal money supply is growing at 6 percent a year while the real money supply is constant at $100 billion, then the "inflation tax" is

a. $100 billion   c. $6 billion
b. $60 billion   d. 0

2. When the rate of inflation is greater than the rate of money growth, the real money supply
a. rises   c. remains constant
b. falls   d. may do any of a, b, or c.

3. A hyperinflation usually ends with
a. a reduction of the budget deficit
b. a reduction in the growth in the money supply
c. a currency reform
d. all the above

4. An increase in the rate of growth of the money supply
   a. raises interest rates
   b. lowers interest rates
   c. first lowers, then raises interest rates
   d. first raises, then lowers interest rates

5. The Federal Reserve is likely to monetize the debt if it targets
   a. interest rates
   b. the money supply
   c. either a or b
   d. neither a nor b

6. The United States came close to suffering a hyperinflation
   a. in 1933
   b. in 1945
   c. in 1979
   d. never

7. As the inflation rate rises, the revenue from the "inflation tax"
   a. rises
   b. falls
   c. rises, but eventually starts to fall
   d. falls, but eventually starts to rise

8. An increase in the rate of money growth will eventually cause the real money supply to
   a. be higher
   b. be lower
   c. remain constant
   d. do any of a, b, or c, depending on the country

9. In the United States, at high inflation rates, we might expect the "inflation tax," as a fraction of GNP, to be around
   a. 0.5 percent
   b. 5 percent
   c. 25 percent
   d. 50 percent

10. Compared with the speed of movement of the economy under adaptive expectations, the speed under rational expectations is
    a. faster
    b. slower
    c. faster, but adjustment is incomplete
    d. slower, but adjustment is more complete

PROBLEMS

1. What rate of money growth can the United States sustain without any inflation?

2. If the annual rate of inflation is 1,000 percent, what is the monthly rate of inflation? If the annual rate of inflation is 19,000 percent, what is the daily rate of inflation?

3. Suppose that the nominal interest rate is 50 percent per year and the inflation rate is 48 percent per year. If you invest $100 today, what will be the real value of your investment in 10 years?

MACROECONOMICS: THE INTERACTION OF EVENTS AND IDEAS

FOCUS OF THE CHAPTER

- Macroeconomic thought has changed over time, at least partially in response to changes in the macroeconomy.
- Major schools of economic thought have included and continue to include Keynesian, monetarist, rational expectations-equilibrium approach, and supply-side. Though there are sharp contrasts among these schools, most economists accept some of the lessons of each.
- The rational expectations–equilibrium approach suggests that markets clear, that most policy is ineffective, and that the economy is, at least in a sense, efficient. New ideas—such as efficiency wage theory and small menu cost theory—have arisen to explain why policy might indeed be effective and why the economy may not always be efficient.

SECTION SUMMARIES

1. During the 1960s, U.S. economic growth was substantially higher, and inflation and unemployment were lower, than the period afterward. Since 1982, growth has accelerated again, and inflation has abated. The behavior of the economy since 1982 is of no surprise, seeing that 1982 marked the bottom of the deepest recession in the United States since the 1930s.

In 1969–1971, the government attempted gradually to reduce inflation with a minimum increase in unemployment. The policy was not very successful at reducing inflation. In August 1971, the Nixon administration temporarily froze wages and prices.

In 1973–1975, the economy experienced simultaneous inflation and unemployment. Many of these developments were due to supply shocks, especially the 1973 Arab oil embargo.

The 1975–1979 period was one of economic recovery, but also one of increasing inflation. High inflation was due to high expected inflation—with some role played by the state of aggregate demand.

The rising inflation of the late 1970s led the Fed to adopt monetary targeting rules in 1979. Inflation was rising so rapidly in 1980 that the Fed and the Carter administration imposed credit controls.

The Reagan Administration proposed and passed the three-year Kemp-Roth tax cuts in 1981. The early result was a large increase in the full-employment deficit. The economy went into a deep recession in 1982, and the Fed abandoned its tight-money policy in an effort to stimulate aggregate demand.

The economy rebounded in late 1982, and experienced rapid growth—though declining inflation—through 1984. Growth slowed in 1985 and early 1986, but there was hope that the decline of the dollar and of oil prices would boost growth soon.

There have been four recessions in the United States since 1969. The poor performance of the economy over this period has been a focal point for debate among macroeconomists. Different ''camps'' emphasize alternative explanations for why the economy has behaved as it has.

2. *Monetarism*, whose foremost spokesman is Milton Friedman, has the central tenet that the money supply is the most important determinant of prices and of economic activity. Friedman has summarized monetarism by saying:

> I regard the description of our position as ''money is all that matters for changes in nominal income and for *short-run* changes in real income'' as an exaggeration but one that gives the right flavor of our conclusions.*

Friedman has also argued that there are ''long and variable lags'' in the connection between the money supply and economic activity. He suggests that because the money supply is so important but its effects so hard to predict, we should use a *monetary rule*. For example, the money supply ought to be increased 4 percent every year without regard to the current state of the economy.

Monetarists have further argued that the Federal Reserve should use a *money supply target* rather than an interest rate target. The three themes which seem to best distinguish a monetarist are:

a. Emphasis on the growth rate of the money stock
b. Arguments against fine tuning
c. A relatively greater weight on the costs of inflation than the costs of unemployment

*''A Theoretical Framework for Monetary Analysis,'' *Journal of Political Economy*, March/April 1970, p. 217.

Many of Friedman's basic propositions are now accepted by the mainstream of American economists.

3. The rational expectations–equilibrium approach to macroeconomics emphasizes the ideas that

1. Individuals use information efficiently and do not (systematically) make forecasting errors.
2. Individuals maximize utility, firms maximize profits, and markets are in equilibrium.

As a theory of expectations, the rational expectations assumption implies that effective policy cannot be based on attempts to systematically ''fool'' the public.

4. Members of the rational expectations–equilibrium school have attempted to explain business cycles while adhering to the notion that all markets clear.

One story offered is the following. Suppose the economy is composed of many markets. A supplier in market i knows the price of his or her own product, but not the aggregate price level. Each supplier's output is an increasing function of the supplier's price relative to the expected aggregate price level.

Shocks to the economy take two forms: shocks to relative prices, which sum to zero across markets, and shocks to the aggregate price level, which affect all prices in the same proportion. An anticipated increase in the money supply is known (by producers) to increase all prices in the same proportion and cannot lead to an increase in output. However, an unanticipated increase in the money supply will raise output in all markets because every producer mistakenly believes that the relative price of his or her product has increased.

Robert Lucas has used such a model to produce a Phillips curve type of relationship between output and inflation. The key feature of Lucas's work is that only unanticipated changes in the money stock (and, thus, the price level) produce variation in output.

Attempts to confirm the proposition that only unanticipated policy changes matter have had mixed results. Evidence seems to suggest that both anticipated and unanticipated policy changes have real effects on the economy.

Equilibrium real business cycle theory takes the view that business cycles are mainly a consequence of real shocks such as shifts in labor productivity and government spending. Equilibrium business cycle theorists believe that business cycles are propagated by large swings in the supply of labor over time, a phenomenon which is known as the ''intertemporal substitution of labor supply.'' According to real business cycle theorists, changes in the money supply are correlated with movements in output because the Fed accommodates movements in GNP. Changes in the money supply are not the cause of, but rather are caused by, changes in GNP.

5. Rational expectations–equilibrium theorists stress that policy will be more effective the more credible it is. They also adopt the view that since the public eventually catches onto the nature of changes in monetary and fiscal

policy, the best policies are stable policies. The rational expectations school argues that stable policy is ensured by effective institutional reform.

7.   Wage contracts, which impart some "short-term" rigidity to wages, negate the strongest implications of the rational expectations–equilibirum models. When wages are "sticky" downward or upward, anticipated changes in policy can have real effects on the economy. Specific explanations for why wages and/or prices might be rigid include efficiency wage theory and small menu costs.

Profit sharing has been suggested as a possible institutional reform for eliminating wage rigidity and, therefore, unemployment.

8.   European unemployment has increased continually since 1960, a phenomenon which appears to stem from downward-rigid real wages (Keynesian unemployment). The downward rigidity of real wages has proved difficult to explain.

9.   There is far less disagreement among macroeconomists than the popular press likes to claim. The evolution of macroeconomic theory since 1960 is best characterized as a series of sophisticated refinements of exiting ideas. The most recent and notable contributions to theory focus on the way in which individuals form expectations and on the incorporation of the role of labor market institutions into macro models. Most macroeconomists put much greater weight on the role of monetary factors in explaining output fluctuations than they did two decades ago.

KEY TERMS

Monetary rule

Rational expectations–equilibrium approach

Credibility

Imperfect information

Real business cycles

Propagation mechanism

Intertemporal substitution of leisure

Supply-side economics

Reaganomics

Efficiency wage

Small menu costs

Profit sharing

GRAPH IT 18

The Federal government entered the 1980s with huge deficits. Since the economy was also in a terrible recession, we know that a large part of the deficit represented cyclical factors. In this Graph It, we make some "back of the envelope" calculations to see the difference between the cyclical and structural deficit.

Both government revenues and government transfer spending vary with the state of the economy. We know that taxes are about 21 percent of GNP. Total transfers are around half of government spending, but not all transfers vary cyclically. Let's guess that transfers minus taxes rises about 1 dollar for every 3 dollars GNP rises. In Table 18-1, you are asked to split the budget into cyclical and structural components using three different assumptions about the natural rate of unemployment. Government estimates use far more detailed figures and therefore can be more accurate, but it's not hard to get a rough idea of how much of any given budget deficit (*BD*) is due to a recession and how much to longer-run fiscal policy.

REVIEW OF TECHNIQUE 18

The Expectations Mechanism

In many chapters we have modeled expectations of some economic variable as depending on past levels of the variable. To see how this works, suppose we have some variable X and that the expectation of X, X^e is based on the last 3 years' value of X according to the following formula:

$$X^e = 0.75X_{-1} + 0.2X_{-2} + 0.05X_{-3}$$

Suppose X rises by one unit for a year and then returns to its original level. What happens to X^e over the next several years?

Nothing happens in the year that X changes, since X^e does not depend on this year's X. Next year, X^e is up by 0.75 units. The year after that, X_{-1} has returned to its original level and X_{-2} is up by one unit, so X^e is up by 0.2 units from its original level and thus 0.55 units lower than it was in the first period following the change in X. In the next period, X^e is only 0.05 units higher than its original level, and thereafter X^e is back to its original level.

Suppose, instead, that X went up one unit permanently. In the first period following the change, X^e is up by 0.75 units, just as in the case of a temporary change. In the next period, X_{-1} and X_{-2} are both up by one unit, and so X^e climbs another 0.2 units to reach 0.95 units above its original level. In the third and following periods, X^e is up by one unit. Notice that we force the long-run change in X^e to be the same as a permanent change in X by making sure that the weights in the expectations equation add to 1.

Figures 18-1 and 18-2 illustrate the changes in X and X^e worked through above.

TABLE 18-1

(1)	1982 unemployment rate	9.7	9.7	9.7
(2)	Guess of natural rate	5.5	6.0	6.5
(3)	Unemployment gap	4.2	____	____
(4)	1982 GNP (billions)	3,058	3,058	3,058
(5)	GNP gap [2.5% × (3) × (4)]	____	____	____
(6)	Cyclical *BD* [.33 × (5)]	____	____	____
(7)	*BD*	148	148	148
(8)	Structural *BD* [(7) − (6)]	____	____	____

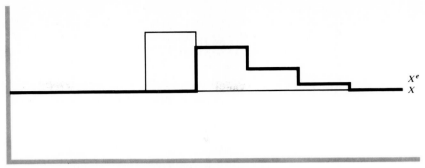

FIGURE 18-1 CHANGE IN EXPECTATIONS (HEAVY
LINE) FOLLOWING A TEMPORARY INCREASE IN X
(LIGHT LINE) .

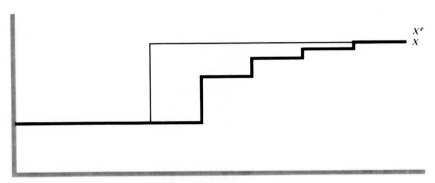

FIGURE 18-2 CHANGE IN EXPECTATIONS (HEAVY
LINE) FOLLOWING A PERMANENT INCREASE IN X
(LIGHT LINE).

FILL-IN QUESTIONS

1. The school of economic thought ''led'' by Milton Friedman is the _____

    _____ school.

2. An example of a _____ is that the nominal money
    supply should grow at a strict 4 percent a year.

3. The relatively new school of economic thought that holds the belief that
    only unanticipated changes in policy have any real effect is the _____
    _____ school.

4. _____ theory suggests that economic fluctuations
    have nothing to do with money, but rather arise from shocks to productiv-
    ity and aggregate supply changes.

5. Recent alternatives to the rational expectations school include _____
    _____ theory . . .

6. . . . and the idea of _____ .

7. The amount by which temporary wage fluctuations affect how much people work depends on the _____ .

TRUE-FALSE QUESTIONS

T   F   1. Monetarists believe that the private sector is inherently unstable.

T   F   2. Monetarists believe in the importance of the money supply for determining real economic activity.

T   F   3. Monetarists believe that the money supply is the primary determinant of nominal GNP in the long run.

T   F   4. Monetarists believe that the money supply is the primary determinant of real GNP in the long run.

T   F   5. Monetarists emphasize the use of a money supply target instead of an interest rate target.

T   F   6. Keynesians believe that anticipated changes in the money supply are a major determinant of economic activity.

T   F   7. *Rational expectations theorists* believe that anticipated changes in the money supply are a major determinant of economic activity.

MULTIPLE-CHOICE QUESTIONS

1. Rational expectations theory suggests that
    a. only unexpected changes in the stock of money affect the price level
    b. only unexpected changes in the stock of money affect the level of output
    c. only expected changes in the stock of money affect the price level
    d. only expected changes in the stock of money affect the level of output
2. The idea that surprise increases in the money supply increase GNP is associated with
    a. Keynesians
    b. monetarists
    c. rational expectations theory
    d. all the above

19

LONG-TERM GROWTH AND PRODUCTIVITY

FOCUS OF THE CHAPTER

- We study here two related topics.

    1. *Potential output*
    - Potential output is determined by *factor inputs* and the state of *technology*
    - Technology is described by a *production function*.
    2. *Long-term growth*
    - By studying how factor inputs change over time, in particular how saving leads to the accumulation of capital, we can predict how potential output will change in the future.

- *In this chapter we always assume that GNP equals potential GNP.* We allow no role for aggregate demand and no role for incorrect expectations.

SECTION SUMMARIES

1. Output depends on factor input and on the technology applied to that input. The *production function* relates output to input. Using Y to represent output and K and N to represent capital input and labor input, respectively, we

can write a production function as

$$Y = AF(K, N)$$

The rate of growth of output can be written as

$$\frac{\Delta Y}{Y} = (1 - \theta)\frac{\Delta N}{N} + \theta\frac{\Delta K}{K} + \frac{\Delta A}{A}$$

where θ is capital's share in income, about 0.25 in the American economy, and A represents the level of technology. Thus the three sources of growth are more labor, more capital, and improved technology. A one percent increase in labor increases output by about three-fourths of one percent, while a one percent increase in capital increases output by about one-fourth of one percent.

2. Since 1929, economic growth has averaged about 3.4 percent per year. Of this, about 1.8 percent has been due to increased input and the remainder to increased output per unit of input. The most important sources of growth have been population growth and increases in knowledge.

3. Supply-side economists argue that potential GNP can be increased by improving incentives to supply labor or to invest in new capital. While such effects clearly exist, they are fairly small and unlikely to have much short-run significance. They may be of greater importance in terms of very long run economic well-being.

4. Potential GNP can be estimated in two ways. First, we can pick a "bench-mark" year, when the economy is believed to be at full-employment, and project trends. Second, we can estimate the production function and the available factor inputs. While neither method is exact, both make it clear that the growth of potential GNP in the 1970s was far below historical trend.

5. Growth theory is the study of the growth of factor inputs and the resultant growth in output. We assume that population grows at a constant percentage rate, $\Delta N/N \equiv n$. We also assume no technological change.

It is sometimes more convenient to think about output *per capita*. (Per capita is Latin for "by head," that is, per person.) We write output per capita as $x \equiv Y/N$ and capital per worker, also called the capital-labor ratio, as $k \equiv K/N$. We assume that the production function has *constant returns to scale*. (See Review of Technique 15.)

The *steady state* of the economy is the position in which capital per worker is constant. Just enough is saved to replace machinery that has worn out and to provide machines for new workers. Output per head is constant whenever capital grows as fast as population.

$$\frac{\Delta K}{K} = n$$

The change in capital is the difference between saving and depreciation. We assume that people save a constant fraction s of their income and that depreciation is a constant percentage d of the existing capital stock.

$\Delta K =$ saving $-$ depreciation
$\Delta K = sY - dK$

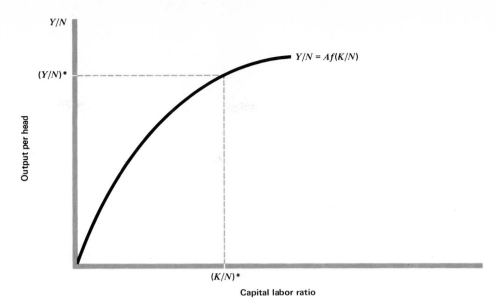

FIGURE 19-1 THE PRODUCTION FUNCTION.

Dividing both sides by K and subtracting n from both sides,

$$\frac{\Delta K}{K} - n = \frac{sY}{K} - n - d$$

Recognizing that the rate of growth of capital minus the rate of growth of labor is the rate of growth of capital per head and that the ratio of output to capital is the same as the ratio of per capita output to per capita machinery,

$$\frac{\Delta k}{k} = \frac{sx}{k} - (n + d)$$

$$\Delta k = sx - (n + d)k$$

This final formula looks formidable. All it says is that the amount of capital each worker has available rises when saving goes up and falls when depreciation rises or when capital must be spread out among more workers.

The growth process can be studied in terms of Figure 19-2 (text Figure 19-4). The x curve gives the level of output per head as a function of the capital-labor ratio. This is a graph of the production function. This sx curve shows the amount saved. The $(n + d)k$ line is the investment requirement, the amount needed to prevent capital per worker from falling.

To the left of point C, saving is above the investment requirement, and so capital per worker is growing. To the right of point C, saving is less than required investment, and so capital is falling. Point C is the steady state of the economy, the point at which the capital-labor ratio is neither rising nor falling.

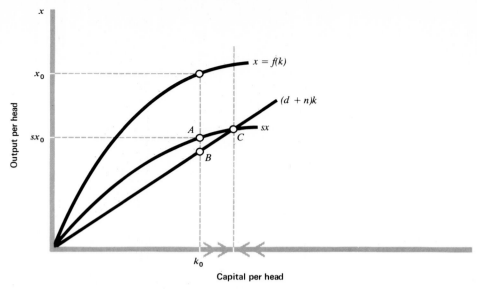

FIGURE 19-2 SAVINGS, INVESTMENT, AND CAPITAL ACCUMULATION.

Steady-state per capita output is found by reading x off the production function directly above point C. Note that while C shows the long-run equilibrium of the economy, nothing prevents the economy from being away from steady-state equilibrium most of the time.

An increase in the saving rate increases steady-state per capita GNP. It does not change the growth rate of per capita GNP permanently. In the steady state, per capita GNP is constant, and so its growth rate is zero. Faster population growth reduces per capita GNP in the steady state. Even though GNP grows faster with higher population growth, it does not grow rapidly enough to keep up with the increasing population. Thus, faster population growth means a lower steady-state per capita GNP.

KEY TERMS

Potential output	Technical progress
Production function	Growth of total factor productivity
Growth accounting	Supply-side economics
Sources of growth	Steady state
Labor productivity	Limits of growth

GRAPH IT 19

We know that an increase in investment increases both aggregate demand and aggregate supply. Aggregate demand rises because of the increase in I in the

TABLE 19-1 SHORT- AND LONG-RUN INCREASE IN AGGREGATE DEMAND

(1)	1979 investment (billions)	———
(2)	20% increase	———
(3)	Increase in GNP [2 × (2)]	———
(4)	Actual 1979 GNP	2,418

$C + I + G$, and aggregate supply rises because of the increase in the capital stock. How do the two effects compare? We'll use 1979 as a base year because 1979 was the most recent year in which the economy was approximately at full employment. Assume that we could increase investment spending by 20 percent and that the aggregate demand multiplier on investment is 2.0.

Fill out Table 19-1. Notice that this table is marked "Short Run and Long Run." If we permanently increase investment, we permanently increase aggregate demand. In other words, aggregate demand goes to a new, higher level and stays there, but it doesn't keep increasing.

In Table 19-2 we try to figure out the increase in aggregate supply. Aggregate supply goes up because increased investment increases the capital stock. We know from studies of the production function that a one percent increase in the capital stock increases output by about one-fourth of one percent. It turns out that the capital stock is roughly three times GNP. Using these facts, fill in Table 19-2 to calculate the supply side of the impact of a 1-year and a 5-year increase in investment. (Use the same annual investment increase as in Table 19-1.)

REVIEW OF TECHNIQUE 19

Levels versus Rates of Change

Economic variables change over time. The difference between the *level* of a given variable and the *rate* at which it *changes* over time is critical. Sometimes the rate of change of an economic variable is itself an important economic variable. For example, the *rate of inflation* is the percentage *rate of change of the price level*. It

TABLE 19-2 SHORT- AND LONG-RUN DECREASE IN AGGREGATE SUPPLY

		1 year	5 years
(1)	Increase in annual investment	———	———
(2)	Cumulative increase in capital	———	———
(3)	Total capital (roughly 3 × GNP)	———	———
(4)	As percentage of capital	———	———
(5)	Relative increase in production [¼ × (4)]	———	———
(6)	Increase in AS [GNP times (5)]	———	———
(7)	As fraction of AD increase [100 × (6)/(3) above]	——— %	——— %

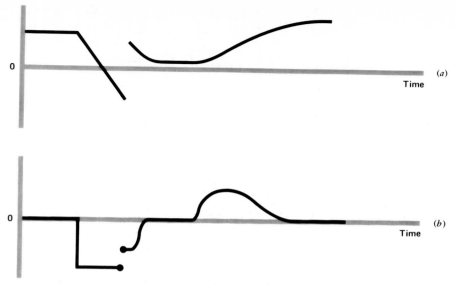

FIGURE 19-3 LEVEL AND RATE OF CHANGE OF A VARIABLE.

is quite possible for the rate of change to be falling while the level of the variable is rising. For example, suppose inflation falls from 13 percent a year to 8 percent a year. The price *level*, of course, keeps rising so long as the inflation rate is above zero.

It is sometimes useful to distinguish between a smooth change in the level of a variable and a sudden jump in its level. If the price level changed from 100 to 110 over a year, the inflation rate over the year would be 10 percent per year. If the same change took place over a month, the inflation rate that month would be 120 percent per year. If the change took only a day, the inflation rate would be 3,650 percent per year. The smaller the time period, the greater the *rate* of change. If an economic variable actually jumps, then the rate of change when it jumps is infinite or, perhaps more correctly, undefined.

Figures 19-3*a* and 3*b* show the level and rate of change of an arbitrary economic variable. Be sure you see how the latter figure is derived from the former.

FILL-IN QUESTIONS

1. When all factors of production are fully employed, we say that the economy is producing _____ GNP.
2. Total output divided by the number of people is _____ GNP.
3. Output per worker is a measure of labor _____.
4. The technological relation between output and inputs is described by the _____.

5. The addition of one unit of capital, with other inputs fixed, increases output by the _____.

6. Payment to capital as a fraction of GNP is called _____.

7. Technology is said to have _____ when a proportional increase in all inputs results in a proportional increase in output.

8. GNP per person is constant in the _____.

9. Continuing growth of GNP per person is due to _____.

TRUE-FALSE QUESTIONS

T F   1. An exogenous addition to the capital stock leads to an immediate increase in per capita GNP.

T F   2. An exogenous addition to the capital stock leads to an increase in steady-state per capita GNP.

T F   3. An increase in the saving rate leads to an immediate increase in per capita GNP.

T F   4. An increase in the saving rate leads to an increase in steady-state GNP.

T F   5. An increase in the saving rate leads to an increase in the steady-state rate of growth of GNP.

T F   6. An increase in the rate of population growth leads to an immediate drop in GNP per capita.

T F   7. An increase in the rate of population growth leads to a drop in steady-state per capita GNP.

T F   8. An increase in the rate of population growth leads to a drop in steady-state GNP.

T F   9. A higher depreciation rate leads to lower steady-state capital.

T F   10. A higher depreciation rate leads to lower steady-state GNP.

MULTIPLE-CHOICE QUESTIONS

1. The most important factor responsible for growth in GNP in the United States has been
   a. population growth
   b. technological change
   c. capital accumulation
   d. stimulative government spending

2. The most important factor responsible for per capita growth of GNP in the United States has been
   a. population growth
   b. technological change
   c. capital accumulation
   d. stimulative government spending

3. Over the last 97 years, per capita GNP has grown about
   a. 0.5 percent
   b. 2 percent per year
   c. 6 percent per year
   d. 8 percent per year

4. Productivity growth has fallen in recent years because
   a. more inexperienced workers have entered the labor force
   b. spending on research and development has slowed
   c. more of GNP is in the service industries
   d. all of a, b, and c combined

5. Assuming everyone is in the labor force, an increase in population causes
   a. an immediate increase in GNP
   b. an immediate increase in GNP per capita
   c. immediate increases in both
   d. no increases in either

6. A 15 percent increase in the capital stock leads to a _____ _____ increase in GNP.
   a. 0 percent
   b. between 0 and 15 percent
   c. 15 percent
   d. more than 15 percent

7. Labor's share of GNP in the United States is approximately
   a. 2 percent
   b. 25 percent
   c. 75 percent
   d. 98 percent

8. If the capital stock increases 15 percent while the labor force increases 7 percent, the capital-labor ratio increases approximately
   a. 2 percent
   b. 4 percent
   c. 8 percent
   d. 15 percent

9. If half the capital in the economy were to be destroyed, per capita GNP would drop
   a. not at all
   b. by less than half
   c. to one-half its original level
   d. by more than one-half

10. If population were suddenly to double, per capita GNP would
    a. remain unchanged
    b. double
    c. drop by less than one-half
    d. drop by more than one-half

PROBLEMS

The Cobb-Douglas production function is

$$Y = AK^aN^{1-a}$$

1. Find the function that gives per capita GNP based on capital per person, using the Cobb-Douglas production function above.
2. Prove that if $a = 0.25$, labor's share of GNP will be 75 percent.
3. Assume that labor's share of GNP is 75 percent and capital's share is 25 percent. If the labor supply increases by 10 percent and the supply of capital increases by 20 percent, by how much does GNP increase? GNP per capita?
4. Assume the economy is initially in long-run equilibrium. Suppose half the capital of society is destroyed. Show the time path of per capita GNP.
5. Assume the economy is initially in long-run equilibrium. Suppose that the saving rate increases. Show the time path of per capita GNP.

MONEY, PRICES, AND EXCHANGE RATES

FOCUS OF THE CHAPTER

- Exchange rates have been allowed to float since 1973. This chapter analyzes the workings of the domestic and world economies when exchange rates are determined by supply and demand.

    1. The model of Chapter 6 is extended to emphasize the role of money.
    2. We look at a world in which all prices are flexible in order to study the determinants of the exchange rate itself.

- Later sections extend these results and consider some of the practical consequences. We explore the role of exchange rate expectations and the relations between interest rates in different countries. We also look at the interdependence between countries and the role of exchange rate intervention by central banks.

SECTION SUMMARIES

1. With a fixed exchange rate and a fixed foreign price level, an increase (decrease) in the domestic price level reduces (increases) foreign demand for domestically produced goods and increases (reduces) the domestic demand for imports.

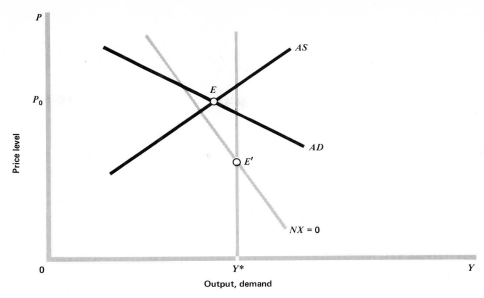

FIGURE 20-1

Aggregate demand is the sum of domestic aggregate demand, A, and net exports, NX. The trade balance schedule, $NX = 0$, is downward-sloping when drawn against the domestic price level and domestic income (Figure 20-1, text Figure 20-1). To the right (left) of the trade balance schedule there exists a current account deficit (surplus).

The short-run equilibrium (point E) in Figure 20-1 shows a situation where the current account is in deficit and the economy is below full employment. With a fixed exchange rate, a current account deficit means that the central bank is depleting its reserves of foreign exchange. This situation cannot persist. A cut in aggregate demand coupled with an increase in aggregate supply can move the economy to full employment and trade balance at the point E'.

Without policy intervention, automatic adjustment mechanisms will move the economy from E to E'. On the aggregate demand side, the central bank's policy of pegging the exchange rate while the economy is running a current account deficit leads to a reduction in the domestic money supply. The result is a leftward shift of the aggregate demand curve. As prices fall, wages fall, and the aggregate supply curve shifts down. The automatic nature of this adjustment process gives it the name "the classical adjustment process."

Sometimes conflicts exist between the goal of achieving domestic full employment (internal balance) and the goal of achieving trade (external) balance. Figure 20-2 (text Figure 20-2) shows the trade balance schedule and a vertical line at full employment. The two lines divide the quadrant into four regions, each region corresponding to some combination of recession/boom and trade surplus/deficit. At point A, policy makers face a policy dilemma. Any policy that shifts the aggregate demand cutting through A moves the

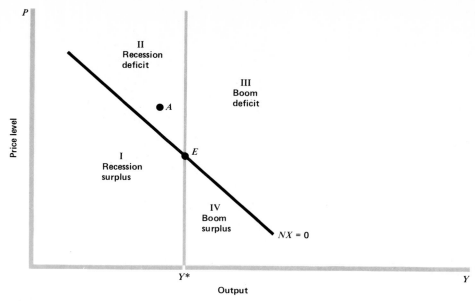

FIGURE 20-2

economy closer to external (internal) balance at the expense of internal (external) balance. The government must find policies to shift the trade balance schedule rightward—for example, by levying tariffs on imported goods or by devaluing the home currency. These are expenditure-switching policies. Whatever the solution chosen, policy dilemmas cannot be solved using one policy instrument. As a rule, policy makers need as many policy instruments as they have targets, to achieve their goals.

2. The monetary approach to the balance of payments is based on the belief that balance of payments deficits are mainly a result of excessive monetary growth. Proponents of the monetary approach charge that central banks often respond to the contractionary effects of a balance of payments deficit (under fixed exchange rates) with a sterilization policy. Sterilization leads to persistent balance of payments deficits.

The monetary approach prescribes a contraction of domestic credit to reduce the balance of payments deficit. Such a policy has a short-run cost of higher domestic interest rates and lower domestic income.

3. In this section, we allow for long-run price flexibility. We also assume that there is perfect capital mobility. This means that in the short run, the economy can be away from potential GNP. We are always on the BB schedule.

We are used to a monetary expansion increasing GNP through a decreased interest rate. The mechanism here is a little different. Since capital is perfectly mobile, the domestic interest rate is fixed equal to the world interest rate. When the money supply increases now, the exchange rate immediately depreciates until the IS curve has moved enough so that it crosses the new LM

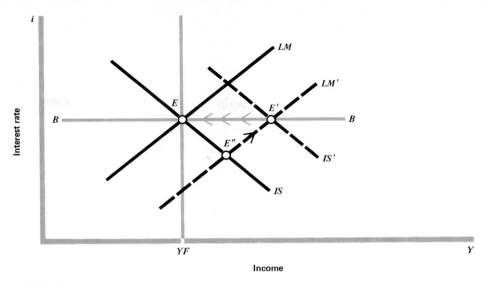

FIGURE 20-3

curve on the *BB* schedule, as in Figure 20-3 (text Figure 20-5). In the long run, prices rise just enough to return the real money supply to its initial level. This increase in the price level also offsets the depreciation of the exchange rate so that competitiveness, eP^*/P, returns to its initial level. GNP returns to potential. Because exchange rates adjust rapidly and prices adjust slowly, the adjustment to long-run equilibrium involves great variations in relative prices and competitiveness.

The concept of *purchasing power parity* (PPP) suggests that the terms of trade, eP^*/P, should remain constant. In our earlier example, we compared the price of German-made and American-made Volkswagens. If the two cars are identical, they ought to sell for the same price. We should have eP^*/P equal 1. If the two cars are truly different, then the relative price might persist at 1.2:1. Purchasing power parity asserts that the terms of trade depend on the true relative values of domestic and foreign goods, not on monetary changes. Purchasing power parity is quite appealing in the long run, but there are substantial deviations from PPP in the short run.

4. Interest rates in different countries are often quite different. This disparity is due to expectations of exchange rate changes. Suppose the U.S. interest rate is 10 percent and the German interest rate is 8 percent, while the dollar is expected to depreciate by 2 percent over the coming year. Investors could invest money in the United States and earn 10 percent directly. Alternatively, they could buy deutschmarks, make a German investment, and earn 8 percent. But now, when the marks are turned back into dollars, they cost 2 percent less, so investors get 2 percent more dollars. The 8 percent plus the 2 percent gives the same 10 percent dollar yield.

5. If real wages are sticky, as they may be in economies with substantial wage indexation, the adjustment mechanisms intended to bring an economy

into equilibrium may break down. Another important qualification to the model of this chapter is the *J curve*. When our currency depreciates, we import fewer goods, but we pay more for each good. Thus, in dollar terms, total imports may increase. The empirical evidence is quite strong that, in fact, in the short run the total value of imports does increase, but in the long run the volume effect is more important and imports do decrease.

6.   In practice, the present system of foreign exchange is one of *dirty floating*. Central banks *intervene* from time to time in order to influence the exchange rate. It is often argued that governments ought to intervene to smooth out temporary fluctuations—unfortunately it is nearly impossible to know whether an exchange rate fluctuation is temporary or permanent.

It used to be argued that floating exchange rates allowed nations to pursue totally independent macroeconomic policies. We now know that *spillover* effects are caused by the changes in a nation's competitive position. Thus *interdependence* suggests that countries can benefit from coordination of macroeconomics policies.

KEY TERMS

Real exchange rate	Exchange rate overshooting
Expenditure switching	Exchange rate expectations
Expenditure-reducing policies	Purchasing power parity
Policy dilemmas	J-curve
Monetary approach	Intervention
Sterilization	Dirty float
Devaluation	Interdependence

GRAPH IT 20

The text tells us that imports rise when GNP rises or when the value of the dollar rises. In this Graph It, we ask you to see whether this is true—but we don't want you to draw a graph. Instead, we ask you to use the computer to examine the relation between imports, GNP, and the value of the dollar. Since you can't draw a three-dimensional graph, we ask you to run regressions on a computer. (If you don't have easy access to a computer with a regression program, just flip to the answer section.)

Estimate the following three relations:

Imports = constant + aY
Imports = constant + b value of the dollar
Imports = constant + aY + b value of the dollar

What value do you find for a and b?

TABLE 20-1

Year	GNP	Exports	Imports	Value of dollar
1967	2,271.4	143.6	160.5	120.0
1968	2,365.6	155.7	185.3	122.1
1969	2,423.3	165.0	199.9	122.4
1970	2,416.2	178.3	208.3	121.1
1971	2,484.8	179.2	218.9	117.8
1972	2,608.5	195.2	244.6	109.1
1973	2,744.1	242.3	273.8	99.1
1974	2,729.3	269.1	268.4	101.4
1975	2,695.0	259.7	240.8	98.5
1976	2,826.7	274.4	285.4	105.6
1977	2,958.6	281.6	317.1	103.3
1978	3,115.2	312.6	339.4	92.4
1979	3,192.4	356.8	353.2	88.1

Source: *Economic Report of the President.*

REVIEW OF TECHNIQUE 20

Triangular Arbitrage

We always quote bilateral exchange rates in terms of the dollar; 60 cents per mark and 20 cents per franc, for example. What is the mark-franc exchange rate? Obviously it must be 3 francs per mark. Suppose it is only 2 francs per mark. You could then take 1 dollar and buy 5 francs. You could take the 5 francs and get 2½ marks. These marks could be turned into $1.50. Now you could take the $1.50 and go around the triangle again and make even more profit. This is called *triangular arbitrage.* If the franc were worth 4 marks, a profit could be made by going around the triangle in the other direction. The only mark-franc exchange rate that prevents infinite arbitrage profits is 3 francs per mark.

FILL-IN QUESTIONS

1. Proponents of the monetary approach to the balance of payments believe that _____ has been a major cause of chronic balance of payments deficits in a number of countries.

2. A _____ exists when a government's goals of internal and external balance are in conflict with each other.

3. It is possible for _____ to improve the performance of a group of interdependent economies.

4. _____ consists of the monetary authority's claims on the public and private sectors.

5. If the relative prices of goods in two countries, adjusted for the exchange rate, are constant, we say there is _____ .

6. The _____ shows the response over time of imports to a devaluation.

7. The value of the dollar relative to its purchasing power in other countries is the _____ .

8. The important linkages between countries cause _____ , or _____ , effects.

9. A policy that aims to encourage consumption of domestic goods and discourage imports is called a _____ .

MULTIPLE-CHOICE QUESTIONS

1. If the typical German good cost 1,000 marks and the typical American good cost $250, and if the exchange rate is 25 cents, the terms of trade are
   a. 4 to 1
   b. 1 to 4
   c. 1 to 1
   d. 16 to 1

2. If German prices increase 10 percent while the dollar depreciates by 10 percent, constant American prices would imply that relative prices
   a. increased 10 percent
   b. increased 20 percent
   c. remained constant
   d. fell 20 percent

3. If the value of the yen increases and the value of the mark decreases, then the effective exchange rate of the dollar
   a. increases
   b. remains unchanged
   c. decreases
   d. cannot be determined from the information given

4. If purchasing power parity always holds, if the current exchange rate is 25 cents per mark, and if the exchange rate in the next year is also expected to be 25 cents, German inflation over the year must be expected to be _____ American inflation.
   a. greater than
   b. the same as
   c. less than
   d. indeterminable because of insufficient information

5. Empirical evidence shows that following a devaluation, the dollar value of imports
   a. rises, then falls
   b. falls, then rises
   c. remains unchanged
   d. rises

6. Capital flows into the United States when the American interest rate (adjusted for expected changes in the exchange rate) is _____ foreign interest rates.
   a. greater than
   b. equal to
   c. less than
   d. capital never flows into the United States

7. With flexible prices and perfect capital mobility, the economy
   a. is always at potential GNP and has current account balance
   b. is always at potential GNP and need not have current account balance
   c. need not be at potential GNP and must have current balance
   d. need not be at potential GNP or have current account balance

8. If the economy is initially in a recession and is running a trade deficit, the economy will eventually return to both internal and external balance without government invervention with
   a. higher prices   c. lower prices
   b. unchanged prices   d. higher imports

TRUE-FALSE QUESTIONS

T F   1. Exchange rates adjust in order to keep the relative price of imports and domestically produced goods from changing.

T F   2. If the dollar appreciates, with prices of domestic goods fixed both in the United States and in Germany, German goods become more expensive in the United States.

T F   3. An increase in the exchange rate increases domestic aggregate demand.

T F   4. An increase in German prices increases American aggregate demand.

T F   5. An increase in world interest rates causes American interest rates to rise.

T F   6. With perfect capital mobility, American interest rates must equal world interest rates.

T F   7. With perfect capital mobility, GNP must equal potential GNP.

T F   8. If purchasing power parity holds, then changes in exchange rates just offset the difference in the inflation experienced in two countries.

T F   9. Given enough time, the economy will reach full employment and balance of trade equilibrium without direct government intervention

PROBLEM

1. The interest rate in Germany is 10 percent, and the interest rate in the United States is 12 percent. If the current value of the mark is 50 cents, what is the exchange rate expected to be in a year?

ANSWERS TO QUESTIONS AND PROBLEMS

CHAPTER 1

Graph It 1

TABLE 1-1

Year	GNP	Percentage change from previous year
1962	1799.4	—
1963	1873.3	4.01
1964	1973.3	5.34
1965	2087.6	5.79
1966	2208.3	5.78
1967	2271.4	2.86
1968	2365.6	4.15
1969	2423.3	2.44
1970	2416.2	−.29
1971	2484.8	2.84
1972	2608.5	4.98
1973	2744.1	5.20
1974	2729.3	−.54
1975	2695.0	−1.26
1976	2826.7	4.89
1977	2958.6	4.66
1978	3115.2	5.29
1979	3192.4	2.48
1980	3187.1	−.17
1981	3248.8	1.94
1982	3166.0	−2.55
1983	3277.7	3.53
1984	3492.0	6.54
1985	3573.5	2.33

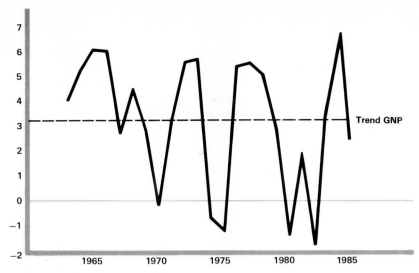

CHART 1-1   PERCENTAGE CHANGE IN GNP

Fill-In Questions

1. potential output
2. output gap
3. trough
4. fiscal
5. monetary
6. stabilization policies
7. Okun's law
8. recovery or expansion
9. recessions
10. aggregate demand

True-False Questions

1. False. Okun's law says that when GNP goes up, unemployment goes down.
2. True.
3. False. It's a "forest" chapter.

CHAPTER 2

Graph It 2

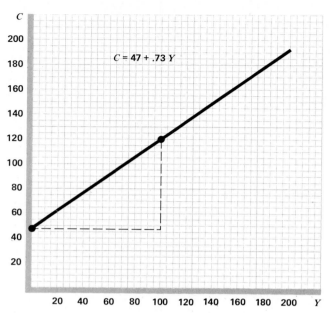

CHART 2-2

Fill-In Questions

1. gross national product (GNP)
2. depreciation (capital consumption allowance)
3. market prices, factor costs
4. consumed, saved
5. transfers, taxes
6. measure of economic welfare (MEW)
7. GNP deflator
8. consumer price index (CPI)
9. the budget deficit, the foreign trade surplus
10. exports, imports

True-False Questions

1. False. Investment equals private savings plus the government budget surplus minus net exports.
2. False. Sale of a home just transfers assets from one person to another. No *new* production is added.
3. True.

4. True.
5. False. An individual can't spend that part of production needed to replace worn-out machines.
6. False. By "investment" we mean buying new productive equipment, not financial investment.
7. True.
8. True.
9. True.
10. True.

Multiple-Choice Questions

1. b   2. c   3. b   4. a   5. d   6. a   7. d   8. d   9. c   10. b

Worked-Out Problems

1. $BD = G + TR - TA = 0$; therefore $G = TA - TR = 300$.
   $YD = C + S = 1,000 + 100 = 1,100$
   $YD = Y - TA + TR = 1,100 = Y - 300$
   Therefore, GNP equals \$1,400.
2. $TA - TR - G = I - S + NX$
   $-50 = I - 200 - 10$
   $I = \$160$

CHAPTER 3

Graph It 3

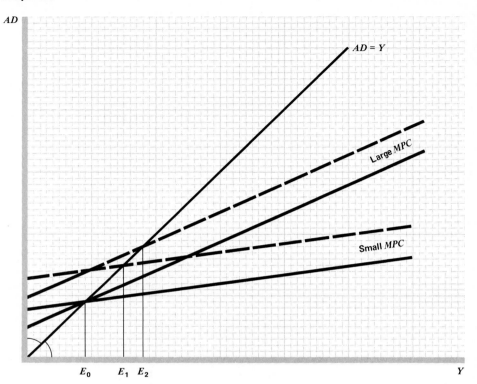

CHART 3-1

Fill-In Questions

1. equilibrium
2. the consumption function
3. marginal propensity to consume (MPC)
4. marginal propensity to save (MPS)
5. multiplier
6. budget deficit (BD)
7. automatic stabilizer
8. full-employment budget surplus ($BS*$)
9. 1
10. planned saving, actual investment

True-False Questions

1. True.
2. False. More taxes mean lower disposable income, less consumption, and thus lower GNP.
3. True.
4. True.
5. False. The budget surplus increases because GNP and thus taxes rise. However, potential GNP doesn't change, and so the *full-employment* budget surplus doesn't change.
6. True.
7. False. The higher MPC means a larger multiplier and thus higher GNP.
8. True.
9. False. GNP will go up by $1/[1 - c(1 - t)] \cdot \Delta G$ because of the increase in G and down by $c/[1 - c(1 - t)] \cdot \Delta G$ because of the drop in TR. Thus the net effect is an increase of $(1 - c)/(1 - c + ct) \cdot \Delta G$.
10. False. This is just the opposite of having a high MPC.

Multiple-Choice Questions

1. c   2. a   3. b   4. b   5. a   6. b   7. c   8. a   9. d   10. b

Worked-Out Problems

1. $C = \overline{C} + cYD$
    $Y_d = Y - TA$, combining these two equations
    $C = \overline{C} + c(Y - TA)$
    $Y \equiv C + I + G$, combining these two equations
    $Y = \overline{C} + c(Y - TA) + I + G$
    $Y - cY = \overline{C} - cTA + I + G$

    $$Y = \frac{1}{1 - c}(C + I + G) - \frac{c}{1 - c}TA$$

    $$Y = \frac{1}{1 - 0.9}(100 + 200 + 500) - \frac{0.9}{1 - 0.9}400$$

    $Y = \$4,400$

2. First, we need to calculate the appropriate multiplier. The income tax is $TA = tY$. Disposable income is $Y - tY$ or $(1 - t)Y$. Thus the consumption function is

    $$C = \overline{C} + c(1 - t)Y$$

    Combining this with the aggregate demand identity gives

    $$Y = \overline{C} + c(1 - t)Y + I + G$$
    $$Y(1 - c(1 - t)) = \overline{C} + I + G$$
    $$Y = \frac{1}{1 - c(1 - t)}(C + I + G)$$

Since autonomous consumption and investment do not change in this problem, we can rewrite the equation as

$$\Delta Y = \frac{1}{1 - c(1 - t)} \Delta G$$

The value of the multiplier is $\dfrac{1}{1 - .9(2/3)} = \dfrac{1}{1 - .6} = 2.5$

$\Delta Y = 2.5 \Delta G$
$750 = 2.5 \Delta G$
$\Delta G = 750/2.5 = \$300$

The change in the budget deficit is the change in government spending minus the change in tax collections. Government spending goes up \$300. Since income goes up \$750 and the marginal tax rate is ⅓, tax collections go up by \$250. The budget deficit goes up by \$50.

3. This problem essentially needs to be worked backward. We start with analyzing the sources of change in the budget deficit:

$BD = G - TA$
$\Delta BD = \Delta G - \Delta TA$

In part a, investment changes. This changes income and tax collections. Government spending does not change.

$\Delta BD = 0 - \Delta TA$
$\quad TA = tY$, so $\Delta TA = \Delta tY = t \Delta Y$
$\Delta BD = -t \Delta Y$
$\quad 15 = -(1/3)Y$

We see that a \$15 increase in the budget deficit implies that GNP fell by \$45. The only remaining step is to see how large a change in investment would cause a \$45 drop in income. From the previous problem, we know that the multiplier on investment is 2.5. Therefore, the change in investment must have been −45/2.5. Investment dropped by \$18.

In part b, government spending and tax collections are both changing.

$\Delta BD = \Delta G - t \Delta Y$

We know from the preceding problem that $\Delta Y = 2.5 \Delta G$.

$\Delta BD = \Delta G - (1/3)2.5 \Delta G = (1 - (1/3)2.5) \Delta G = (1/6) \Delta G$
$\Delta G = 6 \Delta BD = 6(15) = \$90$

This illustrates one of the fundamental findings of macroeconomics. An increase in the budget deficit can result from either a dropoff in economic activity or an increase in government spending.

CHAPTER 4

Graph It 4

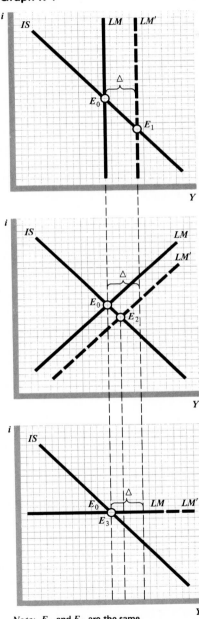

Note: E_0 and E_3 are the same.   **CHART 4-1**

Fill-In Questions

1. income, interest rate
2. goods
3. assets or money
4. open market purchase
5. demand for
6. liquidity trap
7. classical case
8. investment
9. real balances
10. transmission mechanism

True-False Questions

1. True.
2. True.
3. True.
4. False. The *IS* curve has a negative slope.
5. False. Monetary policy has the largest possible effect. See the Graph It.
6. False. Monetary policy has no effect. See the Graph It.
7. True.
8. False. Interest rates go up, and so investment goes down.
9. False. Transfers change *A* by less than government purchases change *A*, and so the *IS* curve is moved farther to the right by *G* than by *TR*.
10. False. Tax rates enter the multiplier and thus affect the slope of the *IS* curve.

Multiple-Choice Questions

1. c   2. b   3. b   4. a   5. c   6. b   7. c   8. b   9. b   10. a

Worked-Out Problems

1. a. IS: $Y = 100 + 0.8(Y - 500) + \bar{I} - 1,000i + 550$
   $$Y(1 - 0.8) = 250 + \bar{I} - 1,000i$$
   $$Y = 1,250 + 5\bar{I} - 5,000i$$

   (Note that we use $\bar{I}$ in place of 200 because autonomous investment changes in part c.)

   LM: $M/P = Y - 1,000i$

   b. Substituting the *IS* curve into the *LM* curve,

   $$M/P = 1,250 + 5\bar{I} - 5,000i - 10,000i$$
   $$i = (1,250 + 5\bar{I} - M/P)/15,000$$
   $$i = 0.09$$

Substituting the equation for the interest rate back into the IS curve,

$$Y = 1{,}250 + 5\bar{I} - 5{,}000(1{,}250 + 5I - M/P)/15{,}000$$
$$Y = (2/3)(1{,}250 + 5\bar{I}) + (M/P)/3$$
$$Y = \$1{,}800$$

Disposable income equals $1{,}800 - 500$, or $\$1{,}300$. Inserting this into the consumption function, we can calculate that consumption is $\$1{,}140$. Putting the interest rate into the investment function, we find that investment is 110. Note that we now have a check on our calculations. $C + I + G = 1{,}100 + 110 + 550 = 1{,}800 = Y$, as it should.

c. Using the formulas derived in solving part b, we see the fiscal policy multiplier is $10/3$. Therefore, GNP drops by $\$300$. The interest rate multiplier of autonomous spending is $1/3{,}000$, and so the interest rate drops by 3 percent. This increases investment by $\$30$. The induced increase of $\$30$ plus the autonomous drop of $\$90$ means that overall investment drops by $\$60$.

d. We need to increase Y by $\$300$. The monetary policy multiplier is $\frac{1}{5}$. Therefore, we need to increase the money supply by $\$900$. Using the equation for the interest rate, we see that this will decrease the interest rate by an additional 6 percent.

e. See Figures a, b, c.

2. a. The consumption function is

$$C = 100 + 0.9(Y - Y/3) = 100 + 0.6Y$$

The IS curve is

$$Y = 2{,}500 - 2{,}500i$$

The equilibrium equations for interest and income are

$$i = 0.20 - 0.00008(M/P)$$
$$Y = 2{,}000 + 0.2(M/P)$$

The initial interest rate is 16 percent. Putting this into the investment function, we find investment equals $\$40$ and GNP equals $\$2{,}100$. Taxes are one-third of income, and so tax collections come to $\$700$. Since government spending is $\$710$, the budget deficit is $\$10$.

b. In order to balance the budget, tax collections would have to rise by $\$10$. This implies GNP would have to rise by $\$30$. Since the monetary policy multiplier is 0.2, the money supply must increase by $\$150$.

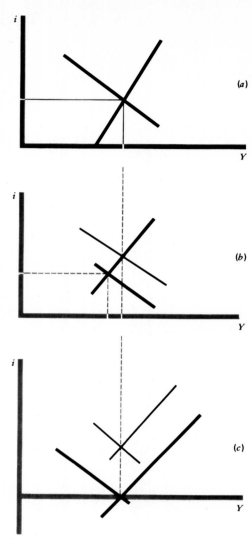

FIGURES *a, b, c*

CHAPTER 5

Graph It 5

Chart 5-1 and the accompanying data table make it pretty clear that loose money is associated with low unemployment, and vice versa.

TABLE 5-1

Year	Unemployment	M1	CPI	M/P
1972	5.60	252.0	125.3	2.01
1973	4.90	265.9	133.1	2.00
1974	5.60	277.5	147.7	1.88
1975	8.50	291.1	161.2	1.74
1976	7.70	310.3	170.5	1.82
1977	7.10	335.3	181.5	1.85
1978	6.10	363.0	195.4	1.86
1979	5.80	389.0	217.4	1.79
1980	7.10	414.8	246.8	1.68
1981	7.60	441.8	272.4	1.62
1982	9.70	480.8	289.1	1.66
1983	9.60	528.0	298.4	1.77
1984	7.50	558.5	311.1	1.80
1985	7.20	624.7	322.2	1.94

Source: Economic Report of the President.

CHART 5-1

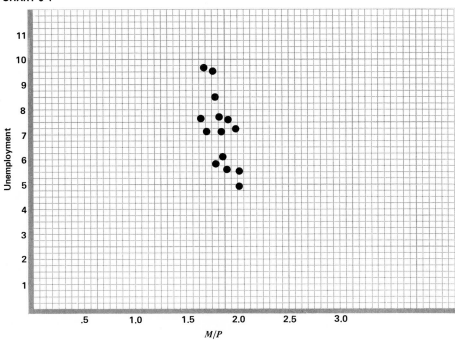

Fill-in Questions

1. Monetary policy multiplier
2. Fiscal policy multiplier
3. Crowding out
4. Monetary accommodation
5. Monetary-fiscal policy mix, composition of output

True-False Questions

1. False. Effectiveness of monetary policy depends on movement of the *LM* and the slope of the *IS*.
2. False. Effectiveness of fiscal policy depends on movement of the *IS* and the slope of the *LM*.
3. True.
4. True.
5. False. At higher GNP, tax collections are higher and thus the budget deficit is lower.

Multiple-Choice Questions

1. b   2. d   3. c   4. b   5. a   6. d   7. c   8. b   9. a   10. c

Problems

1. We know the multiplier on autonomous spending, $\overline{A}$, is given by

$$\frac{h\alpha}{h + kb\alpha}$$

All we need figure out is what happens to A. Transfers enter $\overline{A}$ through the consumption function and are multiplied by the marginal propensity to consume. A goes up by c dollars for each dollar increase in transfers in part a and by $c(1 - t)$ dollars for each dollar increase in transfers in part b. So, the transfer policy multipliers are

a. $\dfrac{ch\overline{\alpha}}{h + kb\overline{\alpha}}$ b. $\dfrac{c(1 - t)h\overline{\alpha}}{h + kb\overline{\alpha}}$

2. a. The increase in government purchases increases GNP by the fiscal policy multiplier. The decrease in transfers cuts GNP by the transfer policy multiplier found in 1a above. The net increase is 1 billion times

$$(1 - c) \cdot \frac{h\alpha}{h + kb\overline{\alpha}}$$

b. Total government spending doesn't change, but tax collections and the budget surplus rise by t times the amount found in 1a.

3. a. The inflation rate over 1985 was $(327.4 - 315.5)/315.5 \times 100 = 3.8$ percent.
    b. The real interest rate is the nominal interest rate minus the actual inflation rate, or approximately 3.7 percent.

CHAPTER 6

Graph It 6

Chart 6-1 shows the relation of exports to the value of the dollar. A 1 percent increase in the exchange rate cuts exports by about 2 billion 1982 dollars.

Fill-In Questions

1. exchange rate
2. current account
3. capital account
4. balance of payments
5. fixed exchange rate regime
6. floating exchange rate regime
7. dirty or managed float
8. depreciation
9. devaluation
10. endogenous
11. balance of payments

True-False

1. False. Expansionary policy increases imports, increasing the trade deficit.
2. False. Interest rates are lower, and so capital leaves the country.
3. True.
4. True.
5. True.
6. False. Our imports rise. German exports and then GNP rise as well.
7. True.
8. True.
9. False. Eventually the bank will run out of reserves.

Multiple Choice Questions

1. b   2. a   3. a   4. c   5. a   6. a   7. b   8. c   9. b   10. d

Worked-Out Problems

1. Initially, there are 4 marks to the dollar. A 50 percent devaluation leaves 2 marks to the dollar. Another 20 percent leaves 1.6 marks per dollar. One mark is now worth 62.5 cents.

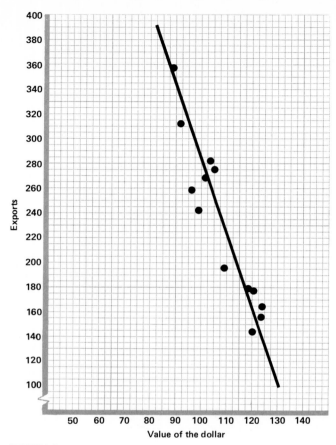

CHART 6-1

TABLE 6-1

Year	Real exports	Value of the dollar
1967	143.6	120.0
1968	155.7	122.1
1969	165.0	122.4
1970	178.3	121.1
1971	179.2	117.8
1972	195.2	109.1
1973	242.3	99.1
1974	269.1	101.4
1975	259.7	98.5
1976	274.4	105.6
1977	281.6	103.3
1978	312.6	92.4
1979	356.8	88.1

2. Negative. The coefficient b is certainly positive, and Y increases with an increase in R, so a (which captures the partial effect of a change in R on Q) *must* be negative.

3. $Y = C + I + G + NX = \overline{C} + 0.9Y + \overline{I} + G + \overline{X} - (\overline{Q} + .1Y)$
   $Y(1 - 0.9 + 0.1) = (\overline{C} + \overline{I} + G + \overline{X} - \overline{Q})$

   The multiplier is thus $1/(1 - 0.9 + 0.1) = 1/.2 = 5$

4. The essential thing is to recognize that our imports are German exports and vice versa. Variables without subscript are for the United States.

   $Y = C + I + G + NX$
   $\quad = \overline{C} + 0.9Y + \overline{I} + G + (\overline{Q}_G + .2Y_G) - (\overline{Q} + 0.1Y)$
   $Y(1 - 0.9 + 0.1) = (\overline{C} + \overline{I} + G + \overline{Q}_G - \overline{Q}) + 0.2Y_G$
   $Y = 5(\overline{C} + \overline{I} + G + \overline{Q}_G - \overline{Q}) + Y_G$
   $Y_G = C_G + I_G + G_G + NX_G$
   $\quad = \overline{C}_G + 0.8Y_G + \overline{I}_G + \overline{G}_G + (\overline{Q} + 0.1Y) - (\overline{Q}_G + 0.2Y_G)$
   $Y_G(1 - 0.8 + 0.2) = (\overline{C}_G + \overline{I}_G + \overline{G}_G + \overline{Q} - \overline{Q}_G) + 0.1Y$
   $Y_G = 2.5(\overline{C}_G + \overline{I}_G + \overline{G}_G + \overline{Q} - \overline{Q}_G) + 0.25Y$

   To conserve on notation, call autonomous U.S. and German spending A and A_G, respectively. Thus several substitutions show

   $Y = 5\overline{A} + Y_G$
   $Y_G = 2.5\overline{A}_G + 0.25Y$
   $Y = 5\overline{A} + 2.5\overline{A}_G + 0.25Y$
   $Y(1 - 0.25) = 5A + 2.5\overline{A}_G$
   $Y = (4/3)(5\overline{A} + 2.5\overline{A}_G)$

   and also that

   $Y_G = 2.5\overline{A}_G + 0.25(4/3)(5\overline{A} + 2.5\overline{A}_G) = (5/3)\overline{A} + (10/3)\overline{A}_G$

   So, the multiplier of the U.S. government's spending on U.S. GNP is 20/3, and the multiplier on German GNP is 5/3. Notice that including all repercussion effects, the estimate of the multiplier rose from question 2 to question 3 from 5.0 to 6⅔.

5. The increase in the money stock is not necessary to maintain the interest rate. Although the increase in G will temporarily raise the interest rate, the money stock will increase automatically as the monetary authority buys foreign exchange and sells dollars in order to maintain the exchange rate. Output, of course, rises.

6. The interest rate falls, the demand for the dollar falls, exports increase (as dollars become cheaper), and imports fall as foreign currency becomes more expensive. That is, the *IS* shifts rightward.

CHAPTER 7

Graph It 7

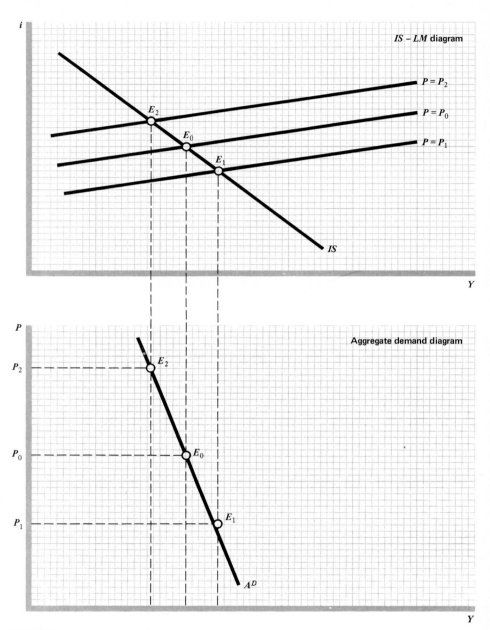

CHART 7-1

Fill-In Questions

1. autonomous spending
2. the money supply
3. *IS-LM*
4. crowding out
5. neutrality
6. aggregate supply
7. aggregate demand
8. horizontal
9. vertical

True-False Questions

1. False. Higher prices mean lower real balances. The *LM* curve moves left, increasing interest rates.
2. False. A low monetary policy multiplier means a steep aggregate demand curve.
3. True.
4. False. Same as question 2.
5. True.
6. False. The aggregate demand curve.
7. True.
8. True.
9. True.
10. False. Prices rise in proportion to the increased money supply, so that real balances are unchanged and the *LM* curve is unmoved.

Multiple-Choice Questions

1. c   2. c   3. b   4. a   5. a   6. d   7. b   8. d   9. b   10. b

Worked-Out Problems

1. $Y = 2(1,500) + 4(50,000/P_{-1}) = 5,000$
$P = P_{-1}[0.2 + 0.8(5,000/4,000)] = 120$

Next year:

$Y = 3,000 + 4(50,000/120) = 4,667$
$P = 120[0.2 + 8(4,667/4,000)] = 136$

Year after:

$Y = 3,000 + 4(50,000/136) = 4,471$
$P = 136[0.2 + 0.8(4,471/4,000)] = 148.8$

2. In the long run, $P = P_{-1}$, and so $Y = Y_p = 4,000$

$4,000 = 3,000 + 4(50,000/P)$
$(1/P) = 1,000/200,000 \qquad P = 200$

Y is at its original level. Consumption must also be at its original level. Since $Y = C + I + G$, if G is up 500, investment must be down 500. Therefore, the interest rate must be up .25.

3. $4,000 = 2,000 + 4(100,000/P)$
$(1/P) = 2,000/400,000 \qquad P = 200$

Investment and the interest rate are unchanged!

CHAPTER 8

Graph It

The completed graph appears below. You should have found the short-run MPC to be about 0.7 and the long-run MPC to be about 0.9. We made up the data by applying the following equation to each group of three points.

$$C = 0.4(Y_1 + Y_2 + Y_3)/3 + 0.5Y$$

CHART 8-1

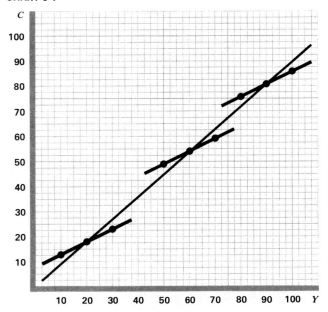

Fill-In Questions

1. life-cycle
2. permanent
3. dissavings
4. 0.90
5. 0.90
6. short-run
7. long-run
8. working, retirement
9. distributed

True-False Questions

1. False. It's just the other way around.
2. True.
3. True.
4. True.
5. True.
6. True.
7. True.
8. False. You have to save in order to have a bequest to leave, and so you reduce current consumption.
9. True.
10. True.

Multiple-Choice Questions

1. b   2. a   3. c   4. b   5. c   6. a   7. c   8. c   9. c   10. a

Worked-Out Problems

1. Total resources are the sum of disposable income over the next 40 years. These resources must be spread out evenly over a 50-year period. A $100 tax cut that is permanent increases disposable lifetime income by a total of 40 times $100, or $4,000. Spread over 50 years, this cut increases consumption by $80 each year.

   A cut that lasts only 1 year increases lifetime disposable income by $100, and so consumption increases by $2. A cut that is not in effect this year but is in effect for the next 39 years yields a total increase of $3,900. Consumption increases $78 each year including the current one.

2. $\Delta C = 0.8(0.75\Delta YD + 0.25\Delta YD_{-1})$
   a. $\Delta C = 0.8[0.75(100) + 0.25(0)] = 60$
      $\Delta C = 0.8[0.75(100) + 0.25(100)] = 80$
   b. $\Delta C = 0.8[0.75(100) + 0.25(0)] = 60$
      $\Delta C = 0.8[0.75(0) + 0.25(100)] = 20$

CHAPTER 9

Graph It 9

TABLE 9-1

Year	GNP	I	$Y_t - Y_{t-1}$	$I_t - I_{t-1}$
1972	2,608.5	465.4		
1973	2,744.1	520.8	135.6	55.4
1974	2,729.3	481.3	−14.8	−39.5
1975	2,695.0	383.3	−34.3	−98.0
1976	2,826.7	453.5	131.7	70.2
1977	2,958.6	521.3	131.9	67.8
1978	3,115.2	576.9	156.6	55.6
1979	3,192.4	575.2	77.2	−1.7
1980	3,187.1	509.3	−5.3	−65.9
1981	3,248.8	545.5	61.7	36.2
1982	3,166.0	447.3	−82.8	−98.2
1983	3,277.7	503.4	111.7	56.1
1984	3,492.0	661.3	214.3	157.9
1985	3,573.5	650.6	81.5	−10.7

Fill-In Questions

1. business fixed, residential housing, inventory
2. flow, stock
3. marginal product of capital
4. rental or user cost of capital
5. expected future
6. investment tax credit
7. depreciation
8. Regulation Q
9. disintermediation
10. inventory cycle

True-False Questions

1. False. High interest rates make capital more expensive and thus lower investment.
2. True.
3. False. If the government pays for part of your equipment, you want to buy more.
4. False. If mortgage rates are high, your monthly house payment is high. People buy less housing, lowering residential investment.
5. True.
6. True.
7. False. If you expect sales to rise, you need more goods on hand, increasing inventory.
8. False. It's the level of investment that's proportional to changes in income.

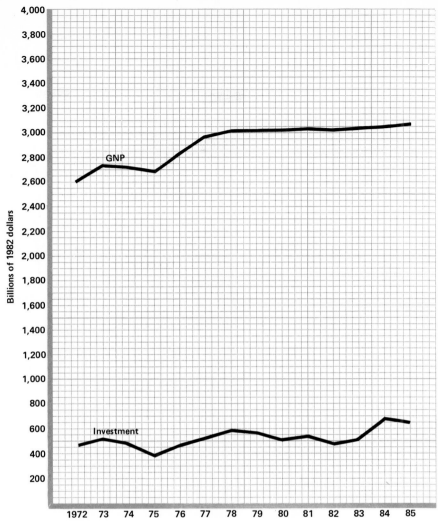

CHART 9-1

9. True.
10. True.

Multiple-Choice Questions

1. d   2. b   3. b   4. c   5. d   6. c   7. a   8. c   9. b   10. a   11. b

Worked-Out Problems

1. $rc = i - \pi + d = 0.12 - 0.06 + 0.10 = .16$
   a. $K^* = 0.25(16,000)/0.16 = 25,000$
   b. $K^* = 0.25(32,000)/0.16 = 50,000$

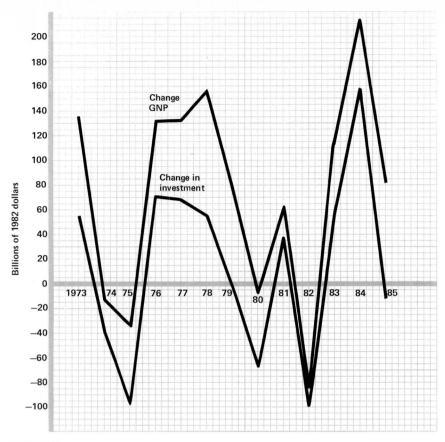

CHART 9-2

c. $I_{net} = (K^* - K_{-1}) = 50,000 - 25,000 = 25,000$
$I_{gross} = I_{net} + dK_{-1} = 25,000 + 0.1(25,000) = 27,500$

2. $I_{net} = K - K_{-1} = 0.5(K^* - K_{-1})$
   year 1: $I_{net} = 0.5(3,600 - 2,000) = 800$; $I_{gross} = 800 + 0.1(2,000) = 1,000$
   year 2: $I_{net} = 0.5(3,600 - 2,800) = 400$; $I_{gross} = 400 + 0.1(2,800) = 680$
   year 3: $I_{net} = 0.5(3,600 - 3,200) = 200$; $I_{gross} = 200 + 0.1(3,200) = 520$

   Notice that each year's net investment is added to the capital stock to determine the following year's capital stock.

3. A "fair" loan is one in which the amount of the loan equals the present discounted value of the payments.

   $$1,000 = \frac{220}{1.1} + \frac{Q_2}{1.1^2}$$
   $$Q_2 = 1.1^2(1,000 - 200) = \$968$$

CHAPTER 10

Graph It 10

Fill-In Questions

1. real balances
2. currency and demand deposits
3. $M1$ plus time and savings deposits
4. transactions
5. velocity
6. velocity
7. precautionary
8. speculative
9. speculative
10. price level

True-False Questions

1. True.
2. True.
3. True.
4. True.
5. False. $M1$ is a strict subset of $M2$.
6. False. To do otherwise would show money illusion.
7. False. The Baumol-Tobin theory says money demand is proportional to the square root of GNP.

CHART 10-1

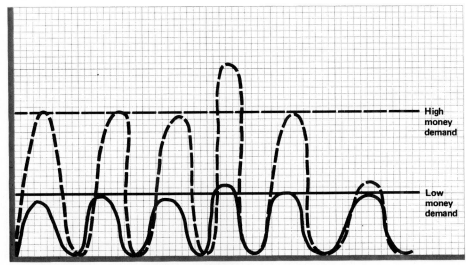

8. True.
9. False. This is just a switch between different components of $M2$.
10. True.

Multiple-Choice Questions

1. c 2. b 3. c 4. a 5. b 6. a 7. b 8. b 9. c 10. b 11. b 12. c

Worked-Out Problems

1. Since the price level doubled, the $220 billion is only worth $110 billion in real, constant dollar, terms. The change from $100 billion to $110 billion is a 10 percent increase. Since the Baumol-Tobin theory says that the income elasticity is ½, real money demand will rise by 5 percent.

2. This problem has to be worked backward. We know the amount we want the interest rate to change. We assume that interest changes by the amount given and see what change in the money stock this implies. We know, then, that if we change the money stock, the desired change in the interest rate will result.

 The interest rate is supposed to go from 4 percent to 3 percent. This is a drop of 25 percent. (The change is 1 percent; 1 percent over 4 percent is one-fourth, or 25 percent. A very common error is to think the change is 1 percent. The change is one percentage point of annual interest, not 1 percent.)

 Since we are told that the interest elasticity is −0.2, one-fifth of one-fourth is 5 percent. Thus, a 5 percent *increase* in the money stock will produce the desired interest rate change.

CHAPTER 11

Graph It 11

FIRST BALANCE SHEETS

Professor B		Bank		
Assets	Liabilities	Assets		Liabilities
Deposit $200	None	Reserves $200 (Required 20) (Excess 180)		$200 Deposit
	$200 Net worth			
$200	$200		$180	$180

SECOND BALANCE SHEETS

Professor B		Bank	
Assets	Liabilities	Assets	Liabilities
Deposit $380	$180 Loan	Reserves $200 (Required) 38) (Excess 162) Loan 180	$380 Deposit
	$200 Net worth		
$380	$380	$380	$380

THIRD BALANCE SHEETS

Professor B		Bank	
Assets	Liabilities	Assets	Liabilities
Deposit $542	$342 Loan	Reserves $200 (Required 54.2) (Excess 145.8) Loan 342	$542 Deposit
	$200 Net worth		
$542	$542	$542	$542

FINAL BALANCE SHEETS

Professor B		Bank	
Assets	Liabilities	Assets	Liabilities
Deposit $2,000	$1,800 Loan	Reserves $200 (Required 200) (Excess 0) Loan 1,800	$2,000 Deposit
	$ 200 Net worth		
$2,000	$2,000	$2,000	$2,000

Fill-In Questions

1. high-powered money, the monetary base
2. required, excess
3. discount rate

4.   federal funds rate
5.   open market sale
6.   money multiplier
7.   sterilization
8.   tax and loan
9.   currency-deposit ratio
10. government bonds

True-False Questions

1.   True.
2.   False. A higher currency-deposit ratio means a lower money multiplier and so a lower money supply.
3.   False. A reserve requirement means a lower money multiplier and so a lower money supply.
4.   False. This also lowers re and thus the money multiplier.
5.   False. Income has nothing to do with the money supply.
6.   True.
7.   False. Regulation Q controls the interest rate banks can pay depositors.
8.   True.
9.   True.
10. True.

Multiple-Choice Questions

1. d   2. a   3. b   4. c   5. d   6. a   7. a   8. c   9. c   10. b

Worked-Out Problems

1. $CU = .4D$
     $M1 = CU + D = .4D + D = 1.4D$
     $H = CU + 0.1D = 0.4D + 0.1 = 0.5D$
     a. $M1/H = (1.4D)/(0.5D)$
        $M1 = 2.8H = 2.8(100) = 280$ billion
     b. $H = 0.5D; \Delta D = 2\Delta H = 2(50) = 100$ billion

2. $M2 = CU + D + T = 0.4D + D + 2.5D = 3.9D$
     $H = CU + 0.1D + 0.04T = 0.4D + 0.1D + 0.04(2.5)D = 0.6D$
     a. $M2 = (3.9/0.6)H = 6.5(100) = 650$ billion
     b. $M1 = [(0.4 + 1)/0.6]H = (1.4/6)(100) = 233$ billion

3. $H = CU + 0.1D = (0.5Y - 495i) + 0.1(Y - 50i) = 0.6Y - 500i$
     $i = (0.6Y - H)/500 = 0.6(2.000) - (1.150)/500 = 50/500 = 10$ percent

CHAPTER 12

Graph It 12

BANK BALANCE SHEET 1

Assets		Liabilities	
Reserves	$ 200	$2,000	Deposit
Treasury bills	400		
Loans	1,600	200	Paid in capital
	$2,200	$2,200	

BANK INCOME STATEMENT

Income		Expenses	
Interest on reserves	$ 0	$110	Deposit interest
Interest on T-bills	38		
Interest on loans	224	40	Stockholders' dividends
		120	Retained earnings
	$260	$260	

BANK BALANCE SHEET 2

Assets		Liabilities	
Reserves	$ 200	$2,000	Deposit
Treasury bills	520		
Loans	1,600	320	Paid in capital
	$2,320	$2,320	

Fill-In Questions

1. inside lag
2. outside lag
3. lags, expectations, uncertainty
4. action lag
5. recognition lag
6. decision lag
7. automatic stabilizer
8. activists
9. decision
10. outside

CHAPTER 13

Graph It 13

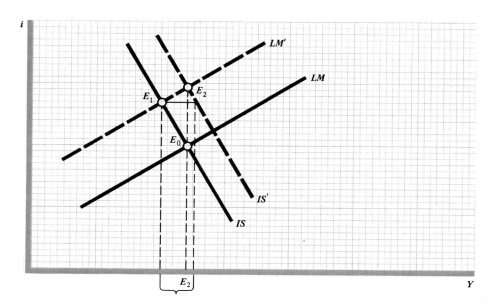

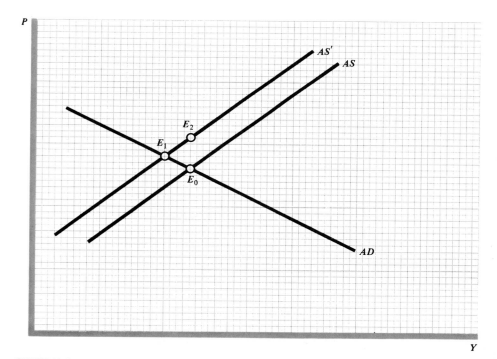

CHART 13-1

Fill-In Questions

1. long-term labor market relations
2. inflation
3. Phillips curve
4. frictionless classical model
5. labor productivity
6. markup
7. supply shocks

True-False Questions

1. True.
2. False. Adding a unit of labor increases output, though each additional unit adds less than the previous unit.
3. True.
4. True.
5. True.
6. True.
7. False. You cannot undo a shock which permanently lowers potential GNP.
8. False. Wages only change slowly.
9. True.

Multiple-Choice Questions

1. b   2. c   3. c   4. a   5. a   6. c

Worked-Out Problems

1. The aggregate supply curve in this case is

$$P = P_{-1}[1 - 2(0.4)(1 - (1.1Y_p)/Y_p)] = P_{-1}[1.08]$$

   Since the initial price level is 100, the price level after 1 year is 108. In the second year, P_{-1} is therefore 108, and so the second year's price level is 116.6.

2. The aggregate supply curve is given above. No inflation means $P = P_{-1}$. Therefore, the term in square brackets must equal 1, and so we must have $Y = Y_p$.

CHAPTER 14

Graph It 14

TABLE 14-1

Asset	Beginning value	End dollar value	End real value	Dollar difference	Real difference
Money	100	100	98.04		6.86
Bonds	100	107	104.90	7	
Corn	100	112.2	110.0	5.2	5.10

TABLE 14-2

Asset	Beginning value	End dollar value	End real value	Dollar difference	Real difference
Money	100	100	89.29		15.17
Bonds	100	117	104.46	17	
Corn	100	123.2	110.0	6.2	5.54

Notice that the real interest rate is approximately 5 percent in each case $(7 - 2$ or $17 - 12)$, but that this is only an approximation.

Fill-In Questions

1. overshooting
2. rational expectations
3. expectations-augmented Phillips
4. Phillips
5. stagflation
6. credible
7. perfect foresight
8. index

True-False Questions

1. False. Rational expectations theory only says that predictable events don't move GNP away from potential.
2. True.
3. True.
4. True.
5. True.
6. False.

Multiple-Choice Questions

1. b   2. b   3. c   4. b   5. a   6. b   7. c   8. a   9. a   10. a

Worked-Out Problems

1. $f = 500$, $m_{-1} = 0$, $\pi_{-1} = 0$ $\Delta\pi^e = 0$
$Y = 4{,}000 + 2(500) = 5{,}000$
$\pi = 0 + 0.8\left(\dfrac{5{,}000 - 4{,}000}{4{,}000}\right) = 0.2$, or 20 percent per year

Next period's expected inflation is this period's actual inflation, 0.2. Next year:

$f = 0$
$Y = 5{,}000 + 0 + 2{,}000(0 - 0.2) + 1{,}000(0.2 - 0) = 4{,}800$
$\pi = 0.2 + 0.8\,\dfrac{4{,}800 - 4{,}000}{4{,}000} = 0.36$, or 36 percent per year

Next year:

$Y = 4{,}800 + 0 + 2{,}000(0 - 0.36) + 1{,}000(0.36 - 0.2) = 4{,}240$
$\pi = 0.36 + 0.8\left(\dfrac{4{,}240 - 4{,}000}{4{,}000}\right) = 0.408$, or 40.8 percent per year

2. $f = 0$ $_{-1}m_{-1} = 0.5$ $\Delta\pi^e = 0$
$Y = 4{,}000 + 2{,}000(0.5 - 0) = 5{,}000$

The rest of the answers are identical to those for problem 1.

3. $Y = 4{,}000 + 2{,}000(0.5 - 0) = 5{,}000$
$\pi = 0 + 0.8\left(\dfrac{5{,}000 - 4{,}000}{4{,}000}\right) = 20$ percent per year

Next year:

$Y = 5{,}000 + 2{,}000(0.5 - 0.2) + 1{,}000(0.2 - 0) = 5{,}800$
$\pi = 0.2 + 0.8\,\dfrac{5{,}800 - 4{,}000}{4{,}000} = 56$ percent per year

Next year:

$Y = 5{,}800 + 2{,}000(0.5 - 0.56) + 1{,}000(0.56 - 0.2) = 6{,}040$
$\pi = 0.56 + 0.8\left(\dfrac{6{,}040 - 4{,}000}{4{,}000}\right) = 96.8$ percent per year

Next year:

$Y = 6{,}040 + 2{,}000(0.5 - 0.968) + 1{,}000(0.968 - 0.56) = 5{,}512$
$\pi = 0.968 + 0.8\left(\dfrac{5{,}512 - 4{,}000}{4{,}000}\right) = 127$ percent per year

CHAPTER 15

Graph It 15

TABLE 15-2 "THE NEW DAYS"

Unemployment rate		Number in labor force	Number employed
Male	2.80	1,000	972
Female	5.50	800	756
Total	4.00	1,800	1,728

The "average" unemployment rate has risen, even though the typical individual, male or female, is less likely to be unemployed.

Fill-In Questions

1. unemployment, inflation
2. natural rate
3. perfectly anticipated
4. imperfectly anticipated, unanticipated
5. distributional
6. gradualist policy
7. cold turkey
8. Okun's law
9. borrowers
10. lenders

True-False Questions

1. False. Aggregate policies have no effect on the natural rate.
2. False. Lost output is gone forever.
3. True.
4. True.
5. True.
6. True.
7. False. Those who are unemployed for a long time make up a large part of the overall average.
8. False. It makes sense for people to spend time looking around for jobs.
9. False. Job creation programs may lower the natural rate, and unemployment insurance programs definitely raise the natural rate.
10. False. Print enough money and you can get as much inflation as you'd like!

Multiple-Choice Questions

1. c   2. c   3. b   4. d   5. d   6. a   7. b   8. b   9. d   10. c

Worked-Out Problems

1. Originally, $\bar{u} = .6(.05) + .4(.08) = 6.2$ percent. Later, $\bar{u} = 0.5(0.05) + 0.5(0.08) = 6.5$ percent. Of course, GNP will be much higher in the latter case, since so many more women are working!

2. The average duration of unemployment is $(2 \cdot 1 + 2 + 12)/4 = 4$ months. In any given month, there will be two people undergoing a 1-month unemployment span, two people with a 2-month unemployment span, and twelve people with a 1-year stretch. Thus, 16 percent of the labor force will be unemployed.

3. At the end of the year you have $107. The price level is now 1.1, and so the real value is $107/1.1 = \$97.27$. In real terms, you have lost $3.

4. In order to gain a 2 percent real return, you need $100(1 + i)/1.1 = 102$, or $102(1.1)/100 = 1.122$, or i is approximately 12 percent.

5. The price of your property will be rising 12 percent per year, so that after 2 years you will sell it for $1.25 on the dollar, though it takes $1.21 to be worth one constant dollar. Your nominal gain is $0.25. The tax on this is approximately $0.06, so that you are left with $1.19, which is worth $0.98 in real terms. Your 4 percent before-tax gain has turned into a 2 percent after-tax real loss.

CHAPTER 16

Graph It 16

Tables 16-1 and 16-2 appear below. In nominal terms, the end of year debt in year 5 was only 530.81 without inflation as opposed to 850.26 with inflation. But as you can see, the real comparison shows little real difference, only 530.81 versus 527.94.

TABLE 16-1

Year	1	2	3	4	5
Spending deficit	100.00	100.00	100.00	100.00	100.00
Beginning debt	100.00	202.00	306.04	412.16	520.40
Interest	2.00	4.04	6.12	8.24	10.41
Price level, end of year	1.00	1.00	1.00	1.00	1.00
Real debt, end of year	102.00	206.04	312.16	420.40	530.81

TABLE 16-2

Year	1	2	3	4	5
Spending deficit	100.00	110.00	121.00	133.10	146.41
Beginning debt	100.00	222.00	369.64	547.10	759.16
Interest	12.00	26.64	44.36	65.65	91.10
Price level, end of year	1.10	1.21	1.33	1.46	1.61
Real debt, end of year	101.82	205.49	311.04	418.52	527.94

Fill-In Questions

1. deficit
2. national debt
3. monetizing debt
4. debt financing
5. money financing
6. bracket creep
7. indexing
8. primary or inflation-corrected deficit
9. Gramm-Rudman-Hollings Act
10. the burden of the debt

True-False Questions

1. True.
2. True.
3. True.
4. False. In the United States, most of the deficit is financed by bond sales.
5. False. The Fed prints high-powered money.
6. True.
7. False. If the tax rates are constant, then nominal tax collections go up with the price level, leaving real tax collections unchanged.
8. True.
9. True.
10. False. The Fed only buys up debt of the Federal government.

Multiple-Choice Questions

1. c   2. d   3. a   4. d   5. b   6. d   7. b   8. b   9. d   10. a

Worked-Out Problems

1. Use the formula $\Delta b = q[(r - y)b - x]$. We want to find the value of x that makes Δb equal to zero, $x = (r - y)b$. The problem specifies $r = 0.02$ and

$y = 0.027$. The national debt is around 1,827.5, and GNP is around 3,992.5 (in current dollars), so $b = 0.46$. Thus the highest sustainable level of x is -0.003204. In other words, the deficit can be 0.3204 percent of GNP without causing the national debt to grow faster than GNP.

2.   This is just a compound interest problem. At the end of 10 years, an amount P has grown to $P(1 + r)10$. $1.0210 = 1.22$, and $1.0510 = 1.63$. The debt will have grown to $244 or $326 billion, respectively.

CHAPTER 17

Graph It 17

Charts 17-1a and 17-1b show the budget deficit and the change in the budget deficit plotted against inflation tax revenue and the change in inflation tax revenues. Inflation tax revenues are computed by multiplying the high-powered money stock by the inflation rate between year t and $t - 1$. The high-

TABLE 17-1a

Year	Deficit	Inflation tax revenue
1959	−1.1	—
1960	3.0	0.758
1961	−3.9	0.496
1962	−4.2	0.555
1963	0.3	0.626
1964	−3.3	0.706
1965	0.5	0.973
1966	−1.8	1.654
1967	−13.2	1.777
1968	−6.0	2.792
1969	8.4	3.687
1970	−12.4	4.274
1971	−22.0	3.308
1972	−16.8	2.770
1973	−5.6	5.518
1974	−11.6	10.147
1975	−69.4	8.869
1976	−53.5	5.967
1977	−46.0	7.211
1978	−29.3	9.267
1979	−16.1	14.599
1980	−61.3	18.698
1981	−63.8	15.276
1982	−145.9	9.826
1983	−179.4	5.662
1984	−172.9	7.923
1985	−197.3	7.430

TABLE 17-1*b*

Year	Change in the budget deficit from previous year	Change in inflation tax revenues from previous year
1960	4.1	—
1961	−6.9	−0.2625
1962	−0.3	0.0596
1963	4.5	0.0710
1964	−3.6	0.0801
1965	3.8	0.2669
1966	−2.3	0.6812
1967	−11.4	0.1231
1968	7.2	1.0142
1969	14.4	0.8952
1970	−20.8	0.5874
1971	−9.6	−0.9666
1972	5.2	−0.5376
1973	11.2	2.7475
1974	−6.0	4.6290
1975	−57.8	−1.2775
1976	15.9	−2.9017
1977	7.5	1.2434
1978	16.7	2.0559
1979	13.2	5.3325
1980	−45.2	4.0993
1981	−2.5	−3.9228
1982	−82.1	−5.4502
1983	−33.5	−4.1637
1984	6.5	2.2616
1985	−24.4	−0.4936

powered money stock is computed by dividing the level of $M1$ by the money multiplier (check the discussion in Chapter 11 if you have forgotten how to compute the stock of high-powered money). It is clear from the charts that there is little association between the size or change in budget deficits and the amount or change in the amount of inflation tax revenues collected.

Fill-In Questions

1. hyperinflation
2. inflation tax
3. seigniorage
4. inflation-corrected deficit
5. Fischer effect
6. monetize
7. liquidity effect
8. income effect
9. expectations effect

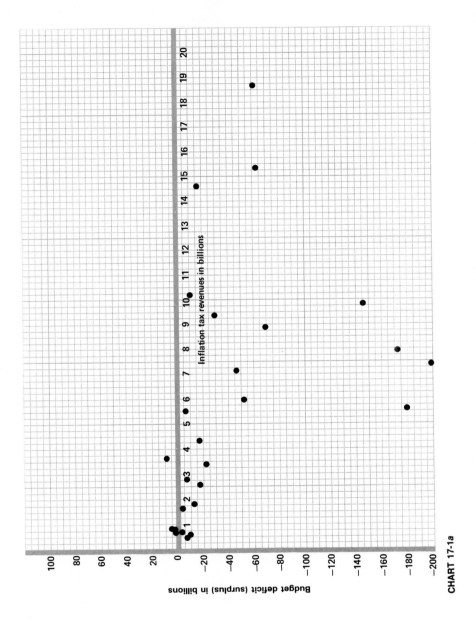

Inflation tax revenues in billions

Budget deficit (surplus) in billions

CHART 17-1a

217

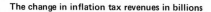

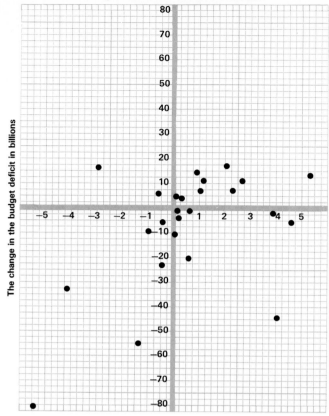

The change in inflation tax revenues in billions

The change in the budget deficit in billions

CHART 17-1b

True-False Questions

1. T
2. False; in the long-run, GNP pretty much stays at potential GNP.
3. T
4. T
5. False; the nominal interest rate adjusts to expected inflation and the real rate is unaffected.
6. T
7. T
8. False; the vast bulk of the deficit is financed by selling government bonds to the public.
9. T
10. False; although they do tend to move together over long periods of time.

Multiple-Choice Questions

1. c   2. b   3. d   4. c   5. a   6. d   7. c   8. b   9. a   10. a

Worked-Out Problems

1. We can use the formula $\pi = m - \eta g^*$, which shows that inflation is the rate of money supply growth less the rate of growth in money demand due to increased GNP. Inflation will be zero if the rate of money growth m equals the income elasticity of money demand, η, times the rate of growth of potential GNP, g^*. A good estimate of the income elasticity (from Chapter 11) is 0.7, with a range being between 0.5 and 1.0. A reasonable estimate for potential GNP growth is 3.0 percent, with a range of about 2.5 to 3.5 percent. So our best estimate of noninflationary money growth is 2.1 percent per year (0.7×3.0) with a range of 1.25 (0.5×2.5) to 3.5 (1.0×3.5) percent per year.

2. First, a minor point: 1,000 percent annual inflation means the price level is multiplied by 11. (A 100 percent increase means something doubles, a 200 percent increase means something triples, etc.) We use the compound interest formula to solve this problem. (See Review of Technique 17.) Thus, $11 = (1 + r)12$. Solving, we write $(1 + r) = 11^{1/12} = 1.221$, or r equals 22 percent per month. We can solve the second question by writing $191 = (1 + r)365$ or $1 + r = 191^{1/365} = 1.014$. The daily inflation rate is 1.4 percent.

3. To be precise, the nominal value will have grown to $\$100 \times (1 + .50)10 = \$5,766.50$ (Wow!). If we take today's price level as 1.0, the price level 10 years from now will have grown to $1.0 \times (1 + .48)10 = 50.42$ (Oh, dear!). The real value of the investment will be $\$5,766.50/50.42 = \$114.37$. A quick and dirty way to find the same answer is to calculate the value of 10 years' compounding at the real interest rate, $.50 - .48 = .02$. $\$100 \times (1 + .02)10 = \$121.90$. You'll note that using the real interest rate introduces a small error in the final answer, but certainly puts you in the right ballpark.

CHAPTER 18

Graph It 18

TABLE 18-1

	(1) 1982 unemployment rate		
(1) 1982 unemployment rate	9.7	9.7	9.7
(2) Guess of natural rate	5.5	6.0	6.5
(3) Unemployment gap	4.2	3.7	3.2
(4) 1982 GNP (billions)	3,058	3,058	3,058
(5) GNP gap [2.5% × (3) × (4)]	321	283	245
(6) Cyclical BD [.33 × (5)]	107	94	82
(7) BD	148	148	148
(8) Structural BD [(7) − (6)]	41	54	66

Fill-In Questions

1. monetarist
2. monetary growth rule
3. rational expectations
4. Real business cycle theory
5. efficiency wage
6. small menu costs
7. intertemporal substitution of leisure

True-False Questions

1. False. They think it is relatively stable.
2. True.
3. True.
4. False. Nominal, not real, GNP.
5. True.
6. T
7. False; they believe that anticipated changes in the money supply are offset by changes in the price level.

Multiple-Choice Questions

1. b   2. d

CHAPTER 19

Graph It 19

TABLE 19-1   SHORT- AND LONG-RUN INCREASE IN AGGREGATE DEMAND

(1)	1979 investment (billions)	423
(2)	20% increase	84
(3)	Increase in GNP [2 × (2)]	168
(4)	Actual 1979 GNP	2,418

TABLE 19-2   SHORT- AND LONG-RUN INCREASE IN AGGREGATE SUPPLY

		1 year	5 years
(1)	Increase in annual investment	84	84
(2)	Cumulative increase in capital	84	420
(3)	Total capital (roughly 3 × GNP)	7,254	7,254
(4)	As percent of capital	1.2	6.0
(5)	Relative increase in production [¼ × (4)]	0.29	1.48
(6)	Increase in AS [GNP times (5)]	7	35
(7)	As fraction of AD increase [100 × (6)/(3) above]	4.2%	20.8%

You can see from Table 19-2 that the aggregate supply effects of an increase in investment take many years to catch up with the aggregate demand effects.

Fill-In Questions

1. potential
2. per capita
3. productivity
4. production function
5. marginal product of capital
6. capital's share of output
7. constant returns to scale
8. steady state
9. technological change

True-False Questions

1. True.
2. False. Eventually, the additional capital stock gets depreciated away unless the saving rate rises.
3. False. It takes time for a higher saving rate to add to the capital stock.
4. True.
5. False. The growth rate depends only on technological change.
6. False. It takes time for the population to grow.
7. True.
8. False. More people, more output, though less output per person.
9. True.
10. True.

Multiple-Choice Questions

1. a   2. b   3. b   4. d   5. a   6. b   7. c   8. c   9. b   10. c

Worked-Out Problems

1. GNP per capita is $y = Y/N$. Capital per worker is $k = K/N$.

$$Y = AK^aN^{1-a}$$
$$Y/N = AK^aN^{1-a}/N = AK^aN^{1-a-1} = AK^aN^{-a} = A(K/N)^a$$
$$y = Ak^a$$

2. Look at Review of Technique 16. You will see there that one can prove directly that the marginal product of labor is $(1 - a)\,Y/N$. Total payments to labor are the marginal product of labor times the total amount of labor, $\{(1 - a)\,Y/N] \cdot N\}$. To find out what share of total GNP this represents, we divide by total GNP; finally,

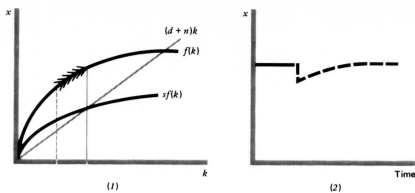

FIGURE d

$\{(1 - a)Y/N] \cdot N\}$. To find out what share of total GNP this represents, we divide by total GNP; finally,

$$\{[(1 - a)Y/N] \cdot N\}/Y = 1 - a = 1 - 0.25 = 0.75$$

3. Apply the formula

$$\frac{\Delta Y}{Y} = \theta \, \frac{\Delta K}{K} + (1 - \theta) \, \frac{\Delta N}{N}$$

where θ is capital's share, 0.25. In this case, $0.25(.2) + 0.75(.1)$ yields a 12.5 percent growth in GNP. Since population has grown 10 percent, per capita GNP grows 2.5 percent.

4. The path of per capita GNP is illustrated in Figures $d1$ and $d2$. $k = K/N$ falls to half its original value. Per capita GNP drops down the dashed line and then gradually returns to the steady state.

5. The path of per capita GNP is illustrated in Figure $e1$ and $e2$. The new saving curve is shown by the dashed curve. Per capita GNP gradually rises from the old steady state to the new steady state.

FIGURE e

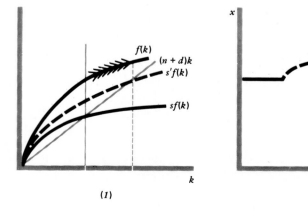

CHAPTER 20

Graph It 20

The regression of imports on GNP looks pretty reasonable. The coefficient a is 0.20. So a 1 billion dollar increase in GNP increases imports by about 200 million dollars. The regression of imports on the value of the dollar gives b equal to -4.5. Oops! The relation should be positive, not negative. This proves you can't always look at one factor at a time in a complex relation. The last regression gives $a = 0.23$ and $b = 0.68$, and so, roughly, a billion dollar increase in GNP increases imports by 230 million dollars and a 1 percent increase in the value of the dollar increases imports by about 680 million dollars.

Fill-In Questions

1. sterilization
2. policy dilemma
3. policy synchronization
4. domestic credit
5. purchasing power parity
6. J curve
7. real exchange rate
8. spillover interdependence
9. expenditure-switching policy

True-False Questions

1. False. Under flexible exchange rates, the terms of trade have fluctuated a great deal.
2. False. If the dollar is worth more, German goods are cheaper in the United States.
3. True.
4. True.
5. True.
6. True.
7. False. This requires flexible prices as well.
8. True.
9. True.

Multiple-Choice Questions

1. c   2. b   3. d   4. b   5. a   6. a   7. a   8. c

Worked-Out Problem

1. An investor could invest a dollar in the United States and end up with $1.12. Alternatively, she could buty 2 marks and end up with DN2.2. For the DN2.2 to equal $1.12, the exchange rate at the end of the year must equal 51 cents.

GLOSSARY

Accelerator model of investment   Theory that investment is proportional to the rate of change in output.

Accessions   People getting jobs.

Accommodation   Use of policy to offset a shock. For example, increase in money supply to prevent increase in interest rate when *IS* curve shifts out. See also *accommodation of supply shocks*.

Accommodation of supply shocks   Use of aggregate demand policy to maintain GNP when faced with a temporary dip in aggregate supply.

Action lag   Period between the time a policy is chosen and the time it is put into effect.

Activist policy   Policy which responds to current state of the economy.

Activists   Economists who believe the government ought to use stabilization policy.

Adaptive expectations   Expectations theory that expectations change gradually over time. Contrast *rational expectations*.

Adjustment of deficits   Alternative to financing deficits with central bank reserves. Policy measures can be used to reduce the deficit.

Adverse supply shocks   Upward movement of the aggregate supply curve; the OPEC oil price increase is the classic example.

Aggregate demand   Sum of all the purchases of final goods throughout the economy.

Aggregate demand curve   Amount of GNP demanded in the economy at a given price level.

Aggregate supply   Total production of all final goods in the economy.

Aggregate supply curve   Amount of GNP supplied by firms at a given price level.

Anticipated inflation   Inflation everybody can predict exactly in advance.

Asset budget constraint A household's investments in different assets must add up to total wealth.

Automatic stabilizer Factors in the structure of the economy which reduce the impact of changes in autonomous spending on the equilibrium level of GNP.

Balance of payments Net flow of dollars into the country from abroad.

Balanced budget amendment Proposed constitutional amendment requiring an annually balanced Federal budget.

Balanced budget multiplier Increase in GNP given equal increases in government purchases and in taxes.

Barro-Ricardo hypothesis Theory that current tax changes do not affect interest rates because people anticipate that the changes must be reversed in the future. Named for Robert Barro and David Ricardo.

Base drift Change over time in initial level of money stock used for money growth calculations. See *fan versus band.*

Beggar-thy-neighbor policy Attempt to increase domestic GNP at the expense of GNP in foreign countries.

Bond Promise by a borrower to repay a loan at a certain date and to pay interest in the interim.

Bracket creep Process through which inflation pushes people into higher tax brackets.

Budget deficit See *government budget deficit.*

Budget surplus Excess of government revenue over government expenditure. (Opposite of *budget deficit.*)

Burden of the debt Share of each individual in the national debt; note also that the "burden" should be corrected for share of each individual in ownership of the debt.

Business cycle Pattern of expansions and contractions of the economy around trend growth.

Business fixed investment Annual increase in machinery, equipment, and structures used in production.

Capital account Net flow of dollars into the country due to investment by foreigners in real and financial assets.

Capital mobility Ability of financial assets to flow between countries.

Classical adjustment process Process by which the economy automatically moves toward internal and external balance.

Classical aggregate supply curve Vertical aggregate supply curve.

Classical case Vertical *LM* curve, due to lack of interest sensitivity of money demand.

Clean floating Pure flexible exchange rate system in which central banks do not intervene. Contrast *dirty floating.*

Cobb-Douglas production function Production function with characteristics of constant returns to scale, constant elasticity of output, and unit elasticity of substitution between input factors.

COLA Cost of living adjustment clause retaining wages along with inflation.

Cold turkey policy Policy strategy of moving immediately to desired target.

Competitiveness Price of foreign goods relative to domestic goods, $eP*/P$

Composition of output Relative amounts of consumption, investment, and government purchases making up GNP.

Consumer durables Consumer goods which yield services over a period of time, for example, washing machines.

Consumer price index (CPI) Price index that measures the cost of goods bought by a typical urban family.

Consumption Purchases of goods and services by households.

Consumption function Equation relating consumption to spending.

Coordination of policies Policies agreed upon by countries. Because of international spillover effects, domestic economies can be best controlled by cooperation between countries.

Costs of cyclical unemployment Principally, the loss of output associated with high unemployment.

Council of Economic Advisers (CEA) The three-person council comprising the President's official economic policy advisers.

Credibility The degree to which the public believes the government will implement announced policies.

Crowding out Displacement of some component of private aggregate demand by government spending.

Currency appreciation Increase in the value of the dollar vis-à-vis other currencies.

Currency-deposit ratio One of the primary determinants of the money multiplier.

Currency depreciation Decrease in the value of the dollar vis-à-vis other currencies.

Currency reform Change in unit of currency, for example, redefinition of Israeli pound to shekel.

Currency account Net flow of dollars into the country due to sales of goods and services and net transfers from abroad.

Cyclical deficit Portion of the budget deficit due to deviation of GNP from potential. Contrast *structural deficit*.

Debt-financed deficits Budget deficits financed through sales of bonds to the public.

Debt-income ratio The ratio of the national debt to GNP. The debt-income ratio cannot grow without limit.

Debt management Policy of dividing financing of the national debt among bonds of various maturities and printing of high-powered money.

Debt problem The inability to pay a debt. A nation has a debt problem when its real interest payments on the national debt, or the portion owed to foreigners, become so large that the nation is unable to meet the payments.

Decision lag Period between the time a disturbance is discovered and the time a policy is chosen.

Depreciation Wearing out of the capital stock.

Desired capital stock Level of capital stock that maximizes profits.

Devaluation of the exchange rate Intentional depreciation of the dollar (or other currency) under a fixed exchange rate system.

Dirty floating Flexible exchange rate system in which central banks intervene in exchange markets to moderate short-run fluctuations in exchange rates.

Discount rate Interest rate charged by the Fed on loans to banks.

Discounted cash flow analysis The method of valuing today cash received in the future, based on applying a discount to future earnings to account for the interest differential between a dollar today and a dollar in the future.

Discretionary spending Portion of the Federal budget under immediate annual congressional control. Contrast *entitlement spending*.

Disintermediation Withdrawal of deposits from financial intermediaries when market interest rates rise above regulated ceiling rates on time deposits.

Disposable personal income Income available for the household to spend.

Dissaving Negative saving, i.e., expenditure out of wealth.

Duration of spells of unemployment Some individuals are unemployed for a very brief period—some for a long time.

Dynamic consistency Being tough when it hurts because you said you would earlier and you want people to believe you next time.

Dynamic multiplier   Response over time of aggregate demand to increase in autonomous spending.

Econometric models   Equation or multiple-equation model used to make quantitative economic predictions.

Econometric policy evaluation critique   Criticism that current econometric models are inappropriate for studying policy changes because the policy changes themselves change the responses of economic agents.

Economic disturbances   Shifts in aggregate demand or supply, or money demand or supply, that cause output, interest rates, or prices to diverge from the target path.

Efficiency wage   Theory attributing wage rigidity to losses in productivity that would occur if wages were cut.

Entitlement spending   Portion of the budget fixed as a result of prior program commitments such as Social Security, unemployment insurance, and student loans. Contrast *discretionary spending*.

Equilibrium output   Level of output when aggregate demand equals the supply of goods.

Excess reserves   Reserves held by banks over and above the level required by the Federal Reserve.

Excess sensitivity of consumption   Evidence that consumption has a larger response to current income than is consistent with the life cycle/permanent income theory.

Exchange rate   Price of foreign currency in terms of the U.S. dollar.

Exchange rate expectations   Anticipated level of future exchange rates.

Exchange rate overshooting   Movement of the exchange rate past its target. Adjustment of exchange rates to long-run equilibrium is frequently accompanied by an interim move of the exchange rate past its final position.

Expansion   See *recovery*.

Expectations-augmented aggregate supply curve   Aggregate supply curve that includes inflationary expectations as a major determinant of the price level.

Expectations-augmented Phillips curve   Phillips curve that includes inflationary expectations as a major determinant of the inflation rate.

Expectations effect   Long-run increase in nominal interest rate following increased growth rate of the money supply due to increased inflationary expectations.

Expected depreciation   Anticipated drop in the exchange rate. (Under perfect capital mobility, the nominal interest differential equals the expected depreciation rate.)

Expenditure reducing (or increasing) policies   Policies aimed at offsetting the effects of expenditure switching policy on aggregate demand.

Expenditure switching policies   Policies aimed at increasing purchases of domestic goods and decreasing imports.

Extended Phillips curve   Expectations-augmented Phillips curve with added term for the rate of change of unemployment.

Factor cost   Cost of goods net of indirect taxes. See *market prices*.

Factor shares   Portion of national income paid to each productive input (labor, capital, etc.).

Fan versus band   Following the band operating procedure, the Fed corrects last year's error in this year's money growth. Following the fan operating procedure, each year starts from a fresh base. See *base drift*.

FDIC (Federal Deposit Insurance Corporation)   Government agency that insures deposits of most commercial banks and mutual savings banks to a maximum of $100,000.

Final goods   Production excluding intermediate factors of production.

Final sales to domestic producers   GNP less net exports and inventory change.

Financing of deficits   Use of reserves by a central bank to pay for temporary imbalances in the balance of payments.

Fine tuning   Continuous attempts to stabilize the economy in the face of small disturbances.

Fiscal policy   Government policy with respect to government purchases, transfer payments, and the tax structure.

Fiscal policy multiplier   Increase in aggregate demand for a 1 dollar increase in government purchases (or other changes in autonomous demand).

Fisher equation   A relation in which the nominal interest rate equals the real interest rate plus the expected inflation rate.

Fixed exchange rates   Exchange rates determined by governments and central banks rather than the free market.

Flexible exchange rates   Exchange rates determined by supply and demand.

Floating exchange rate   Synonym for *flexible exchange rate.*

Frictionless neoclassical model   Model of a world with flexible prices and perfect competition.

Frictional unemployment   Unemployment associated with workers moving in and out of jobs in "normal" times.

Full crowding out   Total displacement of private spending by increasing government spending. See *classical aggregate supply curve* and *classical case.*

Full-employment (high-employment) surplus   What the budget surplus would be (hypothetically) with existing fiscal policy if the economy were at full employment.

GNP deflator   Measure of the price level obtained by dividing nominal GNP by real GNP.

GNP, nominal   Measure of all goods and services produced in the economy in 1 year, measured in dollars.

GNP, real   Measure of all goods and services produced in the economy in 1 year, measured in units of constant value.

Government budget deficit   Excess of government expenditure over government revenue.

Government expenditure   Total government spending; includes both government purchases and transfers.

Government purchases   Government spending on goods and services. Contrast *government expenditure.*

Gradual adjustment hypothesis   Theory that the change in the capital stock responds to the gap between the desired capital stock and the current capital stock.

Gradualism   Policy strategy of moving toward a desired target slowly.

Gramm-Rudman-Hollings Act   Federal law providing for automatic cuts in spending if the President and Congress do not agree on a balanced budget.

Gross domestic product (GDP)   Total goods and services produced physically within the country.

Gross national product   See *GNP, real.*

Growth   Increase in size of the economy.

Growth accounting   The theory of measuring the sources of economic growth.

Growth of total factor productivity   See *Technical progress.*

Guideposts   Advisory rulings for wage and price increases.

High-powered money   Currency plus reserve deposits at the Federal Reserve.

Hyperinflation   Very rapid price increase, usually defined as over 100 percent per month.

Illegal economy   Transactions executed in cash with the intention of screwing up economic statistics.

Imperfect information   Forecasts based on *imperfect information* will be less than fully accurate, though not necessarily biased.

Imported inflation   Inflation due to increase in domestic prices of imported goods following currency depreciation.

Income effect   Increase in interest rate following initial drop (due to *liquidity effect*) after increase in money supply. Not to be confused with income effect of microeconomics as an ''income and substitution effect.''

Income velocity of money   Ratio of income to the money stock.

Incomes policies   Attempts to reduce inflation by wage or price controls.

Indexation   Automatic adjustment of prices and wages according to inflation rate.

Indexation of tax brackets   Automatic adjustment of tax brackets according to inflation rate. Prevents *bracket creep*.

Inflation   Percentage rate of increase in the general price level.

Inflation-corrected deficit   Measure of the budget deficit correcting for effects of inflation, specifically reducing measured budget deficit by the capital gain on nominal bonds.

Inflation tax   Revenue gained by the government through inflation's devaluing money holdings.

Inside lag   Period between the time a disturbance occurs and the time action is taken.

Interdependence   Interconnection between national economies linked through international trade.

Intermediate targets   Policy targets used for control rather than because of their inherent interest. For example, the money supply might be an intermediate target in the attempt to ultimately control inflation. Contrast *ultimate targets*.

Internal and external balance   *Internal balance* occurs when output is at potential GNP. *External balance* occurs when the trade balance is zero.

Intertemporal substitution of leisure   The extent to which temporarily high real wages cause workers to work harder today and enjoy more leisure tomorrow.

Intervention   Sales or purchases of foreign exchange by the central bank in order to stabilize exchange rates.

Inventory cycle   Response of inventory investment to changes in sales that causes further changes in aggregate demand.

Inventory investment   Increase in stock of goods on hand.

Inventory-theoretic approach   Money demand models such as the Baumol-Tobin model.

Investment   Purchase of new capital, principally by the business sector.

Investment subsidy   Government payment of part of the cost of private investment.

IS-LM curves   Goods market and money market equilibrium schedules.

J curve   Curve tracing time path of the response of imports to exchange rate changes.

Keynesian aggregate supply curve   Horizontal aggregate supply curve.

Keynesians   Members of a school of economic thought who argue for active government stabilization policy. Alternatively, those who argue for fiscal rather than monetary policy.

Labor productivity   Average output per worker.

Laffer curve   Relation between tax revenue and tax rates showing that tax revenue is maximized at a tax rate greater than zero and less than 100 percent.

Layoffs   Terms categorizing types of unemployment. A *layoff* occurs when the employer dismisses an employee but promises to recall the worker at a later date.

Life-cycle hypothesis   Consumption theory emphasizing that consumers consume and save out of total life income and plan to provide for retirement.

Limits of growth   Study of whether resource depletion will eventually eliminate economic growth.

Liquidity   A measure of the ability to make funds available on short notice.

Liquidity constraints   Limitations on ability to borrow to finance consumption plans.

Liquidity effect   Initial drop in interest rate following increase in money supply, due to movement in *LM* curve.

Liquidity trap   Horizontal *LM* curve, due to extreme interest sensitivity of money demand.

Long-run aggregate supply curve   Aggregate supply curve showing long-run trade-off between GNP and the price level. Usually assumed to be vertical at potential GNP.

Long-run Phillips curve   Long-run tradeoff between inflation and unemployment (probably none).

Long-term labor market relations   Observation that labor markets rarely clear by day-to-day changes in wages. Employer-employee relations are generally based on understandings over months or years.

*M*1   Currency plus checkable deposits.

*M*2   *M*1 plus small time and savings deposits, overnight RPs and Eurodollars, and money market funds.

Macroeconomic models   Simplified formal models used to study and predict the behavior of the nation's economy.

Managed floating   See *dirty floating.*

Marginal product of capital   Increment output obtained by adding one unit of capital, with factor inputs held constant.

Marginal product of labor   Increment to output obtained by adding one unit of labor, with other factor inputs held constant.

Marginal propensity to consume (MPC)   Increase in consumption for 1 dollar increase in disposable income.

Marginal propensity to save (MPS)   Increase in saving for 1 dollar increase in disposable income.

Market clearing approach   Theory that flexible prices clear all markets. See *frictionless classical model.*

Market prices   Cost of goods including indirect taxes. See *factor cost.*

Markup   Increase of price over cost (often assumed to be constant, as an analytical convenience).

Measure of economic welfare (MEW)   GNP measurement adjusted for nonmarket outputs, economic "bads," and growth in leisure.

Medium of exchange   Asset used for making payments.

Monetarism   See *monetarists.*

Monetarists   Members of a school of economic thought emphasizing the importance of the money supply.

Monetary accommodation   Use of monetary policy to stabilize interest rates during active fiscal policy operations.

Monetary approach to the balance of payments   Theory emphasizing role of the money stock in determining the balance of payments.

Monetary base   See *high-powered money.*

Monetary-fiscal policy mix   Combination of fiscal and monetary policy chosen in recognition of differing effects on interest rates and investment.

Monetary policy   Use of money supply and interest rate changes to influence aggregate demand.

Monetary policy multiplier   Increase in aggregate demand for 1 dollar increase in the money supply.

Monetary rule A rule setting the growth of the money supply; frequently a constant growth rate without regard to current economic conditions.

Monetizing budget deficits Purchase of government debt by the Federal Reserve, indirectly funding the deficit by printing money.

Money (Money stock) Assets that can be used for making immediate payment.

Money-financed deficits Deficits financed by printing of high-powered money.

Money illusion Incorrect belief that the numbers used to express prices have significance.

Money multiplier Ratio of money stock to the monetary base.

Money stock and interest rate targets The Fed can directly target either the money stock or the interest rate, but not both.

Money supply function Function determined by the supply of high-powered money and the money multiplier.

Multiple expansion of bank deposits Process by which 1 dollar of high-powered money supports more than 1 dollar of the money supply.

Multiplier Increase in endogenous variable for 1 dollar increase in exogenous variable. Particularly, increase in GNP for 1 dollar increase in government purchases.

Multiplier uncertainty Uncertainty about effects of policy changes due to uncertainty about value of fiscal policy multiplier, monetary policy multiplier, etc.

Mundell-Fleming model Model first proposed by Robert Mundell and Marcus Fleming exploring economy with flexible exchange rates and perfect capital mobility.

National (public) debt Accumulation of all past deficits; total outstanding government bonds.

National income Total payments to factors of production. Net national product minus indirect taxes.

Natural rate of unemployment The unemployment rate that is permanently sustainable given the institutions of the economy.

Net exports Exports minus imports.

Net national product (NNP) GNP minus allowance for depreciation of capital.

Neutrality of money Proposition stating that equiproportional changes in the money stock and prices leave the economy unaffected.

New classical macroeconomists Economists who believe that the private economy is inherently efficient and that the government ought not attempt to stabilize output and unemployment.

New Deal Slogan for Roosevelt's economic policy reforms.

New Economics Economic policy of the Kennedy-Johnson years emphasizing the use of Keynesian theory to maintain full employment.

Nominal interest rate Stated rate of return—without adjustment for inflation. See *real interest rate*.

Noninterest deficit See *primary deficit*.

Okun's law Empirical "law" relating GNP growth to changes in unemployment; named for Arthur Okun.

Open market operation Purchase or sale of Treasury bills in exchange for money by the Federal Reserve.

Openness Extent to which the economy is involved with foreign trade as measured by the ratio of imports to GNP or GDP.

Output gap Difference between potential GNP and actual GNP.

Outside lag Time required for a policy change to take affect.

Overshooting Movement of an economic variable past its long-run value.

Peak   High points of business cycle.

Permanent income   Estimated lifetime income plus wealth.

Personal income   Income received by households.

Phillips curve   Relation between inflation and unemployment; in a sense a dynamic version of the aggregate supply curve.

Planned aggregate demand   Total planned spending on consumption, investment, and government purchases.

Policy dilemmas   Conflicts between achieving two inconsistent targets. For example, *internal* versus *external balance.*

Policy mix   Combination of fiscal and monetary policy to achieve both internal and external balance.

Policy rule   Activist but nondiscretionary policy guide.

Political business cycle   Theory that politicians deliberately manipulate the economy to produce an economic boom at election time.

Portfolio decisions   Decisions on how to divide wealth among different assets.

Potential output   Output that can be produced when all factors are fully employed.

Precautionary demand   Demand for many held against uncertain expenditure needs.

Present discounted value (PDV)   Value today of a stream of payments to be made in the future.

Price controls   Government-imposed restrictions are raising (and occasionally reducing) prices.

Primary deficit   The budget deficit except for interest payments.

Producer price index (PPI)   Price index based on a market basket of goods used in production. The PPI replaced the older wholesale price index (WPI).

Production function   Technological relation showing how much output can be produced for a given combination of inputs.

Profit sharing   System in which part of workers' compensation is a share of profits rather than an hourly wage.

Propagation mechanism   Mechanism by which current economic shocks cause fluctuations into the future, for example, *intertemporal substitution of leisure.*

Public debt   See *national debt.*

Purchasing power parity (PPP)   Theory of exchange rate determination arguing that the exchange rate adjusts to maintain equal purchasing power of foreign and domestic currency.

q theory   Investment theory emphasizing that investment will be high when assets are valuable relative to their reproduction cost. The ratio of asset value to cost is called q.

Quantity equation   Price times quantity equals money times velocity.

Quantity theory of money   Theory of money demand emphasizing the relation of nominal income to nominal money. Sometimes used to mean vertical *LM* curve.

Quits   A quit occurs when the worker decides to leave.

Rational expectations   Theory of expectations formation in which expectations are based on all available information about the underlying economic variable. Frequently associated with new classical macroeconomics.

Rational expectations–equilibrium approach   See *rational expectations.*

Reaganomics   Slogan describing the Reagan administration's economic program.

Real balance   Real value of the money stock. (Nunber of dollars divided by the price level.)

Real business cycles   Theory that recessions and booms are due primarily to shocks in real activity, such as supply shocks, rather than to changes in monetary factors.

Real exchange rate   Purchasing power of foreign currency relative to the U.S. dollar.

Real interest rate   Return on an investment measured in dollars of constant value.

Real materials prices   Price of raw materials relative to price of output.

Real wage rigidity   Situation in which indexation, formally or informally, of wages to cost of living prevents economic adjustment through changes in real wages.

Recession   Period of economic weakness with GNP below potential.

Recognition lag   Period between the time a disturbance occurs and the time policy makers discover the disturbance.

Recovery   Upward swing in business cycle.

Redistribution of wealth   Desired effect of muggers. Undesired side effect of unanticipated inflation.

Relative-income hypothesis   Consumption theory arguing that consumption is related to previous peak income as well as current income.

Rental cost of capital   Cost of using a dollar's worth of capital for a year.

Repercussion effect   Feedback of domestic economic changes through foreign economies back into the domestic economy.

Reserve-deposit ratio   One of the primary determinants of the money multiplier.

Residential investment   Investment in housing.

Revaluation of the exchange rate   Intentional appreciation of the dollar (or other currency) under fixed exchange rate system.

Rules versus discretion   Argument over whether policy should be on "automatic pilot" or whether (hard-to-predict) human judgment should be used.

Sacrifice ratio   During a period of anti-inflation policy, the ratio of cumulative GNP lost to reduction in the inflation rate.

Seigniorage   Revenue derived from the government's ability to print money.

Separations   People leaving jobs.

Short-run aggregate supply curve   Aggregate supply curve showing short-run trade-off between GNP and the price level. Usually assumed to be quite flat.

Short-run Phillips curve   Short-run tradeoff between inflation and unemployment holding constant anticipated inflation.

Sluggish wage adjustment   Observation that wages adjust slowly rather than instantly, thus preventing labor markets from clearing in a competitive fashion.

Small menu costs   Theory suggesting that very small costs of changing prices and wages may lead to large amounts of price and wage rigidity.

Sources of growth   Increases in factor inputs and improved technology.

Square-root formula   Demand-for-money schedule developed in Baumol-Tobin approach.

Stabilization policies   Use of fiscal and monetary policies to smooth fluctuations in output.

Stagflation   Simultaneous inflation and recession.

Standard of deferred payment   Asset normally used for making payments due at a later date.

Steady state   State in which real (per capita) economic variables are constant.

Sterilization   Open market purchase or sale by the Fed used to offset effects of foreign exchange market intervention on the monetary base.

Sterilized and nonsterilized intervention   See *sterilization* and *intervention*.

Store of value   Asset that maintains its value over time.

Structural deficit   Deficit that would exist with current fiscal policy if the economy were at full employment. Formerly called "high-employment" or "full-employment" deficit. Contrast *cyclical deficit*.

Supply-side economics   School of economics emphasizing changes in potential GNP rather than aggregate demand.

Targeted programs   Employment programs aimed at special subsegments of the work force such as youth or workers having lost jobs to foreign competition.

Targets and instruments of policy   The *target* is the variable of policy instrument. The *instrument* is the variable to be manipulated to change the target variable.

Tax indexation   Under tax indexation, tax brackets move up with inflation. This eliminates *bracket creep*.

Tax surcharge   Temporary increase in tax rate.

Technical progress   Ability to produce more output with a given level of inputs; growth in total factor productivity.

Terms of trade   Ratio of import prices to export prices, a measure of competitiveness.

TIP (tax incentive policy)   Use of tax subsidies and penalties to persuade companies to reduce wage or price increases.

TISA   See Total Incomes System of Accounts.

Total Income System of Accounts (TISA)   System of national income accounting which corrects traditional GNP measures, particularly with respect to measuring "nonmarket" goods.

Trade balance   Net flow of dollars into the country due to sales of goods abroad.

Transactions demand   Demand for money held to minimize costs associated with repeated "trips to the bank."

Transfers   Payments to a household other than in payment for services. Social Security, for example.

Transmission mechanism   Process by which monetary policy affects aggregate demand.

Trend output   See *potential output*.

Trough   Low point of business cycle.

Ultimate targets   Policy targets of inherent interest. For example, the inflation rate might be an ultimate target. Contrast *intermediate targets*.

Unemployment   The fraction of the people in the labor force unable to find work.

Unemployment pool   Group of individuals in transition between jobs.

Unintended inventory accumulation   Increase in stocks of goods when firms are unable to sell output as expected.

Unit of account   Asset in which prices are denoted.

Unit labor cost   Cost of enough labor to produce one unit of output.

User cost of capital   See *rental cost of capital*.

Value added   Increase in value of output at a given stage of production. Equivalently, value of output minus cost of inputs.

Wage and price controls   Regulation of wages and prices by law rather than by supply and demand.

Wage push   Demand for wage increases above inflation rate built into short-run Phillips curve.

ECONOMIC DATA TABLES

TABLE A GROSS NATIONAL PRODUCT 1929–1985

(Billions of dollars)

Year	Gross national product	Personal consumption expenditures	Gross private domestic investment	Net exports	Exports	Imports	Total	Total	National defense	Nondefense	State and local
				NET EXPORTS OF GOODS AND SERVICES			**GOVERNMENT PURCHASES OF GOODS AND SERVICES**	**FEDERAL**			
1929	103.9	77.3	16.7	1.1	7.1	5.9	8.9	1.5			7.4
1933	56.0	45.8	1.6	0.4	2.4	2.1	8.3	2.2			6.1
1939	91.3	67.0	9.5	1.2	4.6	3.4	13.6	5.2	1.3	3.9	8.3
1940	100.4	71.0	13.4	1.8	5.4	3.7	14.2	6.1	2.3	3.9	8.1
1941	125.5	80.8	18.3	1.5	6.1	4.7	25.0	17.0	13.8	3.2	8.0
1942	159.0	88.6	10.3	0.2	5.0	4.8	59.9	52.0	49.4	2.6	7.8
1943	192.7	99.5	6.2	−1.9	4.6	6.5	88.9	81.4	79.8	1.6	7.5
1944	211.4	108.2	7.7	−1.7	5.5	7.2	97.1	89.4	87.5	2.0	7.6
1945	213.4	119.6	11.3	−0.5	7.4	7.9	83.0	74.8	73.7	1.1	8.2
1946	212.4	143.9	31.5	7.8	15.2	7.3	29.1	19.2	16.4	2.8	9.9
1947	235.2	161.9	35.0	11.9	20.3	8.3	26.4	13.6	10.0	3.6	12.8
1948	261.6	174.9	47.1	7.0	17.5	10.6	32.6	17.3	11.3	6.0	15.3
1949	260.4	178.3	36.5	6.5	16.4	9.8	39.0	21.1	13.9	7.2	18.0
1950	288.3	192.1	55.1	2.2	14.5	12.3	38.8	19.1	14.3	4.7	19.8
1951	333.4	208.1	60.5	4.5	19.8	15.3	60.4	38.6	33.8	4.8	21.8
1952	351.6	219.1	53.5	3.2	19.2	16.0	75.8	52.7	46.2	6.5	23.1
1953	371.6	232.6	54.9	1.3	18.1	16.8	82.8	57.9	49.0	8.9	24.8
1954	372.5	239.8	54.1	2.6	18.8	16.3	76.0	48.4	41.6	6.8	27.7
1955	405.9	257.9	69.7	3.0	21.1	18.1	75.3	44.9	39.0	6.0	30.3
1956	428.2	270.6	72.7	5.3	25.2	19.9	79.7	46.4	40.7	5.7	33.3
1957	451.0	285.3	71.1	7.3	28.2	20.9	87.3	50.5	44.6	5.9	36.9
1958	456.8	294.6	63.6	3.3	24.4	21.1	95.4	54.5	46.3	8.3	40.8
1959	495.8	316.3	80.2	1.5	25.0	23.5	97.9	54.6	46.4	8.2	43.3
1960	515.3	330.7	78.2	5.9	29.9	24.0	100.6	54.4	45.3	9.2	46.1
1961	533.8	341.1	77.1	7.2	31.1	23.9	108.4	58.2	47.9	10.2	50.2
1962	574.6	361.9	87.6	6.9	33.1	26.2	118.2	64.6	52.1	12.6	53.5
1963	606.9	381.7	93.1	8.2	35.7	27.5	123.8	65.7	51.5	14.2	58.1
1964	649.8	409.3	99.6	10.9	40.5	29.6	130.0	66.4	50.4	16.0	63.5
1965	705.1	440.7	116.2	9.7	42.9	33.2	138.6	68.7	51.0	17.7	69.9
1966	772.0	477.3	128.6	7.5	46.6	39.1	158.6	80.4	62.0	18.3	78.2
1967	816.4	503.6	125.7	7.4	49.5	42.1	179.7	92.7	73.4	19.3	87.0
1968	892.7	552.5	137.0	5.5	54.8	49.3	197.7	100.1	79.1	21.0	97.6
1969	963.9	597.9	153.2	5.6	60.4	54.7	207.3	100.0	78.9	21.1	107.2
1970	1,015.5	640.0	148.8	8.5	68.9	60.5	218.2	98.8	76.8	22.0	119.4
1971	1,102.7	691.6	172.5	6.3	72.4	66.1	232.4	99.8	74.1	25.8	132.5
1972	1,212.8	757.6	202.0	3.2	81.4	78.2	250.0	105.8	77.4	28.4	144.2
1973	1,359.3	837.2	238.8	16.8	114.1	97.3	266.5	106.4	77.5	28.9	160.1
1974	1,472.8	916.5	240.8	16.3	151.5	135.2	299.1	116.2	82.6	33.6	182.9

236

TABLE A (CONTINUED)

Year	Gross national product	Personal consumption expenditures	Gross private domestic investment	NET EXPORTS OF GOODS AND SERVICES			GOVERNMENT PURCHASES OF GOODS AND SERVICES				
				Net exports	Exports	Imports	Total	FEDERAL			State and local
								Total	National defense	Nondefense	
1975	1,598.4	1,012.8	219.6	31.1	161.3	130.3	335.0	129.2	89.6	39.6	205.9
1976	1,782.8	1,129.3	277.7	18.8	177.7	158.9	356.9	136.3	93.4	42.9	220.6
1977	1,990.5	1,257.2	344.1	1.9	191.6	189.7	387.3	151.1	100.9	50.3	236.2
1978	2,249.7	1,403.5	416.8	4.1	227.5	223.4	425.2	161.8	108.9	52.9	263.4
1979	2,508.2	1,566.8	454.8	18.8	291.2	272.5	467.8	178.0	121.9	56.1	289.9
1980	2,732.0	1,732.6	437.0	32.1	351.0	318.9	530.3	208.1	142.7	65.4	322.2
1981	3,052.6	1,915.1	515.5	33.9	382.8	348.9	588.1	242.2	167.5	74.8	345.9
1982	3,166.0	2,050.7	447.3	26.3	361.9	335.6	641.7	272.7	193.8	78.9	369.0
1983	3,401.6	2,229.3	501.9	−5.3	354.1	359.4	675.7	284.8	215.7	69.2	390.9
1984	3,774.7	2,423.0	674.0	−59.2	384.6	443.8	736.8	312.9	237.0	76.0	423.9
1985^p	3,992.5	2,581.9	670.4	−74.4	370.4	444.8	814.6	353.9	262.0	91.9	460.7

^{p}indicates preliminary.
Source: Department of Commerce, Bureau of Economic Analysis.

TABLE B GROSS NATIONAL PRODUCT IN 1982 DOLLARS, 1929–1985

(Billions of 1972 dollars, except as noted)

		PERSONAL CONSUMPTION EXPENDITURES				GROSS PRIVATE DOMESTIC INVESTMENT						
							FIXED INVESTMENT					
								NONRESIDENTIAL				
Year	Gross national product	Total	Durable goods	Non-durable goods	Services	Total	Total	Total	Struc-tures	Producers' durable equipment	Resi-dential	Change in business inven-tories
1929	709.6	471.4	40.3	211.4	219.7	139.2	128.4	93.0	54.7	38.4	35.4	10.8
1933	498.5	378.7	20.7	181.8	176.2	22.7	33.5	25.8	14.3	11.5	7.7	−10.7
1939	716.6	480.5	35.7	248.0	196.7	86.0	82.1	53.2	25.2	28.0	28.9	3.9
1940	772.9	502.6	40.6	259.4	202.7	111.8	97.4	65.0	28.5	36.5	32.5	14.4
1941	909.4	531.1	46.2	275.6	209.3	138.8	111.1	76.6	33.4	43.2	34.4	27.8
1942	1,080.3	527.6	31.3	279.1	217.2	76.7	64.7	47.4	20.9	26.5	17.3	12.0
1943	1,276.2	539.9	28.1	284.7	227.2	50.4	49.7	39.4	15.6	23.8	10.4	0.7
1944	1,380.6	557.1	26.3	297.9	232.9	56.4	61.6	52.6	20.4	32.1	9.0	−5.2
1945	1,354.8	592.7	28.7	323.5	240.5	76.5	84.9	74.2	27.0	47.2	10.7	−8.4
1946	1,096.9	655.0	47.8	344.2	262.9	178.1	150.2	105.5	50.9	54.7	44.7	27.9
1947	1,066.7	666.6	56.5	337.4	272.6	177.9	178.9	121.7	47.5	74.2	57.2	−1.0
1948	1,108.7	681.8	61.7	338.7	281.4	208.2	196.0	127.4	50.5	76.9	68.6	12.3
1949	1,109.0	695.4	67.8	342.3	285.3	168.8	178.4	114.8	49.3	65.5	63.6	−9.7
1950	1,203.7	733.2	80.7	352.8	299.8	234.9	210.8	124.0	52.8	71.2	86.7	24.2
1951	1,328.2	748.7	74.7	362.9	311.1	235.2	204.3	131.7	56.5	75.2	72.6	30.8
1952	1,380.0	771.4	73.0	376.6	321.9	211.8	201.8	130.6	57.3	73.3	71.2	10.0
1953	1,435.3	802.5	80.2	388.2	334.1	216.6	213.8	140.1	62.3	77.7	73.8	2.8
1954	1,416.2	822.7	81.5	393.8	347.4	212.6	217.3	137.5	64.9	72.7	79.8	−4.8
1955	1,494.9	873.8	96.9	413.2	363.6	259.8	243.5	151.0	69.4	81.7	92.4	16.3
1956	1,525.6	899.8	92.8	426.9	380.1	257.8	244.9	160.4	75.5	84.9	84.4	12.9
1957	1,551.1	919.7	92.4	434.7	392.6	243.4	240.4	161.1	75.2	85.9	79.3	3.0
1958	1,539.2	932.9	86.9	439.9	406.1	221.4	224.8	143.9	70.6	73.3	81.0	−3.4
1959	1,629.1	979.4	96.9	455.8	426.7	270.3	253.8	153.6	71.9	81.7	100.2	16.5
1960	1,665.3	1,005.1	98.0	463.3	443.9	260.5	252.7	159.4	76.1	83.3	93.3	7.7
1961	1,708.7	1,025.2	93.6	470.1	461.4	259.1	251.8	158.2	77.7	80.5	93.6	7.3
1962	1,799.4	1,069.0	103.0	484.2	481.8	288.6	272.4	170.2	81.3	88.9	102.2	16.2
1963	1,873.3	1,108.4	111.8	494.3	502.3	307.1	290.5	176.6	81.6	95.1	113.9	16.6
1964	1,973.3	1,170.6	120.8	517.5	532.3	325.9	310.2	194.9	87.9	107.0	115.3	15.7
1965	2,087.6	1,236.4	134.6	543.2	558.5	367.0	341.8	227.6	101.8	125.8	114.2	25.2
1966	2,208.3	1,298.9	144.4	569.3	585.3	390.5	353.7	250.4	108.0	142.4	103.2	36.9
1967	2,271.4	1,337.7	146.2	579.2	612.3	374.4	345.6	245.0	105.4	139.6	100.6	28.8
1968	2,365.6	1,405.9	161.6	602.4	641.8	391.8	370.7	254.5	108.0	146.5	116.2	21.0
1969	2,423.3	1,456.7	167.8	617.2	671.7	410.3	385.1	269.7	112.9	156.3	115.4	25.1
1970	2,416.2	1,492.0	162.5	632.5	697.0	381.5	373.3	264.0	111.1	152.9	109.3	8.2
1971	2,484.8	1,538.8	178.3	640.3	720.2	419.3	399.7	258.4	107.3	151.0	141.3	19.6
1972	2,608.5	1,621.9	200.4	665.5	756.0	465.4	443.7	277.0	109.5	167.5	166.6	21.8
1973	2,744.1	1,689.6	220.3	683.2	786.1	520.8	480.8	317.3	117.7	199.6	163.4	40.0
1974	2,729.3	1,674.0	204.9	666.1	803.1	481.3	448.0	317.8	115.2	202.7	130.2	33.3
1975	2,695.0	1,711.9	205.6	676.5	829.8	383.3	396.1	281.2	102.8	178.4	114.9	−12.8
1976	2,826.7	1,803.9	232.3	708.8	862.8	453.5	431.4	290.6	104.4	186.2	140.8	22.1
1977	2,958.6	1,883.8	253.9	731.4	898.5	521.3	492.2	324.0	108.3	215.7	168.1	29.1

				FEDERAL				
Net exports	Exports	Imports	Total	Total	National defense	Nondefense	State and local	Percent change from preceding period, gross national product
4.7	42.1	37.4	94.2	18.3			75.9	
−1.4	22.7	24.2	98.5	27.0			71.5	−2.1
6.1	36.2	30.1	144.1	53.8			90.3	7.9
8.2	40.0	31.7	150.2	63.6			86.6	7.8
3.9	42.0	38.2	235.6	153.0			82.6	17.7
−7.7	29.1	36.9	483.7	407.1			76.7	18.8
−23.0	25.1	48.0	708.9	638.1			70.8	18.1
−23.8	27.3	51.1	790.8	722.5			68.3	8.2
−18.9	35.2	54.1	704.5	634.0			70.5	−1.9
27.0	69.0	42.0	236.9	159.3			77.6	−19.0
42.4	82.3	39.9	179.8	91.9			87.9	−2.8
19.2	66.2	47.1	199.5	106.1			93.4	3.9
18.8	65.0	46.2	226.0	119.5			106.5	0.0
4.7	59.2	54.6	230.8	116.7			114.2	8.5
14.6	72.0	57.4	329.7	214.4			115.4	10.3
6.9	70.1	63.3	389.9	272.7			117.3	3.9
−2.7	66.9	69.7	419.0	295.9			123.1	4.0
2.5	70.0	67.5	378.4	245.0			133.4	−1.3
0.0	76.9	76.9	361.3	217.9			143.4	5.6
4.3	87.9	83.6	363.7	215.4			148.3	2.1
7.0	94.9	87.9	381.1	224.1			157.0	1.7
−10.3	82.4	92.8	395.3	224.9			170.4	−0.8
−18.2	83.7	101.9	397.7	221.5			176.2	5.8
−4.0	98.4	102.4	403.7	220.6			183.1	2.2
−2.7	100.7	103.3	427.1	232.9			194.2	2.6
−7.5	106.9	114.4	449.4	249.3			200.1	5.3
−1.9	114.7	116.6	459.8	247.8			212.0	4.1
5.9	128.8	122.8	470.8	244.2			226.6	5.3
−2.7	132.0	134.7	487.0	244.4			242.5	5.8
−13.7	138.4	152.1	532.6	273.8			258.8	5.8
−16.9	143.6	160.5	576.2	304.4			271.8	2.9
−29.7	155.7	185.3	597.6	309.6			288.0	4.1
−34.9	165.0	199.9	591.2	295.6			295.6	2.4
−30.0	178.3	208.3	572.6	268.3			304.3	−0.3
−39.8	179.2	218.9	566.5	250.6			315.9	2.8
−49.4	195.2	244.6	570.7	246.0	185.3	60.7	324.7	5.0
−31.5	242.3	273.8	565.3	230.0	171.0	59.1	335.3	5.2
0.8	269.1	268.4	573.2	226.4	163.3	63.1	346.8	−0.5
18.9	259.7	240.8	580.9	226.3	161.1	65.2	354.6	−1.3
−11.0	274.4	285.4	580.3	224.2	157.5	66.8	356.0	4.9
−35.5	281.6	317.1	589.1	231.8	159.2	72.7	357.2	4.7

Year	Gross national product	PERSONAL CONSUMPTION EXPENDITURES				GROSS PRIVATE DOMESTIC INVESTMENT						Change in business inventories
							FIXED INVESTMENT					
								NONRESIDENTIAL				
		Total	Durable goods	Non-durable goods	Services	Total	Total	Total	Struc-tures	Producers' durable equipment	Resi-dential	
1978	3,115.2	1,961.0	267.4	753.7	939.8	576.9	540.2	362.1	119.3	242.8	178.0	36.8
1979	3,192.4	2,004.4	266.5	766.6	971.2	575.2	560.2	389.4	130.6	258.8	170.8	15.0
1980	3,187.1	2,000.4	245.9	762.6	991.9	509.3	516.2	379.2	136.2	243.0	137.0	−6.9
1981	3,248.8	2,024.2	250.8	764.4	1,009.0	545.5	521.7	395.2	148.8	246.4	126.5	23.9
1982	3,166.0	2,050.7	252.7	771.0	1,027.0	447.3	471.8	366.7	143.3	223.4	105.1	−24.5
1983	3,277.7	2,145.9	283.6	800.7	1,061.7	503.4	508.9	360.1	129.7	230.5	148.7	−5.5
1984	3,492.0	2,239.9	318.6	828.0	1,093.3	661.3	598.6	430.3	148.7	281.6	168.3	62.7
1985P	3,573.5	2,312.6	344.7	847.4	1,120.5	650.6	643.3	471.8	165.7	306.1	171.5	7.3

Pindicates preliminary.
Source: Department of Commerce, Bureau of Economic Analysis.

| NET EXPORTS OF GOODS AND SERVICES | | | GOVERNMENT PURCHASES OF GOODS AND SERVICES | | | | | |
| | | | | FEDERAL | | | | |
Net exports	Exports	Imports	Total	Total	National defense	Nondefense	State and local	Percent change from preceding period, gross national product
−26.8	312.6	339.4	604.1	233.7	160.7	73.0	370.4	5.3
3.6	356.8	353.2	609.1	236.2	164.3	71.9	373.0	2.5
57.0	388.9	332.0	620.5	246.9	171.2	75.7	373.6	−0.2
49.4	392.7	343.4	629.7	259.6	180.3	79.3	370.1	1.9
26.3	361.9	335.6	641.7	272.7	193.8	78.9	369.0	−2.5
−19.4	394.4	368.8	647.8	275.5	207.3	68.3	372.2	3.5
−85.0	370.9	455.9	675.9	292.5	220.3	72.3	383.3	6.5
−105.1	360.2	465.3	715.4	321.3	236.0	85.2	394.2	2.3

TABLE C CIVILIAN UNEMPLOYMENT RATE BY DEMOGRAPHIC CHARACTERISTIC, 1948–1985
(Percent[1])

Year	All civilian workers	WHITE							BLACK						
			MALES			FEMALES				MALES			FEMALES		
		Total	Total	16–19 years	20 years and over	Total	16–19 years	20 years and over	Total	Total	16–19 years	20 years and over	Total	16–19 years	20 years and over
1948	3.8	3.5	3.4			3.8									
1949	5.9	5.6	5.6			5.7									
1950	5.3	4.9	4.7			5.3									
1951	3.3	3.1	2.6			4.2									
1952	3.0	2.8	2.5			3.3									
1953	2.9	2.7	2.5			3.1									
1954	5.5	5.0	4.8	13.4	4.4	5.5	10.4	5.1							
1955	4.4	3.9	3.7	11.3	3.3	4.3	9.1	3.9							
1956	4.1	3.6	3.4	10.5	3.0	4.2	9.7	3.7							
1957	4.3	3.8	3.6	11.5	3.2	4.3	9.5	3.8							
1958	6.8	6.1	6.1	15.7	5.5	6.2	12.7	5.6							
1959	5.5	4.8	4.6	14.0	4.1	5.3	12.0	4.7							
1960	5.5	5.0	4.8	14.0	4.2	5.3	12.7	4.6							
1961	6.7	6.0	5.7	15.7	5.1	6.5	14.8	5.7							
1962	5.5	4.9	4.6	13.7	4.0	5.5	12.8	4.7							
1963	5.7	5.0	4.7	15.9	3.9	5.8	15.1	4.8							
1964	5.2	4.6	4.1	14.7	3.4	5.5	14.9	4.6							
1965	4.5	4.1	3.6	12.9	2.9	5.0	14.0	4.0							
1966	3.8	3.4	2.8	10.5	2.2	4.3	12.1	3.3							
1967	3.8	3.4	2.7	10.7	2.1	4.6	11.5	3.8							
1968	3.6	3.2	2.6	10.1	2.0	4.3	12.1	3.4							
1969	3.5	3.1	2.5	10.0	1.9	4.2	11.5	3.4							
1970	4.9	4.5	4.0	13.7	3.2	5.4	13.4	4.4							
1971	5.9	5.4	4.9	15.1	4.0	6.3	15.1	5.3							
1972	5.6	5.1	4.5	14.2	3.6	5.9	14.2	4.9	10.4	9.3	31.7	7.0	11.8	40.5	9.0
1973	4.9	4.3	3.8	12.3	3.0	5.3	13.0	4.3	9.4	8.0	27.8	6.0	11.1	36.1	8.6
1974	5.6	5.0	4.4	13.5	3.5	6.1	14.5	5.1	10.5	9.8	33.1	7.4	11.3	37.4	8.8
1975	8.5	7.8	7.2	18.3	6.2	8.6	17.4	7.5	14.8	14.8	38.1	12.5	14.8	41.0	12.2
1976	7.7	7.0	6.4	17.3	5.4	7.9	16.4	6.8	14.0	13.7	37.5	11.4	14.3	41.6	11.7
1977	7.1	6.2	5.5	15.0	4.7	7.3	15.9	6.2	14.0	13.3	39.2	10.7	14.9	43.4	12.3
1978	6.1	5.2	4.6	13.5	3.7	6.2	14.4	5.2	12.8	11.8	36.7	9.3	13.8	40.8	11.2
1979	5.8	5.1	4.5	13.9	3.6	5.9	14.0	5.0	12.3	11.4	34.2	9.3	13.3	39.1	10.9
1980	7.1	6.3	6.1	16.2	5.3	6.5	14.8	5.6	14.3	14.5	37.5	12.4	14.0	39.8	11.9
1981	7.6	6.7	6.5	17.9	5.6	6.9	16.6	5.9	15.6	15.7	40.7	13.5	15.6	42.2	13.4
1982	9.7	8.6	8.8	21.7	7.8	8.3	19.0	7.3	18.9	20.1	48.9	17.8	17.6	47.1	15.4
1983	9.6	8.4	8.8	20.2	7.9	7.9	18.3	6.9	19.5	20.3	48.8	18.1	18.6	48.2	16.5
1984	7.5	6.5	6.4	16.8	5.7	6.5	15.2	5.8	15.9	16.4	42.7	14.3	15.4	42.6	13.5
1985	7.2	6.2	5.1	16.5	5.4	6.4	14.8	5.7	15.1	15.3	41.0	13.2	14.9	39.2	13.1

[1]Unemployment as percentage of civilian labor force in group specified.
Source: Department of Labor, Bureau of Labor Statistics

TABLE D GOVERNMENT RECEIPTS AND EXPENDITURES, NATIONAL INCOME AND PRODUCT ACCOUNTS, 1929–1985

(Billions of dollars; quarterly data at seasonally adjusted annual rates)

Calendar year	TOTAL GOVERNMENT			FEDERAL GOVERNMENT			STATE AND LOCAL GOVERNMENT		
	Receipts	Expenditures	Surplus or deficit (−), national income and product accounts	Receipts	Expenditures	Surplus or deficit (−), national income and product accounts	Receipts	Expenditures	Surplus or deficit (−), national income and product accounts
1929	11.3	10.3	1.0	3.8	2.7	1.2	7.6	7.8	−0.2
1933	9.4	10.7	−1.4	2.7	4.0	−1.3	7.2	7.2	−0.1
1939	15.4	17.6	−2.2	6.8	9.0	−2.2	9.6	9.6	0.0
1940	17.8	18.5	−0.7	8.7	10.0	−1.3	10.0	9.3	0.6
1941	25.0	28.8	−3.8	15.5	20.5	−5.1	10.4	9.1	1.3
1942	32.7	64.1	−31.4	23.0	56.1	−33.1	10.6	8.8	1.8
1943	49.2	93.4	−44.2	39.3	85.9	−46.6	10.9	8.4	2.4
1944	51.2	103.1	−51.8	41.1	95.6	−54.5	11.1	8.5	2.7
1945	53.4	92.9	−39.5	42.7	84.7	−42.1	11.6	9.0	2.6
1946	52.6	47.2	5.4	40.7	37.2	3.5	13.0	11.1	1.9
1947	57.8	43.4	14.4	44.1	30.8	13.4	15.4	14.4	1.0
1948	59.6	51.1	8.4	43.9	35.5	8.3	17.7	17.6	0.1
1949	56.6	60.0	−3.4	39.4	42.0	−2.6	19.5	20.2	−0.7
1950	69.4	61.4	8.0	50.4	41.2	9.2	21.3	22.5	−1.2
1951	85.6	79.5	6.1	64.6	58.1	6.5	23.4	23.9	−0.4
1952	90.5	94.3	−3.8	67.7	71.4	−3.7	25.4	25.5	−0.0
1953	95.0	102.0	−7.0	70.4	77.6	−7.1	27.4	27.3	−0.1
1954	90.4	97.5	−7.1	64.2	70.3	−6.0	29.0	30.2	−1.1
1955	101.6	98.5	3.1	73.1	68.6	4.4	31.7	32.9	−1.3
1956	110.2	105.0	5.2	78.5	72.5	6.1	35.0	35.9	−0.9
1957	116.7	115.8	0.9	82.5	80.2	2.3	38.5	39.8	−1.4
1958	115.7	128.3	−12.6	79.3	89.6	−10.3	42.0	44.4	−2.4
1959	130.3	131.9	−1.6	90.6	91.7	−1.1	46.6	47.0	−0.4
1960	140.4	137.3	3.1	96.9	93.9	3.0	50.0	49.9	0.1
1961	145.9	150.1	−4.3	99.0	102.9	−3.9	54.1	54.5	−0.4
1962	157.9	161.6	−3.8	107.2	111.4	−4.2	58.6	58.2	0.5
1963	169.8	169.1	0.7	115.6	115.3	0.3	63.4	62.9	0.5
1964	175.6	177.8	−2.3	116.2	119.5	−3.3	69.8	68.8	1.0
1965	190.2	189.6	0.5	125.8	125.3	0.5	75.5	75.5	−0.0
1966	214.4	215.6	−1.3	143.5	145.3	−1.8	85.2	84.7	0.5
1967	230.8	245.0	−14.2	152.6	165.8	−13.2	94.1	95.2	−1.1
1968	266.2	272.2	−6.0	176.9	182.9	−6.0	107.9	107.8	0.1
1969	300.1	290.2	9.9	199.7	191.3	8.4	120.8	119.3	1.5
1970	306.8	317.4	−10.6	195.4	207.8	−12.4	135.8	134.0	1.8
1971	327.3	346.8	−19.5	202.7	224.8	−22.0	153.6	151.0	2.6
1972	374.0	377.3	−3.4	232.2	249.0	−16.8	179.3	165.8	13.5
1973	419.6	411.7	7.9	263.7	269.3	−5.6	196.4	182.9	13.5
1974	463.1	467.4	−4.3	293.9	305.5	−11.6	213.1	205.9	7.2
1975	480.0	544.9	−64.9	294.9	364.2	−69.4	239.6	235.2	4.5
1976	549.1	587.5	−38.4	340.1	393.7	−53.5	270.1	254.9	15.2
1977	616.6	635.7	−19.1	384.1	430.1	−46.0	300.1	273.2	26.9
1978	694.4	694.8	−0.4	441.4	470.7	−29.3	330.3	301.3	28.9
1979	779.8	768.3	11.5	505.0	521.1	−16.1	355.3	327.7	27.6

243

TABLE D (CONTINUED)

Calendar year	TOTAL GOVERNMENT			FEDERAL GOVERNMENT			STATE AND LOCAL GOVERNMENT		
	Receipts	Expenditures	Surplus or deficit (−), national income and product accounts	Receipts	Expenditures	Surplus or deficit (−), national income and product accounts	Receipts	Expenditures	Surplus or deficit (−), national income and product accounts
1980	855.1	889.6	−34.5	553.8	615.1	−61.3	390.0	363.2	26.8
1981	977.2	1,006.9	−29.7	639.5	703.3	−63.8	425.6	391.4	34.1
1982	1,000.8	1,111.6	−110.8	635.3	781.2	−145.9	449.4	414.3	35.1
1983	1,059.6	1,190.4	−130.8	658.1	837.5	−179.4	487.7	439.1	48.6
1984	1,171.3	1,279.8	−108.5	725.1	898.0	−172.9	539.8	475.4	64.4
1985	1,262.2	1,401.2	−139.0	785.7	983.0	−197.3	575.4	517.1	58.3

[p]indicates preliminary.
Note: Federal grants-in-aid to state and local governments are reflected in Federal expenditures and state and local receipts. Total government receipts and expenditures have been adjusted to eliminate this duplication.
Source: Department of Commerce, Bureau of Economic Analysis.

TABLE E MONEY STOCK MEASURES AND LIQUID ASSETS, 1959–1985

(Averages of daily figures; billions of dollars)

Period	M1 — Sum of currency, demand deposits, travelers checks, and other checkable deposits (OCDs)	M2 — M1 plus overnight RPs and Eurodollars, MMMF balances (general purpose and broker/dealer), MMDAs, and savings and small time deposits	M3 — M2 plus large time deposits, term RPs, term Eurodollars, and institution-only MMMF balances	L — M3 plus other liquid assets	Debt[1] — Debt of domestic nonfinancial sectors (monthly average)	PERCENT CHANGE FROM YEAR EARLIER[2] M1	M2	M3	Debt
December:									
1959	141.0	297.8	299.8	388.7	638.4				8.4
1960	141.8	312.3	315.3	403.7	673.7	0.6	4.9	5.2	5.5
1961	146.5	335.5	341.0	430.8	716.6	3.3	7.4	8.2	6.4
1962	149.2	362.7	371.4	466.1	769.5	1.8	8.1	8.9	7.4
1963	154.7	393.2	406.0	503.8	825.5	3.7	8.4	9.3	7.3
1964	161.9	424.8	442.5	540.4	889.1	4.7	8.0	9.0	7.7
1965	169.5	459.4	482.2	584.5	957.8	4.7	8.1	9.0	7.7
1966	173.7	480.0	505.1	614.8	1,025.1	2.5	4.5	4.7	7.0
1967	185.1	524.3	557.1	666.6	1,102.2	6.6	9.2	10.3	7.5
1968	199.4	566.3	606.2	728.9	1,197.5	7.7	8.0	8.8	8.6
1969	205.8	589.5	615.0	763.6	1,285.5	3.2	4.1	1.5	7.3
1970	216.6	628.2	677.5	816.4	1,375.6	5.2	6.6	10.2	7.0
1971	230.8	712.8	776.2	903.2	1,510.5	6.6	13.5	14.6	9.8
1972	252.0	805.2	886.0	1,023.1	1,670.3	9.2	13.0	14.1	10.6
1973	265.9	861.0	985.0	1,141.8	1,861.4	5.5	6.9	11.2	11.4
1974	277.5	908.4	1,070.4	1,249.2	2,036.9	4.4	5.5	8.7	9.4
1975	291.1	1,023.1	1,172.2	1,367.6	2,225.8	4.9	12.6	9.5	9.3
1976	310.3	1,163.6	1,311.8	1,516.5	2,468.3	6.6	13.7	11.9	10.9
1977	335.3	1,286.6	1,472.5	1,704.3	2,784.1	8.1	10.6	12.3	12.8
1978	363.0	1,388.9	1,646.4	1,909.7	3,157.0	8.3	8.0	11.8	13.4
1979	389.0	1,497.9	1,803.6	2,115.8	3,543.5	7.2	7.8	9.5	12.2
1980	414.8	1,631.4	1,988.5	2,324.8	3,881.7	6.6	8.9	10.3	9.5
1981	441.8	1,794.4	2,235.8	2,596.6	4,255.7	6.5	10.0	12.4	9.6
1982	480.8	1,954.9	2,446.8	2,854.8	4,649.8	8.8	8.9	9.4	9.3
1983	528.0	2,188.8	2,701.7	3,168.9	5,177.1	9.8	12.0	10.4	11.3
1984	558.5	2,371.7	2,995.0	3,541.3	5,927.0	5.8	8.4	10.9	14.5
1985[p]	624.7	2,563.6	3,213.5			11.9	8.1	7.3	

[p] indicates preliminary.
[1] Consists of outstanding credit market debt of the U.S. government, state, and local government and private nonfinancial sectors; data from flow of funds accounts.
[2] Annual changes are from December to December.
Note: The nontransactions portion of M2 is seasonally adjusted as a whole to reduce distortions caused by substantial portfolio shifts arising from regulatory and financial changes in recent years, especially shifts to MMDAs in 1983. A similar procedure is used to seasonally adjust the remaining nontransactions balances in M3.
Source: Board of Governors of the Federal Reserve System.

TABLE F CONSUMER PRICE INDEXES, 1940–1985
(1967 = 100)

Year or month	All items	Year or month	All items	Year or month	All items	Year or month	All items
1940	42.0	1950	72.1	1960	88.7	1970	116.3
1941	44.1	1951	77.8	1961	89.6	1971	121.3
1942	48.8	1952	79.5	1962	90.6	1972	125.3
1943	51.8	1953	80.1	1963	91.7	1973	133.1
1944	52.7	1954	80.5	1964	92.9	1974	147.7
1945	53.9	1955	80.2	1965	94.5	1975	161.2
1946	58.5	1956	81.4	1966	97.2	1976	170.5
1947	66.9	1957	84.3	1967	100.0	1977	181.5
1948	72.1	1958	86.6	1968	104.2	1978	195.4
1949	71.4	1959	87.3	1969	109.8	1979	217.4
						1980	246.8
						1981	272.4
						1982	289.1
						1983	298.4
						1984	311.1
						1985	322.2

Note: Data beginning 1978 are for all urban consumers; earlier data are for urban wage earners and clerical workers.
Source: Department of Labor, Bureau of Labor Statistics.

TABLE G BOND YIELDS AND INTEREST RATES, 1929–1985
(Percent per annum)

Year and month	U.S. Treasury securities, bills (new issues), 3-month	Corporate bonds (Moody's), Aaa	Discount rate, Federal Reserve Bank of New York	Federal funds rate
1929		4.73	5.16	
1933	0.515	4.49	2.56	
1939	.023	3.01	1.00	
1940	.014	2.84	1.00	
1941	.103	2.77	1.00	
1942	.326	2.83	1.00	
1943	.373	2.73	1.00	
1944	.375	2.72	1.00	
1945	.375	2.62	1.00	
1946	.375	2.53	1.00	
1947	.594	2.61	1.00	
1948	1.040	2.82	1.34	
1949	1.102	2.66	1.50	
1950	1.218	2.62	1.59	
1951	1.552	2.86	1.75	
1952	1.766	2.96	1.75	
1953	1.931	3.20	1.99	
1954	.953	2.90	1.60	
1955	1.753	3.06	1.89	1.78
1956	2.658	3.36	2.77	2.73
1957	3.267	3.89	3.12	3.11
1958	1.839	3.79	2.15	1.57
1959	3.405	4.38	3.36	3.30
1960	2.928	4.41	3.53	3.22
1961	2.378	4.35	3.00	1.96
1962	2.778	4.33	3.00	2.68
1963	3.157	4.26	3.23	3.18
1964	3.549	4.40	3.55	3.50
1965	3.954	4.49	4.04	4.07
1966	4.881	5.13	4.50	5.11
1967	4.321	5.51	4.19	4.22
1968	5.339	6.18	5.16	5.66
1969	6.677	7.03	5.87	8.20
1970	6.458	8.04	5.95	7.18
1971	4.348	7.39	4.88	4.66
1972	4.071	7.21	4.50	4.43
1973	7.041	7.44	6.44	8.73
1974	7.886	8.57	7.83	10.50
1975	5.838	8.83	6.25	5.82
1976	4.989	8.43	5.50	5.04
1977	5.265	8.02	5.46	5.54
1978	7.221	8.73	7.46	7.93
1979	10.041	9.63	10.28	11.19
1980	11.506	11.94	11.77	13.36
1981	14.029	14.17	13.42	16.38
1982	10.686	13.79	11.02	12.26
1983	8.63	12.04	8.50	9.09
1984	9.58	12.71	8.80	10.23
1985	7.48	11.37	7.69	8.10

TABLE H EXCHANGE RATES, 1967–1985
(Cents per unit of foreign currency, except as noted)

Period	Belgian franc	Canadian dollar	French franc	German mark	Italian lira	Japanese yen
March 1973	2.5378	100.333	22.191	35.548	0.17604	0.38190
1967	2.0125	92.689	20.323	25.084	.16022	.27613
1968	2.0026	92.801	20.191	25.048	.16042	.27735
1969	1.9942	92.855	19.302	25.491	.15940	.27903
1970	2.0139	95.802	18.087	27.424	.15945	.27921
1971	2.0598	99.021	18.148	28.768	.16174	.28779
1972	2.2716	100.937	19.825	31.364	.17132	.32995
1973	2.5761	99.977	22.536	37.758	.17192	.36915
1974	2.5713	102.257	20.805	38.723	.15372	.34302
1975	2.7253	98.297	23.354	40.729	.15328	.33705
1976	2.5921	101.410	20.942	39.737	.12044	.33741
1977	2.7911	94.112	20.344	43.079	.11328	.37342
1978	3.1809	87.729	22.218	49.867	.11782	.47981
1979	3.4098	85.386	23.504	54.561	.12035	.45834
1980	3.4247	85.530	23.694	55.089	.11694	.44311
1981	2.7007	83.408	18.489	44.362	.08842	.45432
1982	2.1982	81.077	15.293	41.236	.07411	.40284
1983	1.9621	81.133	13.183	39.235	.06605	.42128
1984	1.7348	77.244	11.474	35.230	.05708	.42139
1985	1.6968	73.226	11.220	34.247	.05255	.42248

Period	Netherlands guilder	Swedish krona	Swiss franc	United Kingdom pound	Multilateral trade-weighted value of the U.S. dollar (March 1973 = 100) Nominal	Real
March 1973	34.834	22.582	31.084	247.24	100.0	100.0
1967	27.759	19.373	23.104	275.04	120.0	
1968	27.626	19.349	23.169	239.35	122.1	
1969	27.592	19.342	23.186	239.01	122.4	
1970	27.651	19.282	23.199	239.59	121.1	
1971	28.650	19.592	24.325	244.42	117.8	
1972	31.153	21.022	26.193	250.08	109.1	
1973	35.977	22.970	31.700	245.10	99.1	98.8
1974	37.267	22.563	33.688	234.03	101.4	99.2
1975	39.632	24.141	38.743	222.16	98.5	93.9
1976	37.846	22.957	40.013	180.48	105.6	97.3
1977	40.752	22.383	41.714	174.49	103.3	93.1
1978	46.284	22.139	56.283	191.84	92.4	84.2
1979	49.843	23.323	60.121	212.24	88.1	83.2
1980	50.369	23.647	59.697	232.58	87.4	84.8
1981	40.191	19.860	51.025	202.43	102.9	100.8
1982	37.473	16.063	49.373	174.80	116.6	111.7
1983	35.120	13.044	47.660	151.59	125.3	117.3
1984	31.245	12.103	42.676	133.56	138.3	128.5
1985	30.370	11.672	41.058	129.56	143.2	132.0

Source: Board of Governors of the Federal Reserve System.

Notation in *macroeconomics* 4th edition

1. Some general rules

(a) ′(prime) denotes another value of the same concept. example: t′ means another value for tax rate.

(b) Upper bar means one of the followings.

    (i) The variable is assumed to be constant for the moment.
    (ii) Autonomous portion of the variable.

(c) Δ denotes the change in the variable.

(d) Subscript means one of the followings.

    (i) Subscript 0(zero) usually means an equilibrium level.
    (ii) Date. example: subscript t means that the value is at t. subscript −1 means the value is lagged one.
    (iii) Different schedule. example: AS_1 and AS_2 denote different aggregate supply schedule.
    (iv) A different type of similar notion. example: i_{TD} and i_{CP} denote interest rates on time deposits and commercial paper respectively (chapter 10).
    (v) Subscript f denotes foreign variable.

(e) Notation E is reserved for denoting an equilibrium point.

(f) * denotes one of the followings:
    (i) Some optimal level. example: optimal money demand M*, full employment output Y*, desired capital stock K*.
    (ii) Steady state level. In the following, I suggested that notation with upper bar is used for the steady state.

2. Description and Warning

The list of notation that follows is based on the notation used in the next-to-last version of the manuscript of the fourth edition of Dornbusch-Fischer's *Macroeconomics*. Some small changes may have been made in notation in the final version of the text, particularly in some of the later chapters. We believe this list of notation is highly, but not perfectly, accurate. Please check with the book itself when in doubt.

2. Notation chapter by chapter

Notation	Meaning......

Chapter 2

Y	level of output
Y_0	equilibrium level of income (output)
P_0	equilibrium price level
Y*	full employment income (potential output)
P	price level
AS	aggregate supply
AD	aggregate demand
C	consumption (for individual in chapter 8)
I	investment spending
S	private sector saving
G	government spending on goods and services
NX	net exports
YD	disposable income
TR	transfer payments to the private sector
TA	taxes
BD	budget deficit

Chapter 3

IU	unplanned additions to inventory
$\overline{C}$	autonomous portion of consumption
c	marginal propensity to consume out of disposable

	income
s	marginal propensity to save out of disposable income
$\bar{I}$	investment assumed constant here (autonomous portion of investment in chapter 4)
$\bar{A}$	autonomous portion of aggregate demand
α	simple multiplier
t	average (and marginal) tax rate
$\bar{\alpha}$	multiplier in the presence of income taxes
BS	budget surplus
BS*	full employment budget surplus

Chapter 4

$\bar{c}$	c(1-t)
b	interest response of investment
i	interest rate (nominal rate from chap.8 on)
L	demand for real balances
DB	demand for real bond holdings
WN	nominal wealth
M	stock of nominal money balances (for individual in chapter 10)
SB	real value of the supply of bonds
k	sensitivity of the demand for real balances to the level of income
h	sensitivity of the demand for real balances to the interest rate

Chapter 5

i_0 equilibrium interest rate

Chapter 6

P_f price level abroad

e   dollar price of foreign exchange (nominal exchange rate)

R   real exchange rate

A   spending by domestic residents

X   the level of exports

Q   the level of imports

Y_f foreign income

i*   world interest rate

BoP   balance of payments surplus

CF   capital accounts surplus

i_f foreign interest rate

Y*   full employment output level

Appendix to chapter 6

$\overline{X}$ autonomous export

m   marginal propensity to import

v   coefficient on the real exchange rate in net export equation

Chapter 7

No new notation is introduced in this chapter.

Chapter 8

WR	real wealth
a	marginal propensity to consume out of wealth
YL	labor income
c	marginal propensity to consume out of labor income
NL	number of years in life
WL	number of years working and earning income
WR_{max}	maximum level of assets
T	a point in life
YP	permanent (disposable) income
θ	fraction of change in income which represents the change in permanent income

Chapter 9

K*	desired capital stock
rc	rental cost of capital
γ	share of capital in total income (coefficient in Cobb Douglas production function)
d	rate of physical depreciation
r	real interest rate (*realized* real rate in ch.17)
π^e	expected inflation rate
λ	speed of adjustment of capital stock

K	capital stock
v	desired capital-output ratio
P_H	price of housing
H	housing stock
Q_H	supply of new housing
FS	flow supply curve for housing
q	Tobin's q
RegQ	regulation Q

Appendix to chapter 9

PDV	present discounted value
Q_C	coupon on a bond
i	yield on a bond
P_C	price of a bond
Q_1, Q_2, ...	promised payment on a bond one year from now, two years from now, ...

Chapter 10

M1, M2, M3, L	measures for money supply
Y_N	nominal monthly income of an individual
tc	transaction cost of transferring funds to money
Z	amount of withdrawal from the bond portfolio
n	number of withdrawal from the bond portfolio
MC	marginal cost
MB	marginal benefit

n*	optimal number of transactions
M*	optimal money demand
q	cost of being illiquid
$p(M, \sigma)$	probability of being illiquid
σ	degree of cash flow uncertainty facing the consumer
i_{TD}	interest rate on time deposits
i_{CP}	interest rate on commercial paper
V	income velocity of money
t	time (also t_0)

Chapter 11

CD	quantity of checkable deposits
CU	quantity of currency
LD	quantity of liquid deposits
D	quantity of a uniform class of deposits
cu	currency deposit ratio (CU/D)
RE	quantity of bank reserves
re	reserve deposit ratio (RE/D)
H	quantity of high powered money
mm	money multiplier (M/H)
HD	demand for high powered money
re_R	required reserve ratio

i_D	discount rate
σ	degree of deposit flow uncertainty facing a bank
a	number between 0 and 1 (just in a footnote)

Chapter 12

u	unemployment rate

Chapter 13

ND	demand curve for labor
NS	supply curve of labor
N	employment (or level of labor input)
W/P	real wage
N*	full employment level of employment (employment level consistent with natural unemployment)
W_0	equilibrium nominal wage
gW	rate of wage inflation
ε	responsiveness of nominal wages to unemployment
W	nominal wage
u*	natural unemployment rate
LF	total labor force
WN	wage employment relation given by eq.(4)
a	labor productivity (or input coefficient)
z	markup rate
YF	level of output that would obtain if the entire labor force were employed

λ	responsiveness of price level to output gap
P_m	materials prices
θ	material requirement per unit of output
p_m	real price of materials

Chapter 14

π^e	expected inflation rate
π	inflation rate
SAS	short-run aggregate supply curve
LAS	long-run aggregate supply curve
ϕ	responsiveness of demand increase to the rate of change in real balances
m	growth rate of nominal money stock
σ	responsiveness of the increase of demand to a fiscal expansion
f	change in fiscal policy
DAD	dynamic aggregate demand schedule

Appendix to chapter 14

i_r	real interest rate
γ	$\equiv \overline{\alpha} / [1 + (\overline{\alpha}bk/h)]$
η	responsiveness of the change in aggregate demand to the change in inflation expectation.
x	supply shock

Chapter 15

w_1, w_2, ...	fraction of the civilian labor force that falls within the specific group
u_1, u_2, ...	unemployment rate of the specific group
$\bar{u}$	natural unemployment rate
$\bar{u}_1$, $\bar{u}_2$, ...	natural unemployment rate of the specific group
ß	extent to which changing unemployment affects inflation
gy	actual output growth rate
LPC	long-run Phillips curve

Chapter 16

ΔB_f	value of bond sales to the central bank
ΔB_p	value of bond sales to the public
x	the noninterest or primary budget surplus measured as a fraction of nominal income
gy	growth rate of real GNP
b	debt income ratio

Appendix to chapter 16

B	nominal stock of debt outstanding
q	reciprocal of the growth rate of nominal income $(= [(1+y)(1+\pi)]^{-1})$

Chapter 17

f	function which represents the relation between the change in real balances and the change in

	output
r^e	(expected) real interest rate
$r*$	full-employment interest rate
$gy*$	growth rate of potential output
η	income elasticity of the demand for real balances
AA	schedule showing the relation between inflation rate and inflation tax revenue
IR	inflation tax revenue
IR*	maximum amount of inflation tax revenue
$\pi*$	steady state inflation rate at which IR is at its maximum
td	total deficit as a percentage of GNP

Chapter 18

P^e_t	expected aggregate price level
P_{it}	price of the particular good i at time t
Y_{it}	output of the i'th good at time t
f	supply function

Chapter 19

AF	production function: output as a function of capital K and labor N (A denotes technical progress term)
θ	income share of capital
T	taxes

n	growth rate of labor force
(K/N)*	steady state capital-labor ratio
(Y/N)*	steady state output per head
k	capital labor ratio
x	output per head
k*	steady state capital-labor ratio (k** denotes another steady state)
x*	steady state output per head (x** denotes another)

Appendix to chapter 19

MPK	marginal products of capital
f	production function: output per head as a function of capital-labor ratio
Z	measure of natural resources going into production

Chapter 20

NFA	net foreign assets
DC	domestic credit
ΔNFA*	balance of payment target
ΔH*	planned changes in the stock of high powered money
P_f	price of foreign goods